Rebels at the Bar

Rebels at the Bar

*The Fascinating, Forgotten Stories
of America's First Women Lawyers*

JILL NORGREN

NEW YORK UNIVERSITY PRESS
New York and London

NEW YORK UNIVERSITY PRESS
New York and London
www.nyupress.org

Library of Congress Cataloging-in-Publication Data
Norgren, Jill.
Rebels at the bar : the fascinating, forgotten stories of America's first women lawyers / Jill Norgren.
pages cm
Includes bibliographical references and index.
ISBN 978-0-8147-5862-5
ISBN 978-0-8147-5863-2 (e-book)
ISBN 978-0-8147-5898-4 (e-book)
1. Women lawyers—United States—Biography. 2. Women lawyers—
United States—History—19th century. I. Title.
KF367.N67 2013
340.092'520973—dc23
2012040759

References to Internet websites (URLs) were accurate at the time of writing.
Neither the author nor New York University Press is responsible for URLs that
may have expired or changed since the manuscript was prepared.

New York University Press books are printed on acid-free paper, and their binding materials are chosen
for strength and durability. We strive to use environmentally responsible suppliers and materials to the
greatest extent possible in publishing our books.

Manufactured in the United States of America
10 9 8 7 6 5 4 3 2 1

Dedicated to the memory of

Andrea Horowitz,

John M. Kuldau, and

Philip E. Norgren

Contents

Preface

REBELS AT THE BAR describes the life stories of a small group of nine-teenth-century women who became the first female attorneys in the United States.

In 1865, at the conclusion of the American Civil War, the idea of equal rights found new expression. In the optimistic decade that followed, a handful of women acted on their aspirations to become lawyers. It was a radical ambition. Law was an all-male profession, and most Americans believed that any woman who did not need to work outside her home, or farm, ought not to. Nevertheless, the idea of equality was powerful, and these women marched forward reading law with fathers and brothers, knocking on law school doors, and petitioning county, state, and federal courts for bar privileges.

Progress was usually determined by where the women lived and which law school deans, and judges, they encountered. Columbia University's School of Law refused to admit women when they first applied in 1868 and continued the ban for decades, while not long after the close of the war Washington University in St. Louis, Union College (incorporated in 1891 into Northwestern University), and the University of Michigan permitted female law students to matriculate. In progressive counties and states, judges accepted motions to admit women attorneys to the bar, or did so because of new state laws. In 1869, this opened the way to Arabella Mansfield in Iowa, and shortly thereafter, Lemma Barkaloo and Phoebe Couzins in Missouri, and Ada Kepley in Illinois.

Elsewhere, however, courts declined to extend bar privileges to women, using the dodges of the common law, statutes employing the pronoun "he," woman's proper place, and God's intentions. When Myra Bradwell appealed her exclusion from the practice of law by the state of Illinois, U.S. Supreme Court justice Joseph Bradley, in a concurring opinion, rejected her claim of Fourteenth Amendment rights, declaring it "the law of the Creator" that woman's destiny should be limited to the "noble and benign offices of wife and mother."[1] In 1875, two years after the *Bradwell* decision, Wisconsin Supreme Court chief justice Edward Ryan also invoked Victorian mores in denying Lavinia Goodell's petition for admission to the bar. He wrote that licensing her would mean "a sweeping revolution of social order" and cautioned that it would be "revolting" that "woman should be permitted to mix professionally in all the nastiness of the world which finds its way into courts of justice."[2]

Ultimately, when women faced resistance of this kind, they won admission to law programs and bar privileges only by lobbying state legislatures or, in the case of the federal courts, Congress. In 1877 Lavinia Goodell prevailed at the Wisconsin legislature. In 1879 Congress passed the anti-discrimination legislation long lobbied for by Washington, D.C., attorney Belva Lockwood, a bill that opened the entire federal bar to qualified women lawyers.

Rebels presents the individual but interwoven stories of the women whom historian Virginia Drachman has called "sisters-in-law." It describes their struggle to train and to qualify as attorneys, exploring, in particular, what this first generation of American women lawyers did, after the initial jousting, with their hard-won professional privilege.

Their story is one of nerve and courage, success and frustration. This first generation did everything that law and custom did not prevent to eliminate barriers to equality. They believed that gender equality was guaranteed by natural law and the founding documents of the nation. Yet these women were never given the opportunity to wear the black robes of a judge; they were not invited into the developing areas of corporate or railroad law; and, although male lawyers filled the ranks of legislatures and foreign diplomatic missions, presidents refused to appoint women to diplomatic offices just as the public refused to elect them to assemblies and senates.

The first generation did practice civil and criminal law, solo and in partnership, in both back office and courtroom. They were deeply involved in reform movements, lobbying extensively on the major issues of their day—including suffrage, temperance, race (where Caucasian women lawyers were not always on the side of racial minorities), prison conditions, and international peace and arbitration. They authored countless books, articles, and newspaper columns. They pursued parallel careers as lecturers. In 1876 Belva Lockwood tried but failed to open a law school for women in Washington, D.C.; twenty years later lawyers Ellen Mussey and Emma Gillett succeeded. Several of these women ventured into politics. After each success, the women of the first generation reached higher—expanding their law practices, writing and lobbying more, and looking for ways to use their knowledge of the law to shape and order society.

Myra Bradwell of Chicago made her mark as plaintiff in a case that went to the U.S. Supreme Court, and as an intrepid entrepreneur in the field of legal publishing.[3] Catharine Waite, a law school graduate at the age of fifty-six, also published a legal newspaper. Ada Bittenbender maintained a private practice with her husband and then married her talents and passions, as a lawyer and a reformer, and served as counsel for the Woman's Christian Temperance Union. Kate Stoneman opened the New York State bar to women, and in Albany fought for woman suffrage. Lavinia Goodell, through her wrangling with Justice Ryan, showed herself to be a lawyer with an uncommonly fine theoretical mind. Mary Hall, Connecticut's first woman attorney, practiced law and organized the charitable care of poor working children. She argued against a woman lawyer speaking in court. Her stance, much debated and not infrequently deplored by other women lawyers, prompted Chicago attorney Catharine Waugh McCulloch to urge that "some bristling aggressive woman lawyer . . . ought to stir up those slow moving people [who confine themselves to back office work]."[4] She invited Hall to come visit her in Illinois, "where it is just as honorable for a woman to talk publicly to men as in private."[5]

Lelia Robinson practiced law in Boston and the Washington Territory. She won praise in the courtroom and broke new ground by writing law books for the lay public. Like some, but not all women attorneys, she held special hours for women clients who were too poor to pay or who needed special help. At the end of her (too short) life,

Robinson showed an interest in entering elective politics. In this ambition, she mirrored the daring of Belva Lockwood, who, in addition to practicing law, in 1884 and 1888 ran for the office of U.S. president. Lawyer J. Ellen Foster showed a similar interest in politics, creating considerable controversy among women as a Republican temperance activist.

Lockwood, like McCulloch and California lawyer Clara Foltz, sought out courtroom work despite negative societal attitudes about women working in courtrooms. They were women of considerable ego, talented attorneys who understood societal prejudices but courageously refused to be defeated by them. Foltz, with her friend and colleague, Laura De Force Gordon, opened the California bar to women and at the state supreme court argued successfully that Hastings Law School should not deny admission to women on the grounds of their sex. She and Gordon attracted media attention, even occasioning the production of a rare cartoon lampooning women lawyers. Foltz was, at her core, a reformer. She believed that women attorneys should improve the administration of justice and made good on this belief by lobbying for, beginning in 1890, the new and radical idea of a public defender.

The first generation of American women lawyers was smart, bold, and defiant. Its members were charming, idealistic, and argumentative. They debated seemingly trivial issues such as whether to wear their hats in court as well as fundamental questions of service and professional identity. Would pro bono work be their ruin? (The women divided on this point.) Should they be "*lady* lawyers" or simply "lawyers"? Was a contingent fee case worth the financial risk? And was there any way around the fact that male attorneys had a far easier time making the acquaintance of businessmen in clubs, the business world, and public places? Even the most shy of these pioneering professionals were women of considerable spirit, women who believed that legal training would permit them a new place in the world. What place, of course, was the question.

Rebels, equal part biography and the history of women's earliest inroads into the profession of law, explores the journey taken by several

of these pioneers, their clients, and the men who supported and opposed them. It expands our understanding of the legal profession in
the last quarter of the nineteenth century, creating an additional narrative of what transpired as the profession matured. The book focuses
on the understudied story of women who trained in law and then, like
men, used that education to pursue careers in law, lobbying, politics,
publishing, philanthropy, and teaching.

The struggle for equality frames each woman's biography and is a
core theme throughout the book. The rights vocabulary of the nineteenth century did not include the term "feminism." However, as
chapter 1 illustrates, throughout the nineteenth century ever larger circles of women envisioned a more just American society. Collectively,
in anti-slavery societies, at temperance meetings, or in suffrage associations, and individually, in journeys of personal assertiveness, women
contested the social and legal barriers that obstructed the pursuit of
opportunity and liberty.

The women lawyers described in *Rebels* were Christians. Woman's
struggle to redefine the concept of equality confronted traditional
Christian ideals concerning women's and men's roles. For many
Christians submissiveness, silence, and the hearth defined the ideal
of woman's behavior and place. However, the Society of Friends and
the Methodists, among other denominations, opened up biblical injunctions to new interpretation. Quaker Lucretia Mott spoke and
led. Belva Lockwood permitted the Methodist's belief in individual
responsibility and in faith confirmed by good works to nurture her
sense of personal worth as well as her desire to better the world. Lavinia Goodell, Mary Hall, and several of the women lawyers involved
in temperance organizing, spoke and wrote about the religious beliefs
that motivated their work. Other women lawyers were regular church-
goers but did not leave written records connecting their insistence
on equality to particular theologies. The role of religion among these
women lawyers remains understudied because belief in God was generally taken for granted.

The nature of relationships constitutes another of the themes
found in *Rebels*. Belva Lockwood's family did not encourage her to go

to high school, much less college, but as a young woman she married a man who was liberal and who placed few boundaries on her activities. Widowed in her twenties, she was courted by and again established a marital relationship with a man who was open to her professional ambitions. In contrast to Lockwood's parents, William Goodell fostered his daughter Lavinia's intellectual development. When she became an attorney, she often lived with the senior Goodells. Lavinia did not marry and eventually cared for her aging parents. In contrast, Foltz and Lockwood counted upon mothers, daughters, and female cousins to run their households while they saw clients, went to court, or traveled the lecture circuit. Other women in this story had critically important professional relationships with fathers, brothers, and husbands, apprenticing with them and joining in law partnerships.

Aspiring women attorneys often found that a single man could be counted upon to open or to bar the door to law school, the local bar, or the legislative process by which discriminatory laws might be overturned. Men controlled these institutions and so the establishment of alliances proved critical to women lawyers' success. In the nation's capital, lawyer and former congressman A. G. Riddle stood out as an ally, willing to use his power for women's political and professional rights. In Wisconsin, Judge Edward Ryan held women back with his traditional interpretation of Christian values and legal rights.

Newspaper reporters covered the story of women's entrance into the profession of law. Female applicants and practitioners appreciated the power of the press and cultivated positive relationships that would lead to goodwill on the part of editors and reporters, and affirmative stories. Belva Lockwood shone in her relationships with journalists. Lelia Robinson's 1881 application for admission to the bar in Boston won favor with editors who, for the most part, wrote of her right to choose a profession. Chiding recalcitrant state supreme court justices, the editor of the *Boston Globe* wrote, "We have no doubt that the decision [against Robinson] is based upon the law and constitution as now read. But fifty years from now this decision will be regarded with as much curiosity as knee breeches and buckles. . . . "[6] Women's publications, such as the American Woman Suffrage Association's *Woman's*

Journal, followed the stories of these new professionals. Myra Bradwell never shied away from using the *Chicago Legal News* to champion the cause of a woman lawyer, often printing relevant legal briefs, and judicial opinions, in their entirety.

These women "rebels" practiced alone or in small firms, but their lives present a rich tapestry of social, reform, and professional relationships. Several of these women starred as lobbyists, cultivating support for a host of causes, including women's rights, criminal justice reform, peace, and temperance. They also crafted relationships intended to create a women's legal community: several women lawyers wrote articles in which they identified the first generation of woman lawyers in the United States and described their specialties; graduates and students from the University of Michigan law school founded the Equity Club, a venture encouraging women attorneys to share ideas and problems through circulating letters; and on the east and west coasts women's law clubs were started for the purpose of education and professional networking, several named for Shakespeare's Portia; a woman's law school was established; and a women's bar association was proposed.

Women trained in the law but, like men, did not always practice law—or practice full-time. Some of the time, different considerations drove a woman's decision not to practice. Chapter 2 sketches the nature of the profession of law prior to the entrance of women. Young male attorneys without family money, or community connections, could, and did, have problems earning a living. They supplemented their incomes by giving lectures on the law, writing, and, in a number of instances, running for local, state, and federal elective office. Despite Lockwood's symbolic candidacies, running for political office was generally off limits to women until the 1890s.

Men who practiced law did not need to consider the propriety of arguing in court (although not all men enjoyed trial work). Many women, however, abhorred courtroom work, thinking it indelicate, while others thrived on the challenges of argument and public notice. Foltz, McCulloch, Robinson, Lockwood, and Bittenbender accepted trials as part of their work, and developed reputations for winning.

Thus, an additional theme of this book explores how women interpreted professional opportunities when faced with discrimination and insufficient business or, on the other hand, competing personal views as to whether it was better to serve society as a reformer or as a practicing attorney. Locked out of the judiciary, elective office, corporate law, and diplomacy, early women lawyers were inventive, creative, and thoughtful. Rebuffed by the Illinois bar, Myra Bradwell built a highly successful legal publishing business. Clara Foltz practiced law while fighting fiercely for the institution of an office of public defender. Women began to teach law at institutions of learning in the 1890s shortly after some of their female colleagues turned to writing law books.

Lelia Robinson was one of several women lawyers concerned with the rights of women. She and other of her colleagues held special office hours for women too poor to hire an attorney. In 1886 Robinson wrote *Law Made Easy: A Book for the People*, directed at men and women who needed guidance but could not pay a counselor. Three years later she published *The Law of Husband and Wife. For Popular Use*. A decade later, her friend Mary A. Greene wrote *The Woman's Manual of Law*. Letters from the Equity Club, however, show that women lawyers were not of one mind on the question of helping other women obtain their rights. They were not all what today we might call feminist lawyers.

Chapters 3 through 8 present the biographies of eight "rebels." The lives of Bradwell, Goodell, Lockwood, and Foltz are described in individual chapters. The biographies of Mary Hall and Catharine Waugh McCulloch, however, as well as of Lelia Robinson and Mary Greene, are paired because they raise intersecting professional questions, and because the materials available about their work are limited. African American Charlotte E. Ray, the first woman admitted to the District of Columbia bar, belongs in this story of "rebels." In 1872, after graduating from Howard Law School, Ray began to practice law in the nation's capital. Her name appears as counsel in one or two cases in the docket books of the local courts. Her race, however, combined with her sex, made it impossible for her to make a living as an attorney. Ray quit the law and moved to New York City, where she taught school.[7] Women in the East, Midwest, and West figure in the early history of the legal profession; southern women lawyers come into the story later, and are discussed in the epilogue.

Chapter 9 builds upon these biographies, interweaving the stories of the eight women with those of other women attorneys of the period. From this wider perspective, the chapter appraises law as a woman's enterprise in the late nineteenth century.

* * *

This book grew out of a lecture I delivered on October 27, 2008, at the invitation of the U. S. Supreme Court Historical Society, the Historical Society of the Courts of the State of New York, and Friends of John Jay Homestead. I wish to thank these organizations, along with United States Supreme Court justice Ruth Bader Ginsburg, and Chief Judge (retired) Judith Kaye of the New York Court of Appeals, each of whom offered comments at this talk, held at the Association of the Bar of the City of New York.

Cecelia Cancellaro, my agent, showed enthusiasm for the project, encouraging me to write a book from my original lecture. Many people helped me as I pursued research and writing. Philippa Strum provided friendship and encouragement. She improved the manuscript by reading it, and posing questions. Barbara Allen Babcock and John Phillip Reid graciously reviewed individual chapters. Felice Batlan, Wendy Chmielewski, Elisabeth Gitter, Louise W. Knight, Miriam Levin, and Erika Wayne are some of the scholars who answered my queries, helping to make the book richer in detail, and more accurate. Anonymous reviewers gave careful readings to my proposal, and to the manuscript, improving the final structure and content of the book. Archivists and staff at research collections were generous with their help. These institutions include American University's Washington College of Law, the Hutchins Library at Berea College, the Chapin Library of Rare Books at Williams College, the Evanston (Ill.) History Center, the M. E. Grenander Department of Special Collections and

Archives of the University of Albany Libraries, the New York State Historical Association Library, the Ohio Historical Society, the Prints and Photographs Division of the Library of Congress, the Richmond (Conn.) Memorial Library, the Schlesinger Library, the Collection of the Supreme Court of the United States, and the Wisconsin Historical Society.

Members of New York's Women Writing Women's Lives seminar extended much appreciated friendship and professional advice, as did Sheila Cole and Serena Nanda.

Articles and books have been written about this first generation of women lawyers by a number of authors who are cited in my endnotes and bibliography. I would be remiss, however, if the extraordinary work of the Stanford University Law School Women's Legal History Biography Project was not singled out. Professors Babcock and Wayne and their students have produced papers, available at the project's online website, that have created much new knowledge about the first generation of women lawyers, as well as later generations.

I am grateful to New York University Press for publishing *Rebels*, and to all of its staff. In particular, I was honored to have Deborah Gershenowitz edit this book, helping me, as she did with my biography of Belva Lockwood, to shape the stories of these women into a powerful narrative. Thanks also to Constance Grady, her assistant, and to copyeditor Emily Wright and managing editor Despina Papazoglou Gimbel, who, again, have been loving friends of my work.

Friends and family listened patiently to my endless talk about these smart, gutsy women. To all of you, especially my husband, Ralph, I can only say that "thank you" does not begin to cover my feelings of gratitude.

The Women's War

Let the woman learn in silence with all submissiveness. I do not suffer a woman to teach, nor to usurp authority over men, but to be in silence.

—1 Timothy 2:11-12

Man for the field and woman for the hearth:
Man for the sword and for the needle she:
Man with the head and woman with the heart:
Man to command and woman to obey;
All else confusion.

—Alfred, Lord Tennyson, 1847

ON JUNE 18, 1860, Reverend Theophilus Packard committed his wife Elizabeth to the Illinois Hospital for the Insane. A staunch Calvinist, Theophilus held that his wife's refusal to accept the orthodoxy of his religious views, her refusal to echo his thinking, spoke unequivocally of a deranged mind. Theophilus acted quite legally. Illinois law permitted a husband (but not a wife) to authorize the involuntary commitment of a spouse. Elizabeth Packard, forty-four, the mother of their six children, and completely sane, had not given her consent and was literally dragged off. Elizabeth spent three years imprisoned in the state insane asylum as punishment for her refusal to bend to her husband's commands. She won her release only in 1863 when her eldest son reached the age of majority and asserted legal standing to petition for her freedom. Months later Theophilus again, stubbornly, locked

Elizabeth in a room whose windows had been nailed shut. This time she was freed only after a court trial in which a jury declared her sane.[1]

Elizabeth Packard's fate was the consequence of male action. In addition to her husband's, the decisions of fathers, brothers, sons, male legislators, sheriffs, and doctors contributed to her imprisonment. Even the final—felicitous—ruling of a local jury declaring her sane was a judgment of men. At every step, Elizabeth Packard contended with norms and laws established and carried out by men.

In the eighteenth and nineteenth centuries the power of men was so far reaching that god-fearing Abigail Adams entreated her husband John, later to become the second president of the United States, to join with others at the Continental Congress to shape a code of laws that would expand the rights of women. "Remember the Ladies," she wrote in the spring of 1776, "and be more generous and favourable to them than your ancestors. Do not put such unlimited power into the hands of the Husbands."[2]

The Revolutionary War created opportunities for women to participate in the fight against England. However, neither the Declaration of Independence nor the United States Constitution took note of women's rights. Despite this silence, in 1798 writer Judith Sargent Murray felt confident about the future of her sex, arguing that female rights were now understood and the new nation was now ready "to do justice to women."[3] While it was true that white women shared in many of society's fundamental liberties—including the right to speak, worship, assemble, petition, and protest—custom, and the legal doctrine of coverture (under which a married woman lost much of her individual legal identity to her husband), worked against all women in significant ways: by law, married women could not own property or dispute abusive husbands; they could not sign legal documents, enter into contract, sue in court, or be sued; they could not vote (a short-lived experiment in New Jersey ended in 1807) or serve on juries, and would have been belittled—or worse—had they attempted to run for political office. Before and after the Revolutionary War, they were celebrated as mothers of the republic. In this important domestic and civic role they were expected to uphold the ideals of

republicanism—liberty, inalienable rights, honesty, sovereignty—
to counsel husbands, and to educate their sons and daughters in the
virtues of republican citizenship.[4] Yet in the first decades of the nineteenth century, despite the war for liberty and independence, in the
world of politics traditional male power prevailed and social custom
did not change. The nastiness of political party conflict, the expansion
of male but not female suffrage, and the rise of deal making in smoky
back rooms conspired to marginalize women, at least where electoral
politics were concerned. Men counseled politically inclined women
to become peacemaking negotiators—"non-partisan patriots"—rather
than full-fledged players.[5]

Women were quieted, but this did not end the debate that had flow-
ered during the Revolutionary period about women's role in society.
Ironically, as men pushed women away from electoral politics, nineteenth-century improvements in transportation, increased literacy,
and urbanization encouraged new ideas about what was right, proper,
and possible, opening other roles to women. In the early republic, the daughters of republican mothers, ordinary women, stepped
out of their homes and into their communities ready to expand the
ways in which they improved the lives of their children, their communities, and themselves. This activism was led by a handful of courageous women who proved to be exceptionally able theoreticians,
agitators, and organizers: African American abolitionist and lecturer
Maria Stewart; Quaker minister Lucretia Mott; abolitionists Angelina
and Sarah Grimké; intellectual Margaret Fuller; writer and social reformer Frances Wright. Each asserted the right of respectable women
to talk in public even when what they had to say was controversial.
They insisted that all women had the right and duty, as equals to men,
to speak on matters of public importance. Sarah Grimké argued that
God had created woman equal to man.[6] Fuller made the radical claim
that men "could never reach [their] true proportions while [woman]
remained in any wise shorn of hers."[7]

In the 1840s, in new charitable societies, benevolent organizations,
and nascent social movements, women joined forces, sometimes with
men, to promote temperance, Sabbath observation, and social purity

as well as the abolition of slavery. Many women had come to believe that society could be reformed by renewed religious faith coupled with worldly good works. They claimed the right to control and to change society, and to define the idea, and practice, of fairness and justice. Many, like Elizabeth Packard, turned away from Calvinism and were sustained by the optimism and liberalism of new scriptural interpretations. The Methodists' belief in individual responsibility, divine love freely bestowed upon humankind, and faith confirmed by good works nurtured many a woman's sense of her own worth and desire to improve the world. Unitarianism emphasized the innate goodness of humans, in contradiction to the Calvinist creed of original sin. The 1827 break of Hicksite Quakers from the conservative core of that religion drew the interest of sisters Sarah and Angelina Grimké, who were active in anti-slavery and women's rights politics.

Not surprisingly, taking power out of the "hands of the Husbands" did not come easily. Many women labored under the belief that their sex was governed by emotion rather than reason, and that women were, by God's design, inferior to men. Although they were confident in their homes, self-assurance in public was something women had to, and did gradually, learn. A slow but dramatic transformation in women's civic life began in the 1840s and 1850s, aided by increased access to education and interest in reform causes, among them abolition and temperance. In this coming out, activist women concluded that the perfection of society, including greater equality for women, required their participation in political, civic, and, for some, even professional life. Barred from voting, women nonetheless evaluated political parties and their candidates, and began to investigate the decisions of local tax, zoning, and school boards. Stepping forward even more publicly, the most courageous of these mid-century leaders traveled to conventions and state legislatures where they lobbied for an end to slavery, funds for schools, shorter work weeks, and laws to expand married women's rights to property.

The boldest reformers called for the public discussion of women's rights. Although only one of several local gatherings in this period, the 1848 convention at Seneca Falls, New York emerged as the moment of epiphany and public notice. Meeting on two warm July days, participants drew up, debated, and endorsed a Declaration of Sentiments and Resolutions. The short document took the natural-law language of the Declaration of Independence as its model, thus emphasizing the idea of a universal, unalterable law derived from nature and nature's God, bestowing equal and independent rights to all human beings. The Declaration of Sentiments described women as "aggrieved, oppressed, and fraudulently deprived of their most sacred rights."[8]

The facts submitted "to a candid world" by convention leaders Lucretia Mott, Elizabeth Cady Stanton, and members of the local M'Clintock family, among others, spelled out women's civic, social, economic, and legal disabilities. These included the denial of the right to vote, forced submission to laws they did not make, a double standard in matters of morality, and limited access to education and to well-paying employment. In tough language the authors attacked man's desire to destroy woman's confidence in her own powers, "to lessen her self-respect, and to make her willing to lead a dependent and abject life." The authors took particular care to spell out the abuse of women in marriage, condemning a system of law that gave husbands, like Theophilus Packard, the power to deprive their wives of liberty, property, and wages. One hundred women and men signed the Seneca Falls Declaration. They demanded that women "have immediate admission to all the rights and privileges which belong to them as citizens of these United States."

Women's right to education, fair wages, and a place in the professional life of the country came up five times in this short document. In 1848 the United States was an agricultural society, a way of life increasingly affected by the growth of cities and the expansion of manufacturing industries. Girls and women farmed, served—on farms or in urban settings—and sewed. Women nursed and served local and far-flung communities as midwives, attending a majority of births. With increasing frequency, single young women found employment as factory workers. Some fell into prostitution.

The authors of the Seneca Falls Declaration laid out the stark reality of women's position in the professions, saying simply that their presence was unknown because men had closed to them "all the avenues to wealth and distinction." Communities hired women, at low pay, as schoolteachers, but in 1848 educated women could expect no other professional opportunities: "As a teacher of theology, medicine, or law, she is not known."

Elizabeth Blackwell broke the mold in the field of medicine a year after the Seneca Falls meeting. Rejected from every medical school in Philadelphia and New York City, as well as Harvard, Yale, and Bowdoin, Blackwell had been accepted at Geneva College in New York State, and upon the award of her medical degree in 1849 became the first woman physician in the United States. A biographer describes the difficult decade that followed as one in which the new doctor was "barred from practice in city dispensaries and hospitals, ignored by medical colleagues, and insultingly attacked in anonymous letters."[9]

At the time of the meeting at Seneca Falls, the profession of law was completely closed to women: no woman taught, mentored, or practiced legal work in the United States.

Apart from the Society of Friends, mainstream religious denominations similarly refused to open any calling to the ministry to women. The Quakers had recognized women as ministers since the seventeenth century, but Quaker ministers were called by God, and not ordained. In other mainstream denominations, women wishing the status and authority that accompanied ordination fought deep, longstanding prejudice. Antoinette Brown, later the wife of Elizabeth Blackwell's brother, Samuel, was one of the few to try, and to succeed. In 1847 as a student at Oberlin College, Brown transformed the religious precociousness of her childhood into the insistent intention to take a theological degree. Family and friends, previously pleased by her desire for an education, recoiled. She reported being reasoned with, pleaded with, and told that "masculine headship everywhere was held to be indispensable to morality, and grounded in the inmost fitness of things."[10] Still, she persisted, and finished the program, but was not allowed to graduate. Taking matters into her own hands, Brown arranged professional pulpit engagements and established a successful career as a lecturer who spoke on women's rights, temperance, and abolition. During her speaking engagements fellow clergymen often attempted to shout her down. Brown's spirit was strong, and in 1853 she found a Congregational church whose members understood her vocational calling. In that year she became the first American woman ordained as a minister in the church of a recognized denomination.

In contrast, by the 1840s, the profession of teaching had opened to women, following the enrollment of an ever-growing number of female students who would serve the nation, and commerce, with their literacy and school-instilled discipline. Educator Catharine Beecher, one of the several illustrious Beecher siblings, argued that in addition to their intellect, women instructors would bring a moral sensibility to the nation's classrooms. They would, she said, serve their communities as "a new class of moral guardians."[11] As early as 1830 Beecher wrote that women could achieve the "influence, respectability and independence" inherent in a teaching career without stepping outside "the prescribed boundaries of feminine modesty."[12] School boards quickly discovered that district tax rates could be kept low if they practiced wage discrimination. They commonly offered women instructors half the salary paid to men. Educated women made their pact with the devil and took these teaching positions, being welcome in no other profession.[13]

* * *

Seneca Falls was a call to action. The plan devised in July 1848 proposed that there be more conventions, traveling agents employed to talk up the cause, petitioning, and a campaign to win over ministers and newspaper editors.

The creation of "an equal station for women" meant the reshaping of society with a new balance among marriage, work, and governance. The vision was radical and, not surprisingly, immediately after Seneca Falls the press pilloried the women leaders, describing them as "unwomanly" and "unnatural."[14] Elsewhere, public name calling demeaned outspoken ladies as "personally repulsive."[15] One messenger of reform, who dared to link the future success of temperance to woman suffrage, was attacked in a newspaper editorial as a woman who labored "under feelings of strong hatred toward male men, the effect we assume of jealousy and neglect."[16] While the movement had some supporters in the press and among community leaders, clergy-woman Antoinette Brown's experience of being shouted down was typical of what women endured. Rotten eggs and soft tomatoes were also common weapons of insult.

The work of building a movement benefited from women's energy, intelligence, and determination, but simultaneously bent under prevailing disabilities. Deeply engrained deferential behavior made outreach and networking a challenge, as did the lack of funds for the most basic organizational tasks. An equal station demanded that ideas of obedience and reserve be rethought. Movement leaders were disputing core orthodoxies at a time when advice books told women to be domestic, pious, and submissive, to "avoid a controversial spirit, to repress a harsh answer."[17] Newcomers did not make lightly the decision to join their ranks and to dispute the "inmost fitness of things."[18]

Aspirations, personal slights, and inspirational talks brought girls and women to the movement. Susan B. Anthony said that she became involved after reading reports of activist Lucy Stone's 1850 speech at the first national women's rights convention. Before an audience of one thousand in Worcester, Massachusetts, speaking in favor of women's property rights, Stone insisted,

> [My sisters and I] want to be something more than the appendages of Society; we want that Woman should be the coequal and help-meet of Man in all the interest and perils and enjoyments of human life. We want that she should attain to the development of her nature and womanhood; we want that when she dies, it may not be written on her gravestone that she was the "relict" (widow) of somebody.[19]

A year later abolitionist reformer Wendell Phillips, a prominent male advocate of women's rights, challenged Americans not to be content with the status quo, and to open its institutions to women:

Throw open the doors of Congress; throw open those court-houses; throw wide open the doors of your colleges, and give [women] the same opportunity for culture that men have, and let the results prove what their capacity and intellect really are. When woman has enjoyed for as many centuries as we have the aid of books, the discipline of life, and the stimulus of fame, it will be time to begin the discussion of those questions: "What is the intellect of woman?" "Is it equal to that of man?" Till then, all such discussion is mere beating of the air.[20]

When not being hectored, Antoinette Brown urged women to enter all of the traditionally male professions, including the ministry. The Bible, she lectured, did not forbid it. Along with other women leaders, she raised questions about the ability of a man-made law to represent and protect women. Slights and ambition brought upstate New York teacher and later attorney Belva Bennett Lockwood into the circle. She never worked for a school board willing to match her salary to that paid to male instructors. The discrimination continued even after she reminded board officials that she was a widow with a small child to support. Never altogether content to be a teacher, Lockwood quietly played with the then-absurd idea of becoming an attorney. By 1858 she was ready to take up Susan B. Anthony's proposal that women teachers agitate for equal professional status and pay. In public speeches, Lockwood demonstrated the speaking skills she would later bring to local and federal courtrooms.

Debate about the need for a national woman's rights association began early in the 1850s at the national conventions where Stone, Phillips, and many others spoke. The issue of creating an association at first was sidestepped. These conventions, nevertheless, provided spirited forums for the education of a public still both naïve and at odds over questions of divorce for the wives of alcoholics and abusers, equal inheritance and child custody rights, and trials before a jury of female peers, along with the better-known issues of suffrage, education, and property rights.

The beginning of the Civil War in 1861 quieted talk of women's rights as reformers adopted a dignified silence. Only after Lee's surrender to Grant at Appomattox in April of 1865 were women activists free to pick up the threads of their earlier arguments.

In 1865 most reformers expected that the energy and strategic know-how of the abolitionist and women's movement would be focused upon promoting national legislation, or a constitutional amendment, barring the use of race and sex as a qualification for voting. For more than two decades members of the antislavery and women's movement had worked together, sharing leaders and the common language of natural rights. However, only weeks after the victory of the North, Elizabeth Cady Stanton learned that prominent advocates of African American citizenship and voting rights planned to abandon the fight to enfranchise women, limiting their campaign to black manhood suffrage. Wendell Phillips, president of the Anti-Slavery Society, said that Reconstruction politics could not bear the weight of women's aspirations, declaring that the "hour belongs to the negro."[21] Stanton, a long-time friend, fired off a letter in which she asked Phillips, "Do you believe the African race is composed entirely of males?"[22]

A fight to define the terms of this suffrage-reform debate enveloped the civil rights community. In the course of debate the embryonic women's movement split in two. Lucy Stone, Julia Ward Howe, and Henry Blackwell formed the American Woman Suffrage Association (AWSA), which supported ratification of the Fifteenth Amendment even if it excluded women. Stanton, her close friend Susan B. Anthony, and other proponents of an immediate universal or woman suffrage amendment to the U.S. Constitution created the opposing National Woman Suffrage Association (NWSA).

The fledgling National Woman Suffrage Association held its first annual convention in 1870 in Washington, D.C.'s Lincoln Hall. Belva Lockwood, who had moved to Washington at the end of the Civil War, was one of the activists who joined the Nationals and came to the meeting. She supported immediate voting rights for freedmen and women. The National also attracted Lockwood because its founding members championed equal educational and employment opportunities for women, and for more than twenty years had lobbied for the reform of laws that gave husbands absolute control of their wives' assets and earning. She was typical of the activists who wanted to build more than a suffrage movement. As Lockwood later told an interviewer, she had first taken an interest in woman suffrage because of the "inequality that prevailed between the payment of men and women for identical work."[23]

The 1870 NWSA meeting was a morale-boosting occasion that, to some, must have resembled a revival jamboree. Stanton opened the convention with a speech that rejoiced in the decision of the Wyoming territorial legislature granting women the right to vote. She said that the hour of universal woman suffrage throughout the United States was near, and read a letter of support from the English philosopher John Stuart Mill. Delegate Pauline Davis delivered a lengthy history of the women's rights movement in the United States, Britain, and parts of Europe. Primed with history and exhortation, the delegates listened to Anthony call for the approval of four resolutions. The first requested that members of Congress submit a woman suffrage amendment to the states. A second resolution asked that Congress strike the word "male" from the federal laws governing the District of Columbia, while a third urged officials to enfranchise the women of the Utah Territory as a "safe, sure, and swift means to abolish the polygamy of that Territory."[24] A final resolution petitioned Congress to amend federal law to provide equal pay for women government employees. All of the motions received approval. It pleased Lockwood that she was not alone in wanting to lobby for equal educational, employment, and property rights.[25] For Lockwood, the women's movement would always be about the naturally complementary issues of economic and political rights.

Movement leaders were keeping an approving eye on Lockwood, who, in applying to law school, had challenged what Catherine Beecher called the "boundaries of feminine modesty." Lockwood, and the other members of the first generation of women who sought to open the profession of law, understood the far-reaching power of men but believed, nevertheless, in the possibility of a just society governed by natural law and reform ideals.

❖ 2 ❖

White Knights
and Legal Knaves

[T]here is a suit before the Court which was commenced nearly twenty years ago; in which from thirty to forty counsel have been known to appear at one time; in which costs have been incurred to the amount of seventy thousand pounds; which is a friendly suit; and which is . . . no nearer to its termination now than when it was begun.

—Charles Dickens, 1853

WHEN, AFTER THE CIVIL WAR, a few brave women insisted upon the opportunity to become lawyers, they entered a profession with a decidedly mixed reputation, one populated solely by male practitioners who were responsible for the nature of their profession. By the late 1860s in the United States, significant economic and political changes were in place. Members of the legal profession, which had served rural colonial America and then a small agrarian nation, now understood that they must be capable of addressing the issues created by urbanism, industrial capitalism, and the building of transportation and communication infrastructures. Solo practitioners maintained legal practices in towns and cities, serving more traditional clients, but in the post-war years, law became an increasingly tiered profession, with an ever greater range of fees and status.

* * *

Stretching back to seventeenth-century colonial America, citizens had searched for "justice beyond law"—justice without lawyers or courts.[1] Many of the earliest colonists argued that law, and its servant-lawyers, breached social harmony by promoting contention and un-Christian, self-aggrandizing individualism. Some wags whispered that lawyers were only slightly better than the biblical serpent, and efforts were made in some communities to forbid the practice of law.[2] Puritans contended that "the administration of justice should be based on individual conscience and the word of God rather than legal precedents."[3] Questions of law were presented as theological in nature, rather than legal, and not requiring the counsel of common-law attorneys.[4] In *The Scarlet Letter* adulteress Hester Prynne is examined by a tribunal of magistrates, religious and political leaders charged with enforcing God's will. Lawyers play no role in Hawthorne's drama, set in 1640s colonial Boston, although the crime of which Hester stood accused carried a possible sentence of death.

Despite deep mistrust of the profession, the number of lawyers increased in the eighteenth century. So, however, did the tongue lashings. Near the end of the Revolutionary War naturalized American Hector St. John de Crèvecoeur cautioned that lawyers were "plants that will grow in any soil that is cultivated by the hands of others; and when once they have taken root, they will extinguish every other vegetable that grows around them."[5] He singled out lawyers for the fortunes they acquired from the misfortunes of others. Writer Washington Irving was no less caustic. Satirizing secular New Amsterdam in his biting, 1809 burlesque account *A History of New York*, Irving described the unchecked presence of base lawyers—"caitiff scouts"—who, like Crèvecoeur's "plants," infested the profession and caused the courts to be "constantly crowded with petty, vexatious, and disgraceful suits."[6]

The commentaries were cutting, and after the Revolutionary War calls for abolition of the legal profession continued. Critics wanted "to simplify and Americanize the common law" and to democratize the system.[7] The training of attorneys in English law lent credence to the idea that lawyers were "plotting the downfall of republicanism," while some newspapers voiced the complaint that professions were "out of place in a republican society."[8] Constitutionalism and commerce, however, ultimately provided a safe haven for lawyers, a shelter in which to repair their standing and create a more respectable future. It helped that patriot-essayist Thomas Paine proclaimed that in America, "the Law is King."[9]

In his 1830s travels through the United States, Frenchman Alexis de Tocqueville also praised the rule of law and argued that in this new republic, "[T]he aristocracy . . . is on the bench and at the bar."[10] He argued that the "authority [Americans] have entrusted to members of the legal profession, and the influence that these individuals exercise in the government, are the most powerful existing security against the excesses of democracy."[11] He thought that the study of law cultivated "certain habits of order, a taste for formalities, and a kind of instinctive regard for the regular connection of ideas, which naturally render [lawyers] very hostile to the revolutionary spirit and the unreflecting passions of the multitude."[12] Tocqueville suggested that the profession protected its position by having become "masters of a science which is necessary, but which is not very generally known."[13]

Other nineteenth-century commentators were more frank, and critical. The owner of the *New-Hampshire Patriot*, Issac Hill, lashed out at attorneys, writing that when they moved into towns where peace, quiet, and the absence of litigation had been the norm, "uproar and confusion" suddenly reigned "without any other visible means than the introduction of a lawyer."[14] In an 1830 address to the students of Waterville College, lawyer and novelist John Neal fulminated against the law's uncodified contradictions and incoherencies, which he thought invited manipulation by "scoundrel pettifogger[s]." With less flattery than Tocqueville, he called lawyers "the *unanointed* rulers of the land," again expressing the view that lawyers formed an exclusive group, out of place in a republican society—an aristocracy, whose work was often inconsistent with the values of a free government.[15] Jacksonian reformer Frederick Robinson summed up the anti-monopolists' attack on the profession, writing that while lawyers attempted "the appearance of *Officers*," they were nothing more than followers of a trade that "ought to be left open to competition."[16]

Tocqueville toured the United States during a period of profound change. In 1826, the elderly Thomas Jefferson spoke of feeling lost in a nation that "seemed overrun" by business and banking.[17] A rural economy was yielding to a market revolution in which property rights were becoming a more varied and compelling commodity. Tocqueville observed a nation increasingly divided into city and country, manufacturing and farming, a society whose fault lines were more and more drawn around disparities of wealth.[18] He witnessed economic and political forces pushing the United States toward a system of capitalism in which sellers, lenders, and employers ruled, often at the expense of buyers, borrowers, and employees.[19] Lawyers "were the shock troops of capitalism," and Tocqueville felt it.[20]

The rank assumed by an individual lawyer in this changing world depended upon many factors, including place of practice, wit, ambition, and birth. Beginning in the 1790s, when the rules of business and corporate affairs were altered to permit merchants to testify to the facts or intention of a contract, businessmen who were parties to an action, individuals who had previously favored arbitration because they could tell their side of the dispute, turned to lawyers and courts to draw up their contracts and rule on their quarrels.[21] Meeting them on common ground and seeking fresh opportunities for the legal profession, between 1790 and the 1820s lawyers and judges adopted a friendlier posture toward commercial law, shaping legal doctrine that assisted commercial interests. Quite quickly, "the intellectual foundation was laid for an alliance between common lawyers and commercial interests."[22] Retainers increased, as did damage judgments. In America's great port cities, marine insurance litigation became an important part of commercial practice, making men like Brockholst Livingston and Alexander Hamilton wealthy.[23]

These were years when legislators, an increasing number of whom were lawyers, finally confronted the rather chaotic state of law in the United States. They were citizens of a newly independent nation. They had the task of fashioning civil and criminal legal systems based upon ideas suited to their hearts and minds as Americans rather than subjects of the British Crown. There is little disagreement among historians that as the fledgling nation produced laws in written form, the greatest number addressed the question of regulating property, and did so in such a manner as to make property inviolable.[24] One modern observer has written that "law, once conceived of as . . . paternalistic and, above all, a paramount expression of the moral sense of the community, had come to be thought of as facilitative of individual desires and . . . the existing organization of economic and political power."[25] In small towns people "knew that it was lawyers who served the outsiders reshaping, remaking, and taking over their lives and livelihoods."[26]

Legal change was not universal, and lawyers did not make a place for themselves in all communities. For several decades after the Revolutionary War, state legal systems developed alongside local ones, but, as late as 1840 in places like the Carolinas, state systems had not completely displaced local law that functioned without lawyers.[27] In this part of the South, systems of localized law thrived. Social order was overseen by "ordinary people" who maintained the "peace," while leaving state law—ruled over by professionally trained lawyers—to deliver other forms of rights and justice. The people who tended localized law, led by magistrates who did not have formal legal training, "kept to their own paths, absorbed by what they encountered there and largely oblivious to events at the state level, despite efforts to attract their attention."[28] This process "allowed magistrates to leave Blackstone and the perplexing body of common law behind and adjudicate simply, personally, and pragmatically."[29] Trained lawyers had solidified their hold on property law in the Carolinas even before the Revolution. Crimes and offenses against the public order, however, remained the domain of localized law well into the 1820s and 1830s "largely because they were far less lucrative for lawyers and less important to state leaders, who were often lawyers as well."[30]

Despite localized law, in the Carolinas and elsewhere in the antebellum period, an intelligent and ambitious white man who turned to the law as a profession might reasonably expect respectability, social mobility, and, with luck, financial gain. John Adams recommended the law to his son-in-law as "the most independent place on earth," by which he meant that attorneys did not have to work for other people.[31]

Tocqueville's "aristocracy" often had the advantage of providential birth and institutional schooling. In Massachusetts and Maine nearly three-quarters of the lawyers in practice before 1840 came from a small elite of college-educated men, many of whom were the sons of judges and lawyers.[32]

The system was sufficiently flexible to admit interlopers like William Wirt, who became a member of the early-nineteenth-century "elite" bar that also included John Marshall, Daniel Webster, Horace Binney, Joseph Story, and James Kent. Orphaned as a young child, Wirt had scrambled to provide for himself and to read law as an apprentice. He passed the Virginia bar at the age of twenty and had the good fortune to marry into a gentlewoman's family. Through her, Wirt gained access to Jefferson, James Madison, James Monroe, and other leading men of early American law, politics, and letters. He served as counsel for James Callender in his sensational libel case testing the Alien and Sedition Act, participated in the prosecution of the case against Aaron Burr, and from 1817 to 1829 served as attorney general of the United States.[33]

Early in the nineteenth century practitioners prepared by reading William Blackstone's *Commentaries on the Laws of England* and, later, James Kent's *Commentaries on American Law* and Joseph Story's several *Commentaries* as well as treatises on evidence, equity, commercial law, and pleading.[34] Timothy Walker's *Introduction to American Law*, prepared originally as lectures for his Cincinnati College law students, joined the list of readings in 1837. Walker, a lawyer, educator, and legal reformer who had studied at Harvard with Joseph Story, admired Blackstone. He wrote that Blackstone's *Commentaries* were "without . . . rival [as a] first book on the law" but believed that it contained "much that is inapplicable to this country"[35] (emphasis in original). Walker wrote his textbook to remedy the reliance of American students on a foreign treatise to learn the basics of American law. His text was a great success, widely used as a general introduction into the early twentieth century. Oliver Wendell Holmes Jr. reported that Walker's *Introduction* provided him with the "first clear idea of what law was."[36]

Like Wirt, most men striving to become lawyers apprenticed with an established attorney. In the late eighteenth century, the American legal profession had begun—state by state, sometimes county by county—to shape a system of training and accreditation distinct from the one used in England. Apprenticeship, and later law schools, emerged as the chosen path of training rather than replication of the ancient English "juridical universities," the Inns of the Court and Chancery.[37]

The apprentice ran errands, performed small services, and hand copied endless pages of wills, briefs, pleadings, and other documents, a mind-numbing, rote task. When time permitted, servant and master might discuss points of law. Some mentors accepted an apprentice student's services as pay for the use of his law books and tutoring. Many of the leaders of the bar, however, charged "stiff fees" for the privilege of reading law.[38]

Apprenticeship training varied widely in length of time, quality, and thoroughness. The Massachusetts bar developed a demanding course of apprenticeships and clerkships, hoping to maintain the profitable apprentice system and to control the number of lawyers admitted to its bar.[39] In the Bay State, however, as elsewhere, the number of attorneys increased. In 1818 the editors at *Niles' Register* bluntly reported that "lawyers are as plentiful as blackberries."[40] In 1831 a friend of Timothy Walker's wrote that Boston "is a glutted market—we have . . . more lawyers than wrongs to redress."[41] Walker's Cincinnati, Ohio, also suffered from oversupply. In 1830, Cincinnati newcomer Salmon P. Chase (later chief justice of the U.S. Supreme Court) modestly stated his aspirations amid the competition for clients: "[I]f I can make ten dollars in the first three months, twenty in the next three, forty in the next three, and eighty in the next, I shall do well."[42]

Men of a scholarly bent were not happy with the apprenticeship system. Joseph Story, who served an apprenticeship late in the eighteenth century, thought the system "for the most part a waste of time and effort, at once discouraging and repulsive."[43] Lawyer and law reformer David Dudley Field, born a generation after Story, attacked it for turning out "an undisciplined, half-educated creature, 'the transcriber of legal formulas, the promoter of neighborhood litigation, the unsafe guide, the hopeless bigot.'"[44] Field believed that a true lawyer must know "the law in all its departments" and that the eminent lawyers of his day were "not produced by the system but in spite of it."[45]

New York City attorney George Templeton Strong, proper and elitist, was even more scathing. He faulted changes made in the 1846 state constitution that abolished distinctions among attorneys, solicitors, and counselors and eased licensing procedures as action pushing law in the direction of a technical trade rather than a profession. Strong wrote that, with the new constitutional "reforms," legal practice in New York would soon be reduced "to a Hottentot standard of simplicity."[46] He had nothing but contempt for his own oral bar admission test: "Such a farce of an examination, such an asinine set of candidates."[47] He later added that the legal fraternity was no longer "learned & dignified" but rather ranked "next below that of patent-medicine mongering."[48] Strong's distress was such that he threw himself into developing a law program at Columbia College, his alma mater.[49]

American law schools had an uneven history in the late eighteenth and early nineteenth century. Always small, several were founded and became insolvent. Eleven years after it opened, Harvard Law School was "on the brink of failure" when Nathan Dane's bequest of a chaired professorship and Joseph Story's scholarship revitalized the program.[50] Story sought to create a national law school. He stressed theory, whereas educators like Walker tried to teach both the principles of law and the principles of practice. In New York City, working with others, Strong succeeded in persuading Columbia to start a law program that graduated its first students in 1858. He argued that institutional training would create professionals with higher moral standards and better skills.[51] By 1862 Columbia Law School had 135 students, exceeding the enrollments of Yale and Harvard.

John Adams recommended the profession of law as the most independent place on earth but did not comment on its ability to engage the mind. While Story and Strong worked to draw men of intellect to a career in law, the field was wide open, despite bar examinations and, later, bar associations.[52] As a result, men of varying ability, values, and tolerance for boredom cast their lot with the profession. Compelling cases involving constitutional law, treason, and national power occupied the days of a favored few members of the early American bar. Henry Clay won the enmity of many Americans by defending Aaron Burr. Daniel Webster, a man who frequently appeared before the U.S. Supreme Court, made his reputation arguing the case for enlarging the powers of the federal government. Before becoming an associate justice, Joseph Story appeared before the high court as counsel for land speculators in *Fletcher v. Peck.*[53] In this landmark case, the Supreme Court ruled for the first time that a state law was unconstitutional, lending the weight of its powers to the sanctity of legal contracts. Months after arguing *Fletcher*, Story was nominated for membership on the Court by President Madison, serving from 1811 to 1845. He made his mark as "an aggressive champion of federal jurisdiction" as well as an opponent of slavery.[54] William Wirt ended his career representing the Cherokee Nation against the United States in two landmark cases of national importance.[55]

For the most part, however, well into the nineteenth century—despite local specializations in admiralty, insurance, or land title—lawyers were generalists who might, or might not, have had the good fortune of engaging cases. As the junior member of his New York law firm, George Templeton Strong protested the "endless work on small legal papers . . . a snowbank of mortgages, subpoenas, depositions and polyonymous botherations," carried out in city, state, and federal courts.[56] The actions involved a repetitious mélange of replevin, injunction, partition, ejectment, damages, covenant, assumpsit, and bank foreclosures.

Travel was often an issue. When North Carolina replaced eight district courts with superior courts, local attorneys grumbled about traveling county to county. They preferred the old system of pleasant bonhomie where clients came to them at the district courthouse. More than a few sulked about the change and one said rather grandly, "[T]he prospect [of travel] is dull to men of eminence . . . [U]nder this System Genius will languish, enterprise grow feeble and Petit-fogging become fashionable."[57]

Some men chased criminal cases. Many lawyers, however, resisted work in this area because fees were often low, and the issues tawdry. The attraction was greater if the defendant could pay well, or the case was high profile, with the promise of a courtroom contest that could enhance a good performer's professional standing. Of course, not all lawyers shone in court. As the practice of forming partnerships grew early in the nineteenth century, colleagues divided back-office and courtroom duties and, later, the work of legislative lobbying. This occurred when New Yorkers John Wells and George Washington Strong (father of George Templeton Strong) established a partnership in 1818. After an early, and rather modest, career servicing debt collection, wills, and real estate instruments, Wells came to public notice in court arguing on behalf of James Cheetham in a case testing freedom of the press. His oratorical skills won notice, and when he and Strong founded the law firm of Wells and Strong, their personal talents and business connections dictated a fairly strict division of work. Wells assumed the duties of courtroom advocate while Strong, scion of a distinguished New York family, worked the back office bringing in banking, insurance, and maritime clients.[58]

In 1844 New Yorker David Dudley Field, who spent much of his life working for the codification of the law, observed that his profession had greatly changed from the early years of the republic. Solid learning and decorous manners had been replaced by a bar "now crowded with bustling and restless men."[59] Lawyers with the best practices, he wrote, were "tasked almost beyond endurance. The multiplication of law-books, and, above all, the multiplication of courts, have quadrupled their labors."[60]

Field believed that the growing importance of his profession was inevitable. The reasons were self-evident: "The more numerous and complex the relations of men, the more numerous and complex become the laws, and the more numerous and powerful the profession of the law."[61]

Field approached the law with clear-eyed pragmatism. He wrote that lawyers were distrusted by some while "there are others, who conceive the law is perfect."[62] He saw the need for improvement. One complaint against lawyers was "a vicious system of procedure."[63]

Jurisdictions that sprang out of the English tradition of law had made significant changes. New York State was one. The changes were, to Field, "clumsily devised" and had resulted in an "artificial, complex, technical system . . . now grown obsolete, and so burdensome, as no longer to command the respect or answer the wants of society."[64] If New York State's legal system was "inadequate, uncouth, and distasteful," Field argued that "the remedy . . . is as simple as the evil itself is discernible; and that is, to strike out all the jargon, and substitute a plain and rational system of procedure."[65]

Other lawyers suspected that a plain and rational system would lessen demand for their services. Field recognized this, answering simply, "[T]he occupations of those who remained would be more worthy of the liberal profession they belong to, and would escape the censure which they now receive."[66]

Abraham Lincoln was an attorney of Field's time who rarely experienced censure. As a self-taught prairie lawyer in Illinois he typified the antebellum generalist practitioner. Debt collection figured heavily in his early work, along with land conveyance. At times, he accepted appointment as guardian ad litem in estate settlements. In the 1840s he argued a handful of cases testing various aspects of slavery law. The last of these, *In the Matter of Jane, a Woman of Color*, has long baffled and unsettled scholars because Lincoln represented a slaveholder, suggesting he accepted the role of "hired gun" in defense of a morally repugnant cause.[67] He may have been attracted to the high profile of the case, or felt a professional obligation to provide representation regardless of his personal views. In his personal life Lincoln did argue that slavery was morally wrong. As a Whig Unionist, however, he strongly believed in the authority of the Constitution, which, in the late 1840s, protected the practice of slavery and the return of fugitive slaves.[68]

Lincoln rode circuit like most lawyers in his region. One of his regular circuits covered more than ten thousand square miles across fourteen counties. In autumn and spring he traveled for nine or ten weeks, doubling up at night with other lawyers in cheap hotels. He took criminal cases and won a reputation for effectiveness with juries, but civil law generally filled his caseload. Circuit-riding treks provided no glamour, but after ten years of practice, Lincoln was earning more than two thousand dollars annually (about fifty thousand dollars in 2011), often from five- and ten-dollar cases. A decade later, in the mid-1850s, when he was respected, well known, and often acted as counsel for the Illinois Central railroad, the figure had increased to five thousand a year.[69]

Lincoln shines as the quintessential midwestern self-made man. Other lawyers tried their luck in the West. Hundreds of attorneys crossed the continent, and in the 1850s more than six hundred were admitted to practice in California. By 1870 the state had eleven hundred registered attorneys, far more than were needed.[70] Like their eastern and midwestern brethren, these practitioners negotiated settlement of debt and dealt with crime. The California legislature made bankruptcy easy, and the state earned a reputation as a safe place for debtors. The lawyers were happy for the practice. California attorneys also "transferred property at a feverish pace amid the urban turmoil of the instant cities."[71] Title questions challenged possession everywhere in the new state, with tenure complicated by the presence of squatters. Land titles were fought over every day with lawyers called in to resolve ownership through litigation and the land-claims commission. Practitioners were also called upon to handle personal injury cases arising out of mine accidents, but tort litigation only "exploded in volume and value" with the coming of the railroads.[72]

These western lawyers, like Lincoln in Illinois, traveled on circuit with the district judge. Lincoln and his midwestern colleagues worked within a formal criminal justice system. In California, however, after its admission to the Union as a state in 1850, the bar faced the challenge of replacing frontier justice with institutionalized law, courts, and punishments. They succeeded, bringing "order to law and structure to the legal system in the frenzied instant cities and scrambling mining camps."[73] Streets became safe and criminal proceedings acquired regularity, with the criminally accused having "due process in the courts rather than in popular tribunals," a successful contest between the bar and the people not unlike those carried out in Dodge City and other frontier communities.[74]

For their efforts, early members of the California bar—who tended to be sole practitioners—often received payment in land deeds and gold dust. They also received complaints that the charge of five dollars for twenty or thirty minutes of advice was excessive. Clients whose counsel had pursued losing strategies "submitted" that the recalculation of fees was in order. Presiding judges set the fees in certain litigation, and after 1874 attorneys' fees in mortgage instruments and contracts were fixed by the court.[75] With the exception of a few members of the elite western bar, the prospects for a lucrative practice were rare.

Low fees, contested fees, and economically difficult times often pushed attorneys in California, as elsewhere, to combine the practice of law with other money-making activities. They farmed, ranched, took up journalism, or went into banking and other mercantile occupations. In all corners of the state, but particularly in rural areas, lawyers saw the economic and client-attracting benefits of holding public office. Many served in the legislature, others on the bench or in administrative government positions. One enterprising, perhaps hungry, newcomer in a rural county set up shop in his hotel room and advertised his availability to give "lessons in bookkeeping, penmanship and German," as well advice on the law.[76]

* * *

Historian Rebecca Edwards has written that the Confederate surrender ending the Civil War "did not so much restore the old nation as create a new one, reshaped by not only the war but by economic and political changes that had begun earlier."[77] Years before Jefferson lamented a nation overrun by business and banking. By the end of the Civil War, the small agrarian communities that he so admired had given way to teeming cities, clattering factories, new forms of business financing, and boom-and-bust economic cycles. Law practices built on debt collection and land conveyance adjusted to the new economic age and joined in tackling the complex issues spawned by the frenzied growth of industrial capitalism. Generalists remained, but increasingly men began to see the need, excitement, and profit of specialization. Well before the war William H. Seward, New York governor and later U.S. secretary of state, became an expert in patent law, transforming a small country litigation practice into one of national importance.[78] Railroads, corporate finance, veterans' pensions, and the growth of government regulation expanded and reshaped legal practices. Before the war, Seward's New York firm worked on the financing of railroad consolidation. In the decades after the war few lawyers passed up an opportunity to be general counsel of a railroad. The position marked them as esteemed, as did appointment to railroad and corporate boards.[79]

For some lawyers this transformation brought splendid opportunities, large fees, or, among some railroad and corporate lawyers, attractive fixed salaries. Yet, despite the rise of specialization and the growth of large law firms, throughout the nineteenth century law remained a tiered profession with room for single attorneys and small firms. As in earlier years, however, in the last quarter of the century, not everyone did well practicing law. In the 1880s, of fifteen hundred Philadelphia lawyers "less than one third were said to be self-supporting and not more than 100 were thought to have an income over $5000 a year."[80] Still, ambitious, optimistic young men were not deterred. The number of law school programs increased, and the ranks of the profession swelled.

Women sought to join the profession of law for many, but not all, of the reasons that men had come to the legal bar. Like men, most women needed a source of livelihood. Some applicants were teachers but saw legal work as more interesting, with greater promise of good money and advancement. Several of the earliest women lawyers were attracted by the intellectual challenge of reading law. Others saw the possibility of using law to further reform movement objectives. A small number of optimistic women hoped to establish themselves in elective politics, or as a member of the judiciary. Nearly all of the earliest women lawyers in the United States believed that the nation's ideals of equality, liberty, and justice entitled them to the opportunity to prove that, like men, they could be good members of the legal profession. For all of these reasons, they asked to join with men in the practice of law.

❖ 3 ❖

Myra Bradwell

The Supreme Court Says No

Lex Vincit
  —Myra Bradwell, *Chicago Legal News*

IN 1894, WHEN IT MATTERED VERY LITTLE, the men of the Illinois State Bar Association showered praise on Myra Bradwell. A quarter of a century before she had sought their professional favor and many of them had withheld it. Now she lay on her deathbed receiving tender expressions of respect.

Attitudes had loosened and tempers cooled since 1869 when the Chicago businesswoman, wife of Judge James Bradwell, sought to be licensed as an Illinois attorney. Born in Manchester, Vermont, in 1831, Myra Colby had a New England pedigree and, from the age of twelve, under the watchful eye of four older siblings and activist abolitionist parents, an Illinois upbringing. She attended various schools until the age of twenty, taught briefly, and in 1852 eloped with Bradwell, who, scraping by as a manual laborer while working at a legal apprenticeship, was not viewed by the Colby family as a promising prospect.[1] For a short time the couple ran a school in Memphis, Tennessee, and James continued to read law. Two years after their marriage the Bradwells moved, with their first child, to Chicago. In 1855 James was admitted to the Illinois bar.

In the mid-1850s the people of Chicago were busy, with the help of the railroads, building their young city into an important metropolis.

Myra Bradwell (1831-1894).
(Reprinted from *A Woman of the
Century*, ed. Frances E. Willard
and Mary A. Livermore [Buffalo,
NY: C. W. Moulton, 1893].)

Transplanted New Englander Mary Livermore, later a friend of Myra
Bradwell's, described Chicago at that time as a "somewhat astonish-
ing [place] in which mud, dust, dirt, and smoke seem to predomi-
nate." Only Michigan Avenue was paved and had decent sidewalks.[2]
The impact of the railroads, however, transformed Chicago from a
muddy, rough place whose people thought of themselves as part of
the West into a vibrant urban crossroads soon known, humorously
to some, as "Hog Butcher for the World." A five-thousand-mile network of tracks, reaching in all directions brought business, industry,
and ambitious newcomers like the Bradwells. Myra and James were
anxious to tap into the economic and social possibilities of a town
free from the confining mores and practices of America's older cities.

    James Bradwell initially formed a law partnership with Frank Colby,
his brother-in-law. In the years before the Civil War, despite the birth

of two more children, Myra helped James in the office and made the decision to read law with him. She did not wish to become "an independent practitioner."[3] Rather, Myra said, it was the separation of interests and work that drew couples apart.[4] She wanted to remain close to James and argued that divorce courts would not be needed if couples labored side by side, with wives jointly supporting the family. James, always proud of Myra, felt the same way.

Bradwell's professional aspirations made her the target of gossip, but it took a war to alter her path. At the start of the Civil War Myra stopped reading law, became pregnant with her fourth child, and joined other women in war relief work. She presided over the Chicago's Soldiers' Aid Society, an organization that raised money for Union soldiers and their families.

Bradwell also volunteered to help Mary Livermore and Livermore's friend Jane Hoge when they proposed that the women of Chicago could organize and run a giant two-week-long fair that would benefit the wartime medical care provided by the Union's Sanitary Commission. In Chicago and the nation's capital, the women met disbelief that their "fair sex" would be capable of carrying out so grand and complicated an enterprise. Livermore reported that the men of the commission "laughed incredulously at our proposition to raise twenty-five thousand dollars."[5]

In fact, at the end of the 1863 Northwestern Fair's two-week-run, net receipts reached eighty thousand dollars.[6] The women had commandeered buildings all over Chicago. They ran a wildly popular art gallery, sold donated goods from all over the United States that included rare fabrics, laces, mowing machines, reapers, ploughs, food, and much more. The most noteworthy item was the original manuscript of Abraham Lincoln's "Proclamation of Emancipation," which the president gave as a token of his goodwill. It sold at auction for three thousand dollars.[7]

As her contribution, Myra Bradwell persuaded her husband to turn over the use of the supervisor's hall in the courthouse. James Bradwell, now a judge, adjourned his court for two weeks in order that his wife might transform the hall into the fair's "Curiosity Shop."

In this museum-like space Bradwell laid out shackles and neck irons used on slaves, mounted the battle-torn flags of Illinois regiments, the Union flags unfurled at Vicksburg and Bull Run, and captured rebel weapons and flags—"trophies of victory."[8]

The demands of war gave Bradwell, like other women, the opportunity to show her talents in public and to be in the company of working women, many of whom who were puzzling through questions of woman's proper role and rights. Some of these women were quite political. This included the young Anna Dickinson, a spokeswoman for the Republican Party and an influence on Bradwell, who came to Chicago under sponsorship of the fair and mesmerized audiences talking about the imperative of a Union victory.

Bradwell did not write about how the war affected her political thinking, but her friend Mary Livermore did. In the late 1850s Livermore's husband had become the owner of a small Chicago publishing house as well as *The New Covenant*, the Universalist newspaper of the Northwest. The energetic Livermore, mother of several children, including an invalid daughter, took on partial management of the paper and became associate editor. She was in charge of several departments and was active as a reporter, which brought her the distinction of being the only newspaperwoman to cover the 1860 Republican Party convention that nominated Lincoln for the presidency.

Livermore wrote that before the war she "kept the columns of . . . the paper ablaze with demands for the opening to women of colleges and professional schools [and] for the repeal of unjust laws that blocked [women's] progress."[9] She had publicly argued that women could achieve these goals without suffrage. The war, however, opened her eyes. During business transactions she personally felt the sting of Illinois' married women's property laws, by which the state kept her from entering into contracts. She also found foolish excluding half the population from important responsibilities. "I became aware," she said, "that a large portion of the nation's work was badly done, or not done at all, because woman was not recognized as a factor in the political world."[10] She had come to appreciate the degradation of disfranchisement and women's subsequent inability to act on causes of reform because they could neither vote nor promulgate policy as legislators.

Livermore picked up the banner of suffrage, setting an example for Myra Bradwell and other Chicago women. She wrote pro-suffrage columns in *The New Covenant* and spoke out in Chicago's daily papers and in public lectures. She was well known and highly respected for her war relief work and drew large audiences, expressing views on suffrage, she said, that many men and women had held but not expressed.[11] At one lecture, it was suggested that she arrange Chicago's first suffrage convention. She subsequently filled the platform with prominent woman suffrage advocates from the East who sat alongside important local clergymen and public officials. Judge Bradwell was one of these local dignitaries. During the convention he was called to the podium, where he spoke in favor of women's right to vote and jousted with audience members who opposed such change.[12] In January 1869 Livermore took the additional step of establishing a woman suffrage paper, *The Agitator.*

Myra Bradwell had been a professionally ambitious woman before the war. With the Union victory in 1865 she was free to resume her law apprenticeship with James. However, the experience of her wartime philanthropic work and the company of women like Livermore, Hoge, and Dickinson had enlarged her world, her self-regard, and her opinion of women's civic and political due. Bradwell still intended to take the Illinois bar examination. The objective of sitting beside James as his office helpmate, however, had somehow dulled as she responded to the larger ideas and demands of the women's movement forming around her. It was now Myra's genius to shape a new plan, one in which she would use her training in law as well as management skills acquired during the war to build a national publishing empire specializing in legal materials. The enterprise, built around the *Chicago Legal News*, would make her wealthy while providing a place for the advocacy of women's rights.

Myra Bradwell was an entrepreneur, not an innovator. After the Revolutionary War and beginning early in the nineteenth century, various men in the American legal community had produced law digests and journals, including John Hall's well-known *American Law Journal*.[13] The number of law journals increased significantly by the mid-1840s and, critically, changed in focus. Earlier publications had printed speculative articles and essays of general interest to an educated community. These essays offered theorizing on the law as well as broad discussion of politics. In the two decades before the Civil War, hoping to improve the profession's negative, and often politicized, image, publishers discarded the old format, now giving over the bulk of every issue "to the bare reporting of recent court decisions, in advance of their appearance in official volumes of reports, with heavy emphasis upon law-as-it-is rather than law-as-it-ought-to-be."[14] Not all of these papers survived. They were sometimes the efforts of men who had been scraping by as attorneys, lawyers in search of additional income. California's Bay Area was especially hard on owners of specialized legal newspapers, with one in mid-century lasting only fifteen days and two others failing to last one year.[15]

The October 3, 1868, issue of the *Chicago Legal News* (*CLN*) launched Bradwell's business. The masthead bore her name and title, "Myra Bradwell, Editor," along with the motto *"Lex Vincit"* (Law Conquers). Behind the scenes she was also the paper's owner and business manager. She had watched Mary Livermore work as an associate editor on Daniel Livermore's newspaper and now took professional independence one step further. She would be in charge and answerable only to herself. The money for the paper came from her savings, with some investment, also, from James.

The *News* was an immediate success, quickly building a solid subscription list. On the front page of her first issue Bradwell wrote that it was her objective to do everything "to make it a paper that every lawyer and business man in the Northwest ought to take."[16] *CLN* published news of the Chicago and Illinois legal communities along with summaries of important judicial decisions.

The *Chicago Legal News* did not ignore the social and political world of post-war America. Bradwell shaped the *News* into an important trade publication that also ran articles on controversial issues such as corruption in the court system. She poked and prodded yet never reached beyond intelligent moderation. She was a savvy businesswoman who did not miss opportunities to expand her enterprise. She, therefore, invited only modest risk in the service of reform, thereby keeping this, and later, publications in the mainstream.

As a first act of operating her business Bradwell successfully petitioned the Illinois legislature for a special charter that permitted her to sign contracts in her name and retain her earnings rather than turning them over to James as required by married women's property laws.[17] This action gave her a necessary but unique legal status.

The married women's property laws had long attracted the wrath of the women's movement. Bradwell, like Mary Livermore, wanted to see Illinois laws changed to put women on an equal footing with men, using legislation to mandate the full benefits of the law for women as well as equal obligations. Four weeks after publishing the first issue of the *CLN*, Bradwell used her position as editor to champion reform that would help all of the state's women. She urged changes to the 1861 married women's property law that would protect a woman's earnings as her sole and separate property. In the same editorial Bradwell recommended that mothers be assured of equal guardianship rights to their children.[18] She used her pen repeatedly to attack irresponsible husbands, but tempered the discussion by also printing letters asking for reforms that would protect a husband's liability for his wife's debt as well as the defense of honest creditors.[19]

These editorials won her support in the women's rights community and among liberal male reformers. She also criticized conditions at the county poor house, and at the courthouse. Bradwell was always careful, however, to limit the number of social-commentary articles and to focus on the trade side of information.[20] She used her knowledge of Illinois' courts and legislature, along with the professional comments of James and his colleagues, to fashion services that would make the paper indispensable. For example, like many trade paper owners, Bradwell realized that the substantial lag in time between the enactment of laws and the state's official publication of these laws created an enormous problem for judges and attorneys. To be knowledgeable about newly enacted statutes, law professionals had to journey to the capital at Springfield to read that session's work.

Confident that she could do better, Bradwell arranged with Illinois officials to receive copies of newly enacted legislation immediately after adjournment. In something of a marketing coup, in March 1869 she also received a special charter from the legislature that recognized the laws printed in the *CLN* to be valid as "evidence of the existence and contents of such laws before all courts in Illinois."[21] For more than two decades Bradwell traveled at the end of each legislative session to the office of the state's secretary of state in Springfield to make certain that her galley proofs reprinting these statutes contained no errors.[22] Intent upon marketing the *News* nationally, Bradwell also entered into agreements to receive and reprint federal court opinions, including those of the Supreme Court of the United States.

Within a decade of its founding Bradwell could write that the *Chicago Legal News* had become the most widely circulated legal newspaper in the country.[23] In addition to Illinois and federal court opinions, the paper printed court notices, including chancery and land titles, commentary on recent cases, and ads for attorney services and legal books. In time the high court decisions from nearby states were also picked up and reported. Bradwell, never sentimental when it came to business, even capitalized on the community's losses in the great Chicago fire of October 1871. Realizing that the law libraries of several hundred attorneys had been destroyed, she reeled in advertisements from law book publishers and printed them in the *CLN*. Again working her lobby skills on the state legislature, Bradwell also won the right of her paper to be the official site for the publication of all court records, including land title notices, destroyed in the fire but subsequently recreated. Attorneys and property owners would have to subscribe to the *CLN* in order to learn if any title proceedings had been carried out under the "Burnt Records Act."[24]

Bradwell stepped into the legal publishing business at a particularly felicitous time. She grasped how the changes underway in post–Civil War America would impact the legal community and, therefore, the significance of the business she was building. Government was expanding, laws were passing at record rates, and law offices were growing in number. Bradwell appreciated how these changes were essential to the growth of the *News*, but she quickly saw other profitable opportunities that could expand her publishing empire.

Having invested Bradwell family capital in a printing plant, presses, and binding equipment, Myra made the decision to use the machinery's "down" time to branch out. She began by producing bound pamphlets of recent Illinois statutes. Efficient and accurate, the business attracted the attention of officials and lawyers in other states. From them came pleas "imploring" Bradwell to publish the statutes and judicial decisions of their states.[25] The publication of law books followed, then legal forms—leases, wills, and bankruptcy petitions, and, finally, lawyers' briefs. The company thrived and Bradwell enjoyed considerable wealth, including an impressive home on the shores of Lake Michigan. Where Lydia Pickham, her contemporary, built an empire marketing a "Vegetable Compound" for "woman problems," and later, Madame C. J. Walker fashioned a national corporation out of the sales of women's beauty products, Bradwell had followed her business instincts to create a nationally respected conglomerate in the male world of government and lawyers.

Although the *Chicago Legal News* has been called Myra's "alter ego," she did initially shelter readers from some, albeit not all, of her political views.[26] By 1870, however, the dramatic events of her personal confrontation with state and federal courts as she sought to become a licensed attorney, as well as the success of the paper, made this both impossible and unnecessary.

Myra Bradwell belonged to a small cohort of smart, plucky women who, at the end of the Civil War, sought training to become America's first women lawyers. Their motives for seeking a legal education varied. Some of these women wanted and needed to make a living. Others, buoyed by the women's movement, wished to make the case for women's equal talents and opportunities. Yet others were reform activists who recognized that an understanding of legal codes, legislatures, and judicial opinions would facilitate their work. Easterner Mary A. Greene enrolled in the law program at Boston University in 1886 after realizing that she was "woefully ignorant of the very first principles of our Common law" and therefore at risk in future legal and business dealings.[27]

In 1869 Lemma Barkaloo and Phoebe Couzins were admitted to the law department at Washington University in St. Louis. They were among the very first women to enroll in an American law program. A Brooklyn, New York, native, Barkaloo had been denied admission to Columbia University's law school. Her application caused influential Columbia trustee George Templeton Strong to write in his diary, "No woman shall degrade herself by practicing law . . . if I can save her."[28] Paralleling Barkaloo's and Couzins's success in winning law school admission in St. Louis, it is likely that African American teacher and journalist Mary Ann Shadd Cary enrolled in 1869 at Howard Law School in Washington, D.C., making her, also, one the country's very first women law school students.[29] In 1868 Ada Kepley entered the

MISS PHEBE COUZINS ADDRESSING THE NATIONAL DEMOCRATIC CONVENTION OF 1876, AT ST. LOUIS.

Vol. X., No. 2—10.

Phoebe Couzins was one of the very first women lawyers in the United States. She rose to prominence, however, as a woman suffrage and anti-Prohibition lecturer, and seldom practiced law. (Collection of Jill Norgren.)

law program at Union College (later Northwestern University). She graduated in 1870 (law programs were often only two years long in the nineteenth century), becoming the first woman in the United States to receive a law degree. In that year, in Ann Arbor, the University of Michigan opened its law school for the first time to women. Sarah Killgore, who had been in law school in Illinois with Kepley, took advantage of this reform to transfer to the University of Michigan. She graduated in March 1871, at about the same time as Couzins received her degree from Washington University. Schools opened to women for many reasons: an influential trustee or faculty member, the need for funds, lawsuits, or a sense of fairness.

Other women in this pioneering group, however, emulated Myra Bradwell by reading law in a professional's office rather than attending law school. Alta Hulett was an intellectually precocious teenage teacher in Rockford, Illinois, when William Lathrop, a prominent lawyer, opened his office to her. She passed the state bar examination at the age of seventeen and was admitted to the bar in 1872. Arabella (Belle) Babb Mansfield also chose this route.[30]

After graduating from Iowa Wesleyan College, in the autumn of 1867 Mansfield joined her brother in Mount Pleasant (Iowa) at the firm of H. & R. Ambler, where they both read law. Belle had studied under Henry Ambler in college, where she had taken the valedictorian's prize. Ambler, and later her brother, mentored Belle. They supported her ambition to become an attorney, as did Belle's husband, John, after their June 1868 marriage. Mount Pleasant, a town so saturated in women's rights lectures that the *Des Moines Register* called it an "orator-mill," could not do enough to accommodate Mansfield's professional ambitions.[31] In June 1869 attorneys George B. Corkhill and Edwin A. VanCise examined Belle for bar membership, pleased to be part of a history-making event. They were Radical Republican legal activists interested in using law to improve the rights of women and African Americans. They reported results that were "most eminently satisfactory" and recommended her for a license, commenting that Mrs. Mansfield "has given the very best rebuke possible to the imputation that ladies cannot qualify themselves for the practice of law."[32]

District court judge Francis Springer, a women's rights supporter, liberally interpreted a provision of the Iowa code restricting the practice of law to qualified "white males" and admitted Mansfield to the bar. Springer drew upon a general construction statute to hold (in an unwritten opinion) that "the affirmative declaration that male persons may be admitted is not an applied denial to the rights of females."[33] His legal theory was widely reported in Iowa as well as in eastern, and suffrage, newspapers, encouraging women law graduates for whom bar admission was not to be so easily obtained.[34]

In this early group, not everyone practiced law. Kepley, without being a member of the bar, assisted for several years in her husband's law office but by the 1880s was spending most of her time on temperance and suffrage reform. Phoebe Couzins, an early member of Stanton and Anthony's National Woman Suffrage Association, immediately after graduating took to the lecture circuit, where she earned a national reputation speaking about woman suffrage and temperance. She never practiced law; inexplicably, neither did Belle Mansfield, who also became deeply involved in suffrage activities.[35] Once married, Sarah Kilgore Wertman did back-office real estate law until her children were born. She returned to practice when they reached their teens. Lemma Barkaloo was admitted to the Missouri bar in March 1870 (without graduating from law school), tried one case late that spring, and tragically succumbed to typhoid fever. Alta Hulett, like Barkaloo, followed a career in law. Myra Bradwell noted her rapid success in the *Chicago Legal News*, courtroom victories that included using the Married Women's Property Act to protect women's property. In 1877, Bradwell sadly announced Hulett's death at the age of twenty-three.[36]

The saga of Bradwell's own effort to become a member of the Illinois bar began auspiciously on August 2, 1869, when, at the age of thirty-eight, she passed the required examination with high honors. The Bradwell children were eleven and thirteen, and James was returning to his private law practice. Myra offered no comment on her application to be licensed, nor did she need to. Seeking bar admission was a logical petition for a person who had read law for many years, achieved a high pass on her examination, lobbied for various legal reforms, and published a legal newspaper.[37] For Bradwell, bar admission would be a personal and political victory, reinforcing women in their professional ambitions and quest for rights.

Bradwell quickly discovered that for every Francis Springer anxious to help women with their professional aspirations dozens of others, like George Templeton Strong, stood ready to stop them. Of course Manfield's personal success in Iowa had heartened Bradwell, but she was sufficiently wary of what she might face in Illinois that her application for a license to the state supreme court included a brief normally not required of applicants, an argument in support of her right to bar admission.

Bradwell's intuition was correct. The application failed, with the members of the Illinois Supreme Court invoking the common-law doctrine of coverture (by which upon marriage a woman's legal rights were folded into those of her husband) to justify the denial. Bradwell immediately printed the court's opinion, sent to her as a letter, in her newspaper. The judges had written that Bradwell could not carry out proper attorney-client business because of the disabilities imposed upon her as a married woman (they wrote this despite the special charter that Bradwell had obtained earlier from the legislature permitting her to sign contracts in her own name). They held themselves powerless to grant her a license but suggested that a change in the state's statutory law could trump the problematic common law. Bradwell told her readers that the court was relying upon outdated legal principles that had been invalidated by state legislation enacted in 1861 and 1869.[38]

Undeterred, Bradwell filed an appeal with the Illinois court, including a brief and an affidavit that would establish grounds for an appeal to the U.S. Supreme Court should that become necessary. She argued generally that social conditions had changed and that the law needed to respond to changes in education and employment. More specifically, she claimed that the denial of her application on the basis of her status as a married woman violated citizenship rights established by the Fourteenth Amendment as well as the 1866 U.S. Civil Rights Act. She also argued that the Illinois court had violated the privileges and immunities of her state citizenship (as a former citizen of Vermont) under the fourth article of the U.S. Constitution. The "right to follow a professional pursuit under the law" was, she wrote, one of these "protected privileges."[39]

On February 5, 1870, state chief justice Charles B. Lawrence denied Bradwell's appeal. Reduced to its essence, the court's opinion held that the Illinois legislature had not mandated that women were eligible for bar status because women were not equal with men, and were designed by God for domestic responsibilities.

Bradwell's appeal challenged women's exclusion from the practice of law. Members of the court, however, along with Bradwell herself, understood that the fundamental, highly sensitive issue was the question of women's full and equal citizenship. The judges made this quite clear when they wrote that to grant Bradwell a law license would mean that "every civil office in this State may be filled with women . . . that women should be made governors, judges and sheriffs. This we are not yet prepared to hold."[40]

Bradwell viewed the decision as annihilating the political rights of Illinois women and said so in her *CLN* editorial of February 5, 1870.[41] Citizenship and political rights were very much on Bradwell's mind. On February 3, two days before the Illinois court's second ruling against her, the nation learned that the ratification of the Fifteenth Amendment to the U.S. Constitution had been completed. Explicitly enfranchising only African American men, the amendment assailed the sense of justice of many women who had hoped this final post-Reconstruction change in constitutional law would grant universal suffrage. Rights leader Elizabeth Cady Stanton had long insisted that ratification of the amendment without universal suffrage would establish an "aristocracy of sex."[42] Refusing to leave the determination of women's voting rights to the states, she and other activists, including Isabella Hooker of the famous Beecher family, had already begun speaking of the need for a sixteenth—woman suffrage—amendment, a strategy that antagonized an important part of the women's movement that had accepted a state-by-state approach to winning rights.

Bradwell made the decision to appeal to the United States Supreme Court in this contentious political climate. On its face, *Bradwell v. Illinois* challenged the authority of a state to deny a woman what Bradwell claimed was her Fourteenth Amendment citizen's privilege to pursue a legal career.[43] The failure of the women's movement to win the explicit inclusion of women's rights in the Fourteenth and Fifteenth Amendments also led Bradwell to hope that her case might result in a sweeping judicial decision supporting women's status as full citizens, with all of the rights and privileges of that status. She believed this status had been established *implicitly* under the Fourteen Amendment and the 1866 Civil Rights Act.

Bradwell was one of several activists gamely making this argument and devising strategy to make it a reality. Suffrage advocates Virginia and Francis Minor originated the theory in 1869. They argued that women were citizens of the United States, and of the state of their residence, by virtue of the opening words of the Fourteenth Amendment: "All persons born or naturalized in the United States . . . are citizens of the United States and of the State wherein they reside."

Soon-to-be presidential candidate Victoria Woodhull brought this idea to the public in a November 19, 1870 article in her newspaper, *Woodhull & Claflin's Weekly,* followed by a well-publicized January 1871 appearance before the combined judiciary committees of the U.S. House of Representatives and Senate.[44] Elizabeth Cady Stanton declared that the Minor/Woodhull argument amounted to a "new departure," radically changing the "manner of agitation."[45] The supporters of the "New Departure," appreciating congressional disinterest in taking up the question of a sixteenth amendment, called for a strategy of federal enabling legislation in support of Minor's theory and Supreme Court decisions built on Minor's reasoning. Bradwell's appeal was to be one of those high court cases.

Woman suffrage advocate Matthew Carpenter, U.S. senator from Wisconsin, agreed to take Myra's appeal—without fees or costs. He was politically prominent, an expert on the U.S. Constitution, and well thought of as a courtroom advocate. He was also a pragmatist who, hoping for a favorable decision from the high court, re-fashioned the foundational claims of the case to distinguish the right to practice law (a civil right) from the right to suffrage (a political right). He argued that the denial of membership in the state bar solely on the grounds of sex was a violation of the privileges of citizenship guaranteed as a federal right under the Fourteenth Amendment. In steering clear of any Fourteenth Amendment equal protection claim, he hoped to keep the justices' minds off the question of suffrage. When she found out what Carpenter had done, a furious Susan B. Anthony wrote Bradwell that his Supreme Court argument was "a school boy pettifogging speech—wholly without a basic principle."[46]

Carpenter was no schoolboy. Bradwell had approached him to handle her appeal because of his support for women's rights and his reputation as a smart constitutional lawyer. His professional prominence was considerable. While working her case, Carpenter was also handling a Fourteenth Amendment–based challenge, the *Slaughter-House Cases,* to the creation of state-government-chartered business monopolies. Carpenter argued *Bradwell* and the *Slaughter-House Cases* (on the side of the chartered slaughter-house company) two weeks apart in the winter of 1873.[47] On April 14 the high court handed Carpenter and his *Slaughter-House* clients a narrow five-to-four victory. A day later the court ruled in *Bradwell,* and Myra learned that her attorney's cautious approach had not served *her* cause. The justices had voted against her appeal, eight to one.

Both cases raised the question of the right to work as a federal right immune from state regulation or restriction. In *Slaughter-House* the majority ruled that the Fourteenth Amendment's privileges clause did not insulate the right to labor from a state's right to protect the health and safety of the public, that is, to exercise its police powers. Drawing upon its decision in *Slaughter-House,* and in a stunning defeat for women's rights, the next day the *Bradwell* majority upheld the action of the Illinois Supreme Court on the same grounds, stating that Myra had no federal citizen's right to practice law free from state regulation.

Writing for the majority, Justice Samuel F. Miller said that "the right to control and regulate the granting of license to practice law in the courts of a State is one of those powers which are not transferred [by the Fourteenth Amendment] for its protection to the Federal Government."[48] The decision signaled the Court's restrictive reading of the Fourteenth Amendment's privileges clause and meant that women would have to fight state by state to win the privilege of applying to the bar.

Miller's opinion contained no reference to the law of coverture or the social relations of the sexes. In contrast, Justice Joseph P. Bradley wrote a concurring opinion in which he distinguished his support for a man's right to work unfettered by unreasonable regulation (a "valuable" and "fundamental" right), his position in *Slaughter-House*, from that of a woman. In an opinion that would echo through judicial chambers for years, Bradley argued that women were not covered by his position in *Slaughter-House*. Drawing upon the common law of coverture, and social observation, Bradley wrote that the idea of a woman adopting a "distinct and independent career from that of her husband" was repugnant to the idea of the "harmony" of the institution of the family.[49] "Man is, or should be," he insisted, "woman's protector and defender. The natural and proper timidity and delicacy which belongs to the female sex evidently unfits it for many of the occupations of civil life."[50] While Miller's majority opinion was received soberly and in silence, lawyers in the courtroom laughed out loud as Justice Bradley read his theory of separate spheres.[51]

To some men Bradley was out of step with changes in post–Civil War America. Bradwell's and Ada Kepley's early efforts to join the bar already had received encouragement from the editors of various law periodicals, including the *American Law Review* and the *Albany Law Journal*.[52] Even in Bradwell's home state, pragmatic politics were resulting in new opportunities for women. While Myra's case was on appeal, she and James, Kepley and her husband, and the precocious Alta Hulett drafted a broadly worded bill, submitted to the Illinois legislature, to prohibit the use of sex to bar women from any occupation. The legislature responded to their lobbying, and the public's support, by passing an amended bill that allowed women the right to work in most fields, and to practice law, exempting entrance into the military, road construction, and service on juries.[53] Myra was a force behind the successful bill but, willful and principled about her own situation, refused to reapply for bar admission, maintaining that the Illinois Supreme Court had been mistaken in turning her down. She asked the court to admit her on the basis of her original application, which it would not do.[54] Prejudice—Bradwell called it "deep-rooted"—remained. After Hulett's 1873 admission to the Illinois bar one of the state court judges remarked that "if she were his daughter, he would disinherit her."[55] In the same year, however, the lawmakers conferred on Illinois women a limited right to run for public office, passing legislation permitting single and married women, twenty-one and older, to hold any office under the school laws of the state. The following November nine women were elected county superintendents of instruction. This mirrored reform in other parts of the country. In 1873 several women were elected to the Boston school board. Challenged on the grounds of their sex, they successfully lobbied the state legislature for a law permitting elected women to serve on school boards.[56]

Bradwell's growing success as a publisher kept her out of the orbit of these grumblings. She spent her time expanding the reach of her commercial empire while drafting and advocating reforms concerning the legal system, including jury packing and corruption, guardianship, treatment of the insane—prompted by her friendship with Mary Todd Lincoln, who had been hospitalized involuntarily in an asylum—suffrage, and married women's property rights.[57] She encouraged her daughter to study law, and stood by proudly in 1882 when Bessie graduated from Chicago's Union College of Law, having been chosen orator in a class of fifty-five. Bessie married lawyer Frank A. Helmer and joined him in his practice. She also helped in her mother's company, compiling at least ten volumes of Bradwell's Appellate Court Reports.[58]

Bradwell's harshest critics portrayed her as "a fanatic destroyer of domesticity."[59] This was, of course, the curse directed at virtually any middle-class married woman of the time who wanted a career. In Wisconsin, however, Lavinia Goodell, another ambitious woman, discovered that being single and free from the law of coverture by no means granted her easy admission to the profession of law.

❧ 4 ❧

Lavinia Goodell

"A Sweeping Revolution of Social Order"

If nature has built up barriers to keep Woman out of the legal profession, be assured she will stay out; but if nature has built no such barriers, in vain shall man build them, for they will certainly be overthrown.

—Lavinia Goodell, 1876

LAVINIA GOODELL, BORN IN 1839, learned about the power of law at an early age. Slavery and temperance were everyday topics of conversation at her parents' dinner table. By the age of nineteen Lavinia imagined law as a profession through which she could do good and not lose her moral bearings. From the same age, she also imagined herself happily, forever, unmarried.

Moral bearings were everything in the world of Rhoda Lavinia Goodell. The second surviving daughter of William and Clarissa Goodell, Lavinia, or Vinnie as she was called, began life in Utica, New York. The area was a stronghold of religious revival, and earnest social and moral reform. Earlier, while earning a living as a merchant trader, William found himself "tugged at" by the slavery question and "the Drink Demon."[1] He put commercial life behind him and began working for the cause of abolition, and for temperance.

By the year of Lavinia's birth, William had been writing and publishing reform newspapers for more than a decade. He was on his way to building a national reputation as an abolition and temperance activist.

Rhoda Lavinia Goodell
(1839-1880). (Reprinted
by permission from the
William Goodell Papers,
Historical Collections,
Berea College, Berea,
Kentucky.)

Along with her father, her more conservative and conventional mother, and a much-loved sister, Maria, twelve years her senior, Lavinia shared in a daily routine of prayer, dinnertime debate, and adherence to the vegetarian diet prescribed by wellness reformer Sylvester Graham. Maria said that the household lived by "regularity," yet on any given day guests might include well-known anti-slavery agitators as well as the "poor and defenseless . . . without distinction of color or sex."[2]

William and his colleagues set a high moral bar for the members of their community. Clarissa Goodell struggled, once telling a neighbor,

"[M]y selfishness is every day rebuked by his [William's] higher life."[3] Lavinia, a quick study from an early age, knew her own mind. She developed predictably strong feelings in support of the abolition of slavery, but by the time she was eight or nine, according to her sister, had adopted "entirely independent views from her family" with respect to organized religion and making public professions.[4] Later, she would not join a church just to help her business.

Maria married and moved away when Lavinia was eleven and the family had established a residence in Brooklyn, New York. The separation, one that lasted virtually all of Lavinia's life, encouraged the two to exchange letters containing everyday news as well as deeply felt meditations about how to live a decent and principled life. In March 1858, Lavinia sent Maria a letter full of pain and pleading, one seeking an ally for an audacious plan. Lavinia was nearly nineteen and ready to graduate from Brooklyn Heights Seminary.

> Dear Sister,
>
> You know I expect to graduate . . . and I must have some life plan. I don't believe in living to get married, if that comes along in the natural course of events—very well, but to make it virtually my end and aim, to square all my plans to it, and study and learn for no other purpose, does not suit my ideas. . . . This would be different if women would learn to depend more on themselves, instead of thinking it devolves on the other sex to support them. We want self-reliance. . . . I would not counsel neglect of such accomplishments as are necessary in a wife and mother, but they are not reliable capital to un-engaged, unlikely to be engaged girls, who want to be true to themselves.
>
> I think the study of law would be pleasant, but the practice attended with many embarrassments. Indeed I fear it would be utterly unpracticable [sic]. Our folks would not hear to my going to college. I should not mention it. Momma is being much afraid I shall become identified with the women's rights movement. . . . In all probability I must teach, that is about all a woman can do, and now the profession is over crowded with women.

I do hope that you can give me some suggestions. I have only you to advise me, as our folks think of me only as a child and don't think I need ever do any thing.

Your loving Sis,
Lavinia[5]

Maria, thirty-one, the wife of a minister and a mother, had listened to Lavinia's ruminations during a visit the previous summer. At that time she had dismissed her younger sister's ideas as ones "founded on a false and vain ambition."[6] Lavinia's letter did nothing to change Maria's mind or to win her as an ally. Despite Maria's stance, Lavinia maintained good spirits and shortly wrote again. She said that her first duty was to make a cheerful and pleasant home for their parents, and not to do anything to which they would object. The senior Goodells were unwilling to have Lavinia leave home to teach. Lavinia told Maria, "I have not the slightest desire to do anything out of the common cause."[7] Her sensibilities as a dutiful daughter intersected with her interest in the law, and she concluded, "I shall wait eight or ten years before deciding and see how matters stand."[8]

The wait, in fact, proved to be a dozen years, time in which Lavinia matured as a woman who was concerned about duty, but also personal growth. At twenty-two she told her trusted cousin, "You know we reached the conclusion last summer that the object of life is discipline, not happiness; viewing matters in that light we can not wonder that all our wishes are not gratified."[9] Her independent views about religion had not been resolved. In her late teens she had written Maria, "I hope I may be coming nearer that 'higher life,' but theory is so much easier than practice. I don't want to make any professions. I think God has given me a great deal more light on some things."[10] In her early twenties, despite working alongside her father at his newspaper, she was no closer to that higher life.

Lavinia stayed in New York during the Civil War. She liked the "stir and excitement of city life" and the mental challenges of journalism. When her father was ill, she sat in for him at his reform newspaper as editor-in-chief.[11] At the end of the war, her parents retired from the city. At the age of twenty-six, for the first time, Lavinia was alone and "beginning life for herself."[12]

She had written that teaching was the only calling for an educated woman, and when her father closed the newspaper, she hired herself out as an instructor. For two years, Lavinia tutored a dozen students in the home of a Brooklyn family. To Maria, the mother of four boys, she expressed very mixed feelings about this calling. When the children were good, Lavinia enjoyed her days, but when they fell into tantrums, she was reduced to despair.

The weight of teaching ill-behaved children and dealing with their parents sparked many conversations between the sisters. In the summer of 1866 Lavinia wrote, agreeing with Maria, who had commented that "the manner in which we have been raised has unfitted us for contact with the world"; Lavinia added, "[A]t the same time it has molded our characters, so that we are less liable to yield to temptation."[13] The moral rectitude expected of a Goodell daughter did not, however, seem entirely disagreeable. "The memory of what our parents have been through, of what they are," Lavinia asserted, means "I can not be sufficiently thankful for that rare house training which I have received even if it does make my subsequent life harder. It is a selfish world and sometimes I think there is no way to go through it but to be selfish too, but we will try, to be actuated by high motives."[14]

While teaching, Lavinia had written stories, and in 1868 she was taken on as an assistant in the editorial rooms of the new *Harper's Bazaar* fashion magazine. Children's tantrums were now a thing of her past. The work of recommending which stories to reprint from other publications required discrimination and judgment. She found the position congenial and so well-paying that she was able to visit her sister in Janesville, Wisconsin, while also making investments and sending money to her parents and Maria. At night Lavinia, the intellectual daughter who had not been permitted to attend college, began to study German. To sharpen her spoken Deutsch, she moved into a boarding house run by a German family. In letters from this period Lavinia admitted to Maria that she shocked people "by not keeping

Good Friday"; she also asked if her sister had been reading Tennyson and encouraged her to make time for Charlotte Brontë.[15]

Lavinia loved journalism and hoped that her position at *Harper's* would be permanent. Mr. Harper had "spoiled" her for any other boss, and she told Maria that if she should have to leave, "it would be to go into business for myself" but did not let slip what this work might be.[16]

The senior Goodells had been thinking about moving to Janesville—childhood home of temperance leader Frances Willard—to be near Maria. This unsettled Lavinia. She told her sister that if William and Clarissa left the East, she would think about resettling in Chicago or even Janesville. In 1870 the Goodells made the move to Janesville. A year later Lavinia, thirty-two, joined them, once more making her home with her parents. Maria thought that this was an entirely good arrangement. William was nearly eighty and Clarissa had health problems. She divulged that their parents now had "a competence, and were able to give [Lavinia] such a home without labor, as she had not enjoyed for many years; [a household that permitted] leisure to follow her literary tastes."[17]

Lavinia, however, had never lost interest in the idea of becoming a lawyer. Before she resettled in Janesville, small items had appeared in the press about the first women to make their way into legal sanctuaries. It is probable that Lavinia knew that Lemma Barkaloo had been denied admission to New York's Columbia Law School but had succeeded, along with Phoebe Couzins, Ada Kepley, and Sarah Killgore, in winning admission to midwestern university law programs. She might also have learned about the welcome given Belle Mansfield when she began to read law as an apprentice in Iowa. With Columbia, her home-town school, as off-bounds to Lavinia as it had been to Barkaloo, a move to Illinois or Wisconsin was not an unreasonable strategy despite her happiness as a Manhattan career woman.

When Lavinia finally settled in Janesville she spoke of the move as her good fortune, an act of "Special providence."[18] Maria still saw folly and vain ambition in her sister's desire to become an attorney, speaking about it as an "indulgence."[19] For practical reasons as well as the sake of propriety, Lavinia spent her first Wisconsin year making acquaintances, looking after her sometimes problematic health, and doing the necessary housekeeping. At the age of nineteen Lavinia had professed that she would be content never to marry. In early January 1872, now thirty-three years of age, Lavinia appears to have opened her mind to the possibility of marriage only to find herself in a community where there were few single men. She wrote to Maria, "[Y]ou need not worry about my getting married. I haven't gone far enough west yet."[20]

Maria, who later in life wrote her sister's biography, controls the story, and she casts Lavinia's choice to read law as a decision that could not, or would not, be made without the permission of relatives. Lavinia had, Maria writes, put off her studies while settling in but then "father and sister encouraged her, the former because of his conviction that she was 'cut out for a lawyer.' . . . The latter because Lavinia could not live without some high aim, and the study of the profession would occupy her mind, and make her happy."[21] Maria appears dyspeptic and condescending. Surely, Lavinia wanted the approval of her family, but many things about her move to Wisconsin suggest she had set an independent course of action in leaving New York, one that would permit her to read law. And that is what she began to do in January of 1872.

Lavinia went to Janesville, the county seat, hoping to find a culture of liberality. She encountered a community that, believing law to be men's work, nevertheless met her halfway in terms of her professional plan—that is to say, nobody shunned her, and a few members of the local legal fraternity even lent her their law books. She built upon her family's good name as reformers and temperance activists. The community knew her to be a decent and proper Christian woman.

Goodell's own temperance activism burnished her image, as did her willingness to make and receive conventional social calls, and to teach Sabbath school. The community's positive view of her was no small accomplishment at a time when another Wisconsin woman commented in the *Woman's Journal*, "I never before found myself settled in the midst of such a conservative society. To affirm one's faith in woman suffrage is about as much as one's social position is worth,

and for a woman actually to declare that she desires to go to the polls
and vote, produces an effect not unlike that which might be produced
should she express a desire to commit burglary or arson."[22]

* * *

By 1872 several dozen law school programs existed in the United
States, but none was near Janesville. Young Janesville men wishing to
learn the law apprenticed with local attorneys, but none of the town's
more than two dozen lawyers was willing to give Goodell a desk and
make her an apprentice in the traditional manner. However, A. A.
Jackson agreed to direct her reading, which she did at home five or
six hours a day.[23] Jackson, she said, was "one of the pillars of the Cong.
Church, and a good woman's rights man."[24]

In March 1872 Lavinia wrote to Maria that she had been studying
law for six weeks and liked it "ever so much."[25] She had already read
through *Warren's Law Studies* and two volumes of Blackstone. Opening her heart to Maria, she confided that if something would happen
in the family, her studies would have to be stopped temporarily, so

> I don't like to tell what great things I'm going to do, but wait and see
> whether I can do them. I think the information I shall acquire will always
> be of great use to me, even if I never should practice. If I succeed in get-
> ting creditably thro' my studies, tho', I think I shall try to get admitted to
> the Bar, if only for the precedent. (How would it look—Lavinia Goodell,
> Counselor at Law.)[26]

By the spring of 1873 Goodell reported reading "no books now but
law books."[27] Three volumes of Greenleaf's *Treatise on the Law of Evidence* took her several months, after which she moved on to real estate
subjects. Blackstone and Kent were always on her table. Even when
the Wisconsin weather turned harsh, Lavinia continued what had become regular visits to the local circuit court, where she scrutinized the
presentations of the attorneys and the rulings of Judge Herman Conger, a former New York State attorney and two-term congressman.[28]

Goodell was not put off by this world of men and spittoons and found, in the courtroom, that the sheriff was "delightfully polite" to her.[29] She wrote to Maria—now living in Michigan—that her recent observation of cases involving counterfeit money and burglary had been "interesting." Intrigued, but sensitive that Maria's concerns were those of family and housekeeping, she finished off, "[T]here has been a very amusing case about seventeen dead hogs, also some horse cases, but I presume a detailed account of them would not interest you."[30]

Goodell understood that tolerance was the best she might expect from the locals. She told her sister that it was "quite an innovation" for her to go into court as Janesville was a "small, conservative, gossipy town."[31] To make these visits, she drew on reserves of "moral courage," all the while thinking of the "primitive Christians, who had to fight with wild beasts in the amphitheatres, or live in the catacombs, or be beheaded, or burned alive."[32] Thus fortified, she managed her courthouse visits and appreciated that while the local people did not comprehend her ambitions, if she dressed well, attended an orthodox church, made cake and preserves, and developed "no other alarming eccentricity than a taste for legal studies" she would be fine and would not antagonize the gossips.[33] Indeed, she wrote to her cousin, Sarah Thomas, "nobody seems shocked" by her studies.[34]

Initially thankful not to be a pariah, Goodell nonetheless wanted intellectual companionship. She enjoyed her legal reading and the fact that she paid no tuition but, intellectually isolated (lonesome, she said), Lavinia desperately hoped for a community of people with whom she could talk over Blackstone, Kent, and the other jurists. She continued to hope for hands-on experience in an office, like a male student, cautiously sounding out Janesville's attorneys, hoping, without success, for an apprentice's desk. She wrote facetiously that these men had no "particular prejudice against strong minded women, but that the superior masculine mind, has a terror of being laughed at."[35] A practical woman, she was appalled that even when there were no male apprentices in town, the attorneys would not take her on although they needed help copying papers, and keeping their offices open when they were in court. Goodell was outright furious when she saw that these lawyers "would sooner hire shiftless, incompetent boys, that are continually bringing them to grief, than take my services gratis, when they know how steady I am, and anxious to learn."[36]

All of this gnawed at Goodell's pride, and challenged the idea of fair play instilled by her parents and their reform movement friends. Most of all, however, her failure to win an apprenticeship troubled her because she wanted to become the best possible lawyer, with the best possible training. When the members of one Janesville partnership took on a young gentleman scholar only a few months after telling Lavinia that they had no work for her, she was openly envious of the apprentice's good fortune, sitting in his nice little anteroom "with every advantage, getting an insight into practical law, through their cases learning more in a week than I could in a month of unaided study."[37] Strong-willed and cheerful, she sized up the rebuffs, called them "a good tonic," and predicted that adversity would stimulate even greater effort on her part.[38]

Goodell was not without hope, or allies. The two local attorneys who lent her law books occasionally, privately gave her bits of instruction and advice. They admired her intelligence but did not wish to be identified in public as supporters of women's rights. As they got to know Goodell better, the same men employed her every once in a while as a clerk when, in Goodell's words, "an indolent boy leaves."[39] Predictably, infuriatingly—they let her go as soon as "any kind of young boy" appeared.

By February of 1874 Lavinia felt that she would be ready in June to be examined for the bar. She related to Maria that, summoning much courage, she had "consulted a popular lawyer here, and told him definitely what I wanted to do, and that I wanted him to help me. Have never been so frank before but concluded to make the plunge, hit or miss."[40] Her candor won a pledge of aid from local attorney and civic leader Pliny Norcross, who, in June, would sponsor Goodell for the bar by filing her application.

The winter and spring of 1874 passed quietly with small pleasures, and a few vexations. Some mornings she cleaned house, then permitted herself, after lunch, to rest on a bed and read "Revised Statutes."

The discovery that the mother of a Sunday school student was a suffragist delighted her, while in the same weeks she chafed and complained about faint-hearted temperance supporters.

And then it was June, and time for battle. Goodell was ready to be
examined by a panel of local attorneys and Judge Harmon Conger but
was told that Conger and the lawyers were busy trying a case in justice
court, "and can not attend to it."[41] Days later she pushed Norcross to
submit her application but he "failed" her.[42] Norcross explained that
other lawyers, who knew the judge well, reported that Conger intended to refuse her admission, on account of her sex. He asked if she
would prefer to back out. "Steamed up" by this piece of news and in
a "martial state of mind," Goodell said that she would be admitted to
the bar of Wisconsin and that if Judge Conger "refused me, I would
make him very sorry for it before I had done with him."

Goodell first thought she would apply at once, despite what she had
been told, face Conger's judgment, and "then make a row about it."
Then she stopped to reflect and decided to proceed more cautiously.
Norcross agreed to interview Conger in private to find out what he
intended to do. For her part, Goodell agreed to hunt up precedents.
She wrote to suffrage leader Lucy Stone and several women lawyers in
different parts of the country intending to compile a list of judges who
had permitted women to be examined, as well as legislation explicitly
allowing qualified women to be admitted to the bar. She also tried to
find out if Milwaukee law student Lilly Peckham had applied to the
bar before her untimely death.

Several days passed with no call asking her come to the courthouse.
Norcross had learned that Judge Conger was nervous, uncertain
whether he was allowed to admit women. Finally, word came that the
judge would be examining "a couple of young men from Beloit within
a few weeks [and if she had] a mind to come in and be examined with
them [she] might!" Rolling out a bit of cheek, the would-be candidate
commented, "Very kind! I shall do so . . . study up . . . and come down
on him with what thunder I can command."

Goodell did not feel she could lower her defenses. Contemplating the possibility of rejection at the courthouse, she noted, "[I]f he

refuses me I shall try all the other courts in the State, and if I can not get admitted shall have a bill introduced into the next Legislature and make a fuss generally till I get in." Like other women in her position, Goodell did not fail to observe that making a fuss might be for the best, as it would "advertise me."

Happily, all of this proved to be unnecessary, and on June 18 Lavinia shot off an ecstatic letter, as she often did, to Sarah Thomas: "The middle aged, grey headed individual who now addresses you is an honorable member of the Wisconsin bar."[43] On the previous night, after the court had adjourned, she and a young man from Beloit, "also nervous and friendly," were summoned before the judge and several "old and able lawyers."[44] The judge, admitting that he initially doubted the legality of admitting a woman, told of having studied up on the question. He gave everyone in the room, including Goodell, a chance to express an opinion. Her letters and diary do not mention whether any of the attorneys, or Conger, knew about the Illinois law that had been lobbied by the Bradwells—and Alta Hulett's subsequent admission—or that nine months before, in Washington, D.C., Belva Lockwood had become a member of the local bar. Whatever Conger had learned "studying up" on the issue apparently helped him to overcome his reservations, and after rigorous questioning by three attorneys and Conger, Goodell and the nervous young man received favorable evaluations. They were sworn in as members of the Rock County (circuit court) bar, and signed their names on the roll of attorneys. Goodell was thirty-five years old. Without knowing the names of all of the other rebels, she had become one of the ten or so women in the United States admitted to a local or county bar. The *Rock County Recorder* and the *Milwaukee Sentinel* posted short, positive notices about the lady whom the *Recorder* predicted would "no doubt be a shining light among the legal profession. Success to her."[45]

Sixteen years had passed since Lavinia first told Maria of her desire to become an attorney. Once licensed, she did not miss a moment in establishing herself. Hours after being sworn in she rented professional rooms near Norcross's office and arranged for them to be painted and papered and for street signs to be made advertising her practice. She also had business cards printed. Weeks later Lavinia resolved to add "Miss" on these cards because correspondence directed to "Mr." had been coming to her office.[46] Like any male attorney new to the profession, she was reasonable about her finances. Decades before, the future Supreme Court chief justice Salmon P. Chase had been modest in hoping to earn eighty dollars after a year of practice.[47] Four decades later, Goodell wrote, "If I pay expenses the first year or two I shall be satisfied."[48]

At the end of June Goodell sent a happy but somewhat curious letter to Maria, a wife for more than twenty years: "I feel very much as if I had been married, receiving so many congratulations, and sending out cards. Don't see but it is just as good! I think I stand quite as good a chance of future happiness and prosperity."[49]

Goodell had good reason to be pleased. She reported that the majority of women in Janesville were "delighted and enthusiastic" with her pathbreaking accomplishment, although a few tried to "snub" her.[50] Some men saw her success as a joke, and one facetiously called her his "sister-in-law," but most local people accepted it "in a more rational light," and the sheriff took pleasure in calling her "squire." The Janesville press had favorable notices and Gerrit Smith, an old family friend and social reformer, sent her twenty dollars for the purchase of law books. Learning that she had done better in the exam than most candidates, Goodell could not help but cluck, "I think it is pretty good if my admission raises the standard of scholarship."

By July her office was ready—furniture in place and looking pleasant. Indeed, the space was so pleasing that after debating with herself, Goodell decided not to "furnish a spittoon for the use of future clients."[51] She had never seen a law office without one but decided "not to mar my pretty rooms with such an unsightly object."[52]

Thus, with the hissing "quite faint, and the applause loud and long," along with thoughts of Blackstone—who was said to have waited four years for his first case—Goodell sat back and watched for clients, writing that she would be "consoled" if she did not get a case at once.[53]

Goodell left no office logbooks. Her letters, however, suggest the slow shaping of a general law practice typical of a solo male practitioner without family or political connections, or a specific expertise. One week after her admission to the bar, she earned a dollar completing a title search. Debt collections followed. She prepared guardianship papers for a "country client," but he failed to come back to get them.[54]

In early August Goodell had her first taste of a significant case—or cases. Temperance women in nearby Fort Atkinson wanted action taken against two men for the illegal sale of liquor. The local prosecutor was a "liquor man," and so they approached Lavinia, hoping she would have the courage to take on the saloon keepers.[55] Goodell was pleased to accept the two cases. They promised good fees and the work was a perfect fit for the child of nationally acclaimed temperance activists, herself a strong advocate of the temperance pledge.

After making preliminary preparations in Janesville, Goodell boarded a train for the twenty-five mile journey to Fort Atkinson, rounded up her witnesses, and sailed through her arguments in the local justice court. She wrote Maria that it "was real fun. I knew just what to do and was not a bit frightened and do not think now I should be afraid to run any case through Court, having time enough before to prepare."[56] In her words, she "beat" in both cases, and was paid twenty dollars and train fare.

When the defendants—Goodell called them "the Dutchmen"—appealed the verdict, Lavinia's clients retained her to argue at the court in Jefferson, where she won the first case and lost the second. Goodell wrote that it was "exciting" and that the liquor men had tried to win by circulating false information that there was to be a postponement.[57] Goodell uncovered the ruse and wrote Maria with no little amount of pleasure that they were "taken back when they saw us women." The courthouse was full of men and Goodell admitted to being "considerably scared" but added charmingly, "not so much as Mr. R—— [opposing counsel][who] was so flustered and nervous and 'mad,' that it tickled me immensely."

Maria confided in her sister that she would find it "dreadful" to confront men in court on her own.[58] Lavinia shot back that she did not find it difficult to work in the company of men, and that so far "masculine lawyers have been a good deal more afraid of me, than I have of them," perhaps because they were "teased about being beaten by a woman."[59] She was referring to her success against her mentor, Pliny Norcross, in a case involving a shipment of rotted peanuts.[60] Norcross barely forgave Goodell for whopping him in front of his colleagues.

* * *

In 1875, a bright and ambitious Wisconsin lawyer appealing a client's case before the state supreme court could not avoid Edward G. Ryan, the new chief justice. Lavinia Goodell came before Ryan's court that year as the first woman lawyer in Wisconsin seeking admission to the high court's bar. The liquor suit she won in Jefferson had been appealed to Ryan's court along with an estate settlement case. Goodell was "quite delighted at the prospect" of appearing there, but first she needed to be admitted.

Edward Ryan immigrated to the United States from Ireland in 1830, a twenty-year-old with seven years of Jesuit education followed by a bit of legal reading, a man determined to become an American citizen and a member in the New York bar.[61] As a newcomer, Ryan taught, read law, and joined the Democratic Party. Five years later, he was a citizen and a member of the bar. He then moved west, first to Chicago, then Racine, Wisconsin, and, finally, Milwaukee. He practiced law, sought judicial appointments with mixed success, and impressed everyone who listened to him that he was smart, loved a platform for his ideas, and was in no way scared off by controversy.[62]

Ryan was interested in politics and first earned public notice at the 1846 Wisconsin constitutional convention. As a delegate, he espoused strong positions on many issues, including regulation of banks and opposition to the direct election of judges. He voted against a proposal that would grant women suffrage and another that would provide a state constitutional guarantee for married women's property rights. In Ryan's reading of the Bible (Mark: 10), neither was necessary because upon marriage "the two shall become one."[63] Husbands were obliged to protect wife and family.

Wisconsin Supreme Court chief justice Edward G. Ryan (1810-1880) opposed Lavinia Goodell's application to become a member of the state supreme court bar, arguing that admitting women would create a "sweeping revolution of social order." (Photograph WHi-24975 courtesy of the Wisconsin Historical Society.)

Traditional views about women's rights dominated most Americans' thinking in the 1840s and 1850s. The very fact that there was support for such reform, however, demonstrated to conservatives like Ryan that there was a chink in society's social armor. After seeing how proponents of women's rights—among them Mathilde Anneke, Amelia Bloomer, and Clarina Nichols—were winning converts on the local lecture circuit, Ryan decided to fight back by writing a talk of his own.

The lecture, "Mrs. Jellyby," thirty-one pages when later typed, took hours to deliver.[64] Ryan used a minor character from Dickens's *Bleak House*—a woman who neglects her family in order to engage in philanthropy and argue for women's rights—as a device to draw in the crowds and mock "strong-minded women" who, in his telling, endangered society by urging members of the fair sex to abandon their proper, pure, God-given role. Ryan did not present men as intellectually superior. Rather, he argued that each sex was endowed with unique abilities and roles. Reproduction, he insisted, "is the duty of all God's creatures."[65] Almost anticipating Lavinia Goodell and the inapplicability, in her case, of coverture, Ryan admitted that there were "old maids," but immediately restated that "marriage is the duty and natural condition of both sexes . . . and we are to reason with the sex and not with its exceptions."[66] A woman could "accomplish her social destiny" only by marrying because it is "the achievement of her sphere of action, her compact of duty with society, the seal of her life."[67] Delivering the *coup de grâce*, he pronounced that "every position of woman in Society, which essentially severs her from home, or gives her functions or interests conflicting with the duties of home, or lessens her peculiar adaptation to the refined charities of home, is a prostitution of her sex and a heresy to nature. . . . [and she an] apostasy to her sex."[68]

Governor William R. Taylor appointed Ryan to fill out the term of Chief Justice Luther Dixon on June 16, 1874, a day before Lavinia Goodell was admitted to the circuit court bar in Janesville.[69] Ryan's private law career had careened between singular successes—he appeared before the U.S. Supreme Court eleven times between 1865 and 1872—and periods when his office door seldom opened.[70] His unyielding views and hot-headed disposition affected business, and eventually caused his wife to leave him. He was said to have "colossal frailties" of temper; those who wished to be kinder described him as possessing a "petulant temper."[71] Still, Ryan's views on ethics and the need for honest government as well as his stance on banks, railroads, and credit got him through the vetting process and put him on the bench that would decide whether Goodell would be admitted to the

Wisconsin Supreme Court bar and, therefore, permitted to represent her Fort Atkinson clients at the appeal of their liquor case.

Although Goodell did not know it, she stood no chance of admission. Customarily, male attorneys who had been admitted to a circuit court bar were granted the privilege of admission to the high court bar without pause. But Goodell was not male, and that was really all Edward Ryan needed to know.

There was, in fact, little about Goodell or what she requested of the court that resonated with Ryan. He stood by the opinions expressed in his "Mrs. Jellyby" talk as much in 1875 as when he wrote the lecture in 1854. (He delivered it regularly until his appointment as chief justice.) As a leader of the state Democratic Party, he had strongly opposed temperance, dry candidates, and activists like the Goodells who supported both.[72] Ryan viewed Lavinia as an old maid, an apostate to her sex as described so maliciously in "Mrs. Jellyby."

Goodell made her petition for admission in the summer of 1875 without revealing to Maria, or anyone else, whether she expected trouble. She did not let on whether she knew about Ryan's conservative views, or whether he had ever given the "Jellyby" talk in Janesville. Instead, she continued with a busy year of practice, and lobbying on behalf of temperance laws.

By the request of women in Whitewater, twenty miles away, Goodell had prepared a petition to submit to the state legislature for a prohibitory law. In February she went to Chicago for a national temperance meeting where the question of political action and woman suffrage dominated many contentious discussions. After a full suffrage resolution was tabled, Goodell proposed that temperance women support woman suffrage because "women ought to vote on the liquor question."[73] Well-known activist Anna Dickinson backed her, and after more hot debate, Goodell's resolution was adopted by a vote of 108 to fourteen. Keeping the Goodell family tradition alive, she was often lecturing on temperance to various groups—in October touring the circuit for eight days.

Goodell busied herself with the preparation of wills, and smaller cases in justice and circuit court. In August she wrote Maria about a "vicious" husband case, a suit that "convinced me of the necessity of women jurors, for more reasons than one."[74] This may be a reference to the Leavenworth divorce case, argued before Judge Conger, who subsequently refused to grant the divorce, claiming that the treatment of the plaintiff, represented by Goodell, had not been "cruel and inhuman," according to his understanding of those words.[75] Goodell wrote to Sarah Thomas that the decision "surprised and outraged every unprejudiced person." In Goodell's view Conger's decision "in effect [says] that a husband may abuse and ill treat his wife all his life and then turn her adrift in her old age, penniless, when he is wealthy; and the Courts will sustain him in it. It is as atrocious as the Dred Scott decision."

Goodell had many female clients whose legal concerns involved divorce proceedings or probate matters, and occasionally, criminal charges such as shoplifting. While she did not consider herself a woman's lawyer, women who hoped to be lawyers were drawn to Goodell, and wrote for advice. She corresponded with a young Pennsylvania woman caught in a typical tug and pull of ambition. The would-be student told of her lawyer friends trying to dissuade her, getting up "all sorts of bugbears to frighten her off."[76] Goodell found it amusing. As time went on Lavinia became friends with Angie King and Kate Kane, each of whom studied law in Janesville, although not with Goodell, and became attorneys.

Two weeks before Christmas, with appeals work piling up, Goodell went to Madison to attend the December 14 hearing in Ryan's court concerning her admission. She hired I. C. Sloan, once Judge Conger's Janesville law partner, to represent her and to make the arguments that she had written out but was not permitted to stand and make. The points were simple and compelling. First, Sloan said, Wisconsin statutes, which used the word "person," not "men," did not state that women could not be lawyers. Next, he argued that courts were meant to be fair and just but would not be as long as women clients could not have women attorneys available to argue for them in court. Third, Sloan told the court that women were entitled to earn a good living as attorneys. And, finally, the attorney concluded by reminding the court that some states and territories had begun to allow women to practice law. Goodell liked what she heard, but Ryan clearly did not and now she knew it. Lavinia told Maria, "The Chief Justice is an old fogey and quite opposed to me. He bristled all up when he saw me, like a hen when she sees a hawk. . . . If they don't admit me . . . [I d]on't much care! It will advertise me splendidly and 'the blood of the martyrs is the seed of the church.'"[77]

Although her bar status had yet to be resolved, a legal event of another sort provoked a profound change in Goodell's life when Judge Conger appointed her to represent two criminal defendants in his court. She won the first man a reduced charge for stealing a watch, and brought in a verdict of innocent for the second defendant, also charged with theft. Goodell became "quite interested" in her second client, visiting him several times before his trial, and concluded that he was "smart, bright, intelligent and witty, with many excellent qualities."[78] He had, she wrote her sister, no parents or family, and so Goodell did not "think it so strange that he went astray." Bringing together the sympathies of a liberal, the skills of a teacher, the beliefs of a Christian, and the aspirations of a temperance activist, Goodell contended, "[H]e can be reclaimed."

From November 1875, until her premature death in March 1880, the men of the Janesville (Rock County) jail became Goodell's flock and surrogate family. In letter after letter, and in her diary, she poured out thoughts about these men—that she was proud to have the confidence of a criminal, that they could "yet" be useful men, that in helping them she was doing no more than Maria would want for her boys "if you should be taken away," that "jails are schools of vice and crime."[79] In a very short moment, she had turned mind and heart to the cause of prison reform while acknowledging, with honesty, that she appreciated the fees paid by the county (fifteen dollars for each day she worked on a case).[80]

On Christmas Day, 1875, Goodell ate oysters with her elderly parents, took care of some matters at her office, and then went to the jail with good books and magazines, beginning what would become a prison literacy program. Despite her relatively short exposure to the jailhouse men, Goodell already had a theory of penal reform. The "schools of vice and crime" could be righted, would be righted, when "women learn to assume their duties as citizens."[81] On New Year's Day, she wrote Maria that

> the element of motherhood is the one thing needful in the administration of our public affairs. . . . I believe I could run that jail so as to turn out every man better than he came in. Jails and prisons could just as well be made schools of virtue as vice if people chose to have it so, and would give a very little thought to the subject.[82]

She admitted to Sarah Thomas that the sheriff "had no faith in her efforts" and considered the visits a bit of a nuisance.[83] She also mused about becoming a chaplain in a state's prison: "I think that would be a good opening for women; they would do a sight better than men in such a place and have lots of influence over the criminals."[84]

Weeks later Goodell's optimism turned to fury when, on February 16, the Ryan court finally handed down its ruling on her petition to join the bar. The three judges not only voted against her right to be admitted but postponed their decision until it was too late in the term to submit a bill of remedy to the state legislature. Goodell had planned, should her petition be denied, immediately to ask the state assembly for a law allowing women to practice law, a strategy similar to Bradwell's and, in Washington, D.C., a tactic adopted by Belva Lockwood. Outmaneuvered, she would have to wait a year to approach the legislature.

Goodell saw summaries of the opinion in the newspapers before reading it in full. On the basis of these sketches she wrote, "I should judge that, that august body had descended to throw dirt in a way which the lowest thief and tramp would be ashamed. If I don't come out and give old Ryan a skinning over this, it will be because I can't and I think I can."[85] A week later, in a letter to Sarah Thomas, she called "Old Ryan's" opinion a "disgrace to the Bench—real Smutty."[86] During the week, however, Lavinia had reflected on her situation, and also told her cousin that she would not say anything to Ryan because "my Mrs. Burrington case" is before him and she did not wish him "to revenge himself on me by going against her."[87]

Lavinia tried to be optimistic, struggling to push aside hurt, and the loss of professional status: "Perhaps it will be the best thing that ever happened, as creating thought and discussion."[88] Still, Goodell was not naïve. At least in the near term, the denial meant that two cases she had in the supreme court would have to be "run" without her by male co-counsel. She also had the prospect of two or three cases in the next term of the circuit court, and two in justice court late in February, and admitted to not knowing what effect the decision would have on the future of her practice. "Time," she said, "would determine."[89] She would lose the fees from the supreme court appeals but hoped that the publicity would create a reaction in her favor.

Ryan authored the opinion of the unanimous court. His associate justices, Orsamus Cole and William Lyon, were happy to let him write for the court and agreed, at least in public, with his conclusions.[90]

Anticipating that Goodell would appeal to the legislature for redress, Ryan began by asserting the exclusive jurisdiction of courts to admit and expel individuals from the bar.[91] He further argued that women would lower professional standards, that the rules guiding bar admission among Wisconsin's circuit courts did not bind his court, nor did he find any statutory authority for the admission of females to the bar of any Wisconsin court.[92] Then the author of "Mrs. Jellyby," perhaps emboldened by Justice Bradley's concurring opinion in *Bradwell*, moved to the heart of his argument: Victorian mores by which he would save Lavinia Goodell from herself, and by extension, save society.

Ryan contended that licensing Lavinia Goodell would mean "a sweeping revolution of social order."[93] Nature had not, he argued, "tempered woman for juridical conflicts," and he believed that it would be "revolting" that

> woman should be permitted to mix professionally in all the nastiness of the world which finds its way into courts of justice; all the unclean issues, all the collateral questions of sodomy, incest, rape, seduction, fornication,

adultery, pregnancy, bastardy, illegitimacy, prostitution, lascivious cohabitation, abortion, infanticide, obscene publications, libel and slander of sex, impotence, divorce: all the nameless catalogue of indecencies . . . with which the profession has to deal, and which go toward filling judicial reports which must be read for accurate knowledge of the law. . . . [R]everence for all womanhood would suffer in the public spectacle of woman so instructed and so engaged.[94]

Ryan was thought by most lawyers to be a brilliant jurist who wrote thoughtful, well-researched opinions. *In the Matter of . . . Miss Lavinia Goodell* was an exception. Many of his arguments were not carefully researched, and his personal views influenced the screed that he wrote concerning the purity of woman. Goodell attacked its sources and reasoning as soon as a complete copy came into her hands. By the end of March, she had a lengthy brief in reply to submit to Wisconsin newspapers, Myra Bradwell's *Chicago Legal News*, and the American Woman Suffrage Association's publication, the *Woman's Journal*.

Goodell began by refuting Ryan's contention that the admission of women to the bar would "lower the standard of professional excellence."[95] Besotted and "imbruted" attorneys of meager mental qualification and scholarship were, Goodell argued, admitted to the bar and rarely dismissed. The bar needed mature citizens of high moral repute, and a full and fair competition: "If one-half the human race is shut out from competition, just so much mental and moral ability is excluded and the standard is necessarily lowered." Set the bar high, she suggested, let women "scale those heights," and if they can they have the right to be admitted.

Ryan was committed to the paramount power of courts in bar admission. Goodell destroyed his argument, showing that at the time of the adoption of Wisconsin's constitution, the establishment of the bar was a legislative function and that the current licensing powers of the judicial branch were enumerated and limited.

Goodell next rebutted Ryan's assertion that the common law had always excluded women from the bar, and that the statutes of

Wisconsin did not modify the common law on this question. She reminded readers that at common law,

> Woman has always been admitted to the bar, if she chose to plead there in
> her own behalf, as a party to the suit. Such being the common law, previ-
> ous to any statutory enactment, it would seem that it would have required
> a statutory prohibition to have excluded her from practicing as an attor-
> ney. No such statutory prohibition appears ever to have been enacted.

Morever, she continued, four states had ruled in favor of women's admission to the state high court bar.

Goodell also attacked Ryan's labored interpretation of the legislature's intent in opening the state university to women. She wrote that
the state university admitted women, by statute, and did not bar them
from applying to its law department. Law, and logic, she contended,
argue that the legislature saw no reason for women graduates to be
barred from actually entering the profession.

In contesting Ryan's last, social argument, Goodell permitted herself a touch of sarcasm: "His honor with a humility at once touching
and *naïve* assumes that matrimony is so undesirable a state for Woman
that, were she allowed freely to earn an honorable and lucrative support in any other manner, she would never enter it." She maintained
that "possibly this is so, though I confess I am slow to believe it." She
suggested that life for married women would be made more attractive
"by according her fuller rights." Goodell would have nothing of Ryan's
insistence that opening the bar would "force" women into a profession for which she is "utterly unfitted." Rather, she maintained, "[T]he
force is in refusing her." A local paper argued that if woman's "purity is
in danger, it would be better to reconstruct the court and bar, than to
exclude the women."[96]

In her last paragraphs, Goodell meditated on Ryan's screed, offering, in its place, her eloquent understanding of law and courts:

> The learned judge declares that the legal profession "has essentially and
> habitually to do with all that is selfish . . . knavish . . . coarse . . . and brutal

in human life," forgetting that this is but the reverse side of the picture, and that the theory of law, has, and its practice should have . . . essentially and habitually to do with all that is unselfish and noble, honest and honorable, high and holy, refined and pure in human life. The object of law is the administration of justice, and the righting of wrongs, and carries with it a consideration of very many of the most-weighty and important questions affecting the welfare of humanity. . . . In the consideration of these questions, the peculiar qualities of womanhood which the honorable court sets forth . . . are needed no less than the sterner and hardier traits of manhood.

Goodell returned to everyday life while her brief circulated in the media. She relaxed by reading the British novelists George Eliot and Anne Manning.[97] She anticipated winning state legislators to the cause of women attorneys at the next session. The Ryan court decision limited her practice and earnings, but Goodell did not permit it to drive her from the profession, or otherwise restrict her life. She corresponded with suffrage leaders like Lucy Stone, went east for a temperance convention, and followed the lives of her "prison boys." She started jailhouse prayer meetings and a jailhouse Bible class, and kept her law practice active. Her work remained general law—replevy (recovery of goods), deeds, wills, loans and collections, divorce, mortgage complaints, habeas corpus, chancery letters, and, whenever possible, criminal defense. She was pleased that, in a sign of changing times, Kate Kane, who had come to Janesville, perhaps after hearing about Goodell, had been taken on as an apprentice by A. A. Jackson.[98]

On March 22, 1877, Wisconsin enacted a law prohibiting denial of admission to the bar on account of sex. Goodell had drafted the bill, "induced" local attorneys to sign a petition in favor of it, and then worked with Janesville state assemblyman (and speaker of the assembly) John B. Cassoday to win its passage.[99] Jubilant over her victory, she puckishly related to Maria that "Judge Ryan takes it quite hard that I beat him. . . . One man who argued against my bill, used it as an argument that the passage of the bill would probably be a death blow to Judge Ryan who was in feeble health. They passed it notwithstanding but he still survives!"[100]

Goodell's merriment softened the pain of her letter's opening words. The previous summer she had been diagnosed with an ovarian tumor and, although in constant pain, delayed surgery because of her mother's declining health. Now she gave Maria the "dreaded" news, adding, "[D]o not feel blue. . . . I have hope and courage, and feel perfectly reconciled to any fate."[101] A short time before she had also revealed her illness to cousin Sarah Thomas, admitting the possibility that she might not get better: "Of course I believe in God; but I have been thinking of Chloe's remark in *Uncle Tom's Cabin* [that] 'The Lord lets drefful things happen sometimes.'"[102]

Maria later wrote that "the dark clouds around Lavinia got darker."[103] Her sister finally underwent an operation in the late spring of 1877. She recovered slowly and began taking on legal work as her health permitted, as well as lobbying temperance issues. In November Goodell had an interview with the governor where she argued that the "community were responsible for most of the crime, when they licensed saloons." He replied that licensing was "a difficult question."[104] Lavinia repeated to Maria, and others, this belief that society was responsible for crime. She singled out liquor and parents "who fail to train their children wisely," whether because they were intemperate, severe, or indulgent, and continued to maintain that giving women the ballot "would be a powerful weapon" in diminishing crime— "women," she insisted, "should make a dive for the ballot rather than shrinking from it."[105] Her views corresponded to those of national temperance leader Frances Willard, who was now espousing the "home protection ballot."

Early in 1878 Goodell's parents died, and she underwent yet another operation. Again, after recovering, she resumed her law practice. In a New Year's letter to Sarah Thomas, Lavinia described how she had rearranged the furniture in the Goodell's front parlor to better suit her while at work.[106] She was making more time for her jailhouse men who, after the death of the elder Goodells, became even more important to her. She explained to Maria, "As I have no boys of my own to bring up, it is my duty to do what I can for the boys of other women."[107] And, indeed, she allowed the young men of the jail to call her "mother."[108]

In January 1879 Goodell sent Sarah Thomas a letter that revealed the tension involved in wanting to help another woman lawyer while not necessarily liking her. She wrote that Miss Kane and Angie King had just been admitted to the bar. She then confided to her cousin that "King is going to open an office, but Kane is still drifting along in a vagabond way. She does not seem to know how to plan for the future. If only she suited me I would open an office and take her in partner and give her a start; but she will do so many things that I don't like."[109] After complaining that Kane had been at the Janesville jail with several reformers, where she spoke "sneeringly" of temperance and religion, Lavinia asked her cousin, "Is it for such as these that I went thro' the agony of breaking my way into a new profession for women?" She concluded on a note of dismissal, writing that "Miss K. means well enough, but she certainly lacks judgment, principle, and refinement. I am getting to like her less and less, and I am sorry for it, for she has some desirable qualities. Angie has a good deal more sense, & I hope she will do well."

Shortly after sending this letter, Lavinia and Angie King formed a partnership, Goodell & King, Attorneys at Law.[110] Goodell helped the novice lawyer and King aided Goodell, whose health was deteriorating. A letter to Sarah Thomas two months later reveals that Lavinia may have been wrong in her professional appraisal of Kane, who had opened a law practice in Milwaukee: "[J]udge, officers, and lawyers have welcomed her very warmly . . . [S]he is energetic and getting paying clients at once. . . . I shouldn't wonder if she beat Angie and I all out yet; especially as the Milwaukee folks take to her so."[111]

The prospect of an appeal to the state supreme court on behalf of one of her clients gave Goodell the opportunity to renew her petition for bar admission. She spent the early part of April 1879 preparing an argument for Ryan's court. This included a new survey of precedents. The best, she knew, was Belva Lockwood's admission to the United States Supreme Court bar only weeks before, following the passage of anti-discrimination legislation by Congress. Goodell thought that Ryan "will fight to the last" but that the other judges (the associate judges now numbered four) would go against him.[112] Although she believed that Ryan would fight, Goodell would not consider that he would "dare disregard" the Lockwood precedent. Happily, she predicted that it would be "delicious to make him admit me after the way he has acted; and if he should refuse, I think I can compel him to do it by a mandamus issued by the U. S. Supreme Court—which would be still better fun. Ryan had his little day, and now I think my hour has come!"

She went to Madison on April 22 to make her application and, again, to listen to I. C. Sloan argue on her behalf. Sloan admired Goodell, but told her to anticipate opposition.[113] She was not surprised when the court reserved its decision. Less than two months later, however, on June 18—over Ryan's protest—Lavinia Goodell was admitted to the Wisconsin Supreme Court bar, the first woman in the state to win this privilege. Justice Orsamus Cole wrote for the court, conceding deference to the new legislative rule.[114]

Happy and empowered, Goodell set to work on the first appeals brief that she would submit to the state supreme court.[115] The case involved one of her jailhouse boys, Tom Ingalls, who had previously served time for stealing a coat. In October 1878 he was accused of stealing clothes from a tailor shop. Ingalls said he had been drinking with friends. In Judge Conger's court Goodell argued that Ingalls had been too drunk to carry out a theft involving a precisely cut hole in the shop's window. The jury disagreed and returned a verdict of guilty. A second-time offender, he was sentenced to five years in the state prison. Goodell wrote the appeals brief by herself. Over the summer of 1879, she and Angie King had a falling out, perhaps over the firm's finances, and by late summer the partnership had been dissolved.[116]

The death of her parents and the failure of the law partnership pushed Goodell to look elsewhere to live. Early in the autumn of 1879 she walked around Milwaukee, now Kane's home, but decided upon Madison because of its law library. In November Lavinia wrote Sarah Thomas that she was living in a boarding house and had been "the bluest and lonesomest dog" since arriving.[117] She was despondent that the only law office within her means was an "unlovely" back room with no view.[118] It was there that Goodell completed the Ingalls appeals brief, while trying a few cases in justice court.

One of these justice court cases provided Goodell with a final "ray of sunlight." In court, she argued and won in front of a group of visiting law students who were delighted to see her "give it to Carpenter [their professor]," laughing and applauding. Her success galled Carpenter as he opposed the idea of women lawyers and had "spoken disparagingly" of Goodell's abilities.[119]

By the New Year cancer was severely limiting Lavinia's activities. Over the winter, she pursued cures and the alleviation of pain—Turkish baths, homoepathic treatments, and, finally, morphine. On March 11, 1880, she learned that the Ingalls case had been decided in her favor. She had handled the case without the aid of men and called it "a pure woman's victory."[120]

Goodell died days later on March 31, a month shy of age forty-one. Thanks to the articles published by Myra Bradwell, Lucy Stone, and others, reformers in the women's rights community knew about both the obstacles Goodell had faced and the victories she had wrenched from the legal system using intellect, patience, and alliances with sympathetic male attorneys and legislators.[121] Those who knew her best undoubtedly imagined that had Goodell lived she would have pushed limits, and opened more doors. Many of her male lawyer acquaintances had served in the Wisconsin legislature, or Congress. Perhaps she would have worked to break the barriers keeping women from elective office. Or perhaps, following the example of her father's life, she might have formed a penal reform organization.

Goodell spelled out her values and aspirations in her last will and testament: family, friendship, learning, and reform. She left money and jewelry to her cousin, Sarah Thomas, and her friend Sarah Case. She willed her law books to Angie King, "provided she shall be engaged in the practice of law . . . otherwise to Miss Kate Kane."[122] Maria received the bulk of her estate. This included money and investments to be managed by an uncle in a way that would keep both out of the reach of Maria's nearly estranged husband, to make certain that Maria did not deny herself "the comforts of life for the sake of others."[123] Goodell instructed that upon Maria's death, this trust fund would not be conferred upon Maria's sons but, rather, used equally "for the advancement of the cause of woman suffrage . . . the advancement of the cause of temperance . . . and the advancement of the cause of prison reform."[124] Lavinia had affection for her nephews but said that they already had been sufficiently provided for in their grandmother's will, and "for the further cause that as boys they are better able to provide for themselves than women are."[125]

Goodell had a profound understanding of the trials women faced in providing for themselves. Edward Ryan's pronouncement that the "fair sex" should not be permitted to mix professionally in "all the nastiness of the world which finds its way into courts of justice" was only one of the many barriers thrown in her way as she tried to earn a living as an attorney. Yet, like other women who wished to be admitted to the legal bar, she finally found tolerance, if not complete acceptance, among legislators who were willing to grant women the equal opportunity to prove themselves. Goodell had won over Wisconsin's representatives in March 1877, two years before Belva Lockwood, locked into a similar struggle in Washington, D.C., prevailed before the U.S. Congress.

❖ 5 ❖

Belva A. Lockwood

The First Woman Member of the U.S. Supreme Court Bar

I have been now fourteen years before the bar, in an almost continuous practice, and my experience has been large, often serious, and many times amusing. I have never lacked plenty of good paying work, but, while I have supported my family well, I have not grown rich. . . . There is a good opening at the bar for the class of women who have taste and tact for it.

—Belva A. Lockwood, 1888

BELVA LOCKWOOD, like Lavinia Goodell, dreamed of a life in law long before she could make that ambition a reality. Lockwood was the second child, born October 24, 1839, of Hannah and Lewis J. Bennett, farmers who eked out a modest living in the Niagara County town of Royalton, New York. The Bennetts were removed from the cosmopolitan world of professions, and wedded to the conservative words of scripture in the matter of woman's submissiveness. Social status was not theirs to bestow, nor the higher education that their bright, assertive daughter craved.

With her family in need of money, at fourteen Belva stopped her own schooling and became a rural teacher. As a female instructor she received half the salary paid to her male counterparts. Young Miss Bennett complained to the wife of a local minister that this was "odious," and was counseled that such was the way of the world.[1] The bitter taste of this experience never left her. Later in life, she used it as an example of the kind of economic discrimination that women must end.

Belva Ann Lockwood
(1830-1917). (Collection
of Jill Norgren.)

Belva had a large, closely knit, extended family but she found no
role models among its members. Turning inward, as an eighteen-year-
old she began to imagine a life different from that of her mother and
aunts—the life of a great man. Belva asked her father's permission to
return to school but Lewis Bennett refused her request. He had little
money and did not believe that women needed a higher education.[2]
Defeated, his daughter did what was expected of her: on November 8,
1848, at the Bennett home, Belva married Uriah McNall. The 22-year-
old groom was a promising local farmer and sawmill operator.

The couple appears to have worked well together. Belva helped
with accounts at the mill and, after July 31, 1849, took care of their

infant daughter, Lura. She said, however, that Uriah had joined with an unconventional wife who did not wish marriage to be "the end of her personality, or individuality of thought and action."[3] As Mrs. Mc-Nall, Belva had little time to find the permanent direction of her domestic star. Uriah suffered a mill accident, and by the spring of 1853 Belva McNall was a widow with a three-year-old daughter to care for.

Tragedy freed Belva McNall from the comforts of a settled arrangement and challenged her to act on long-buried ambitions. At first, the responsibility of caring for Lura made her indecisive. As she gradually formed a plan to return to school, friends and family ridiculed her, saying her desire for education was improper and unwomanly.[4] At eighteen she had yielded but now she persisted, catching up on high school classes, taking on a teaching job in order to save money, and, finally, in 1854, being accepted at Genesee Wesleyan (Women's) Seminary sixty miles away in Lima, New York. Using powers of persuasion that would later win her court cases, Belva arranged for Lura to stay with the Bennetts, on their way to relocating in Illinois, while she went to live in a women's dormitory for nearly three years.

On June 27, 1857, Belva graduated with honors from Genesee College, having been admitted soon after her arrival into the newly coeducational college program. Reunited with her daughter, she began eight years of teaching in various New York State schools. She again experienced wage discrimination because of her sex but fought back, agitating for equal professional status and pay at upstate teachers' conventions with her new friend Susan B. Anthony, with whom she also designed curriculum to give girls some of the same learning opportunities as boys.[5]

While at Genesee College, Belva had attended law lectures in the town of Lima conducted by a local attorney. Her fascination with law had been growing, but her responsibility for Lura, the public's attitude toward anything as unheard of as a woman lawyer, and then the Civil War made it impossible to devise a plan for regular study. Months after the northern victory, however, Belva decided to visit the nation's capital. It was a natural destination for a woman long active in local civic issues, restless, and fascinated with politicians and power.

She stayed in Washington for a few months, keeping herself by working as a teacher, used the summer of 1866 to visit her family in Illinois, and by autumn had settled on the capital as her new home. Belva later wrote in an autobiographical *Lippincott's* article that she came "to see what was being done at this great political centre,—this seething pot,—to learn something of the practical workings of the machinery of government, and to see what the great men and women of the country felt and thought."[6] The city throbbed with political ego and the demands of a wounded nation. The outspoken schoolteacher, the woman whose secret dream was to live the life of a great man, sensed that in this place she could break the restraining bonds of custom and forge a new identity.

Belva was ambitious, but she was no fool. While she shaped her dreams into a concrete plan, she opened McNall's Ladies' Seminary in downtown Washington. Lura, who had gone to school at Genesee Seminary, assisted her mother by conducting French and Latin recitations. When Congress and the Supreme Court were in session, Belva, perhaps with Lura, walked up Capitol Hill and listened to political and judicial arguments. Belva ran the school to make a living, but her heart and mind were already elsewhere, engaged by other, more provocative plans.

One of these endeavors involved an effort to open the American Foreign Service to women. She had been told about a vacancy at the U.S. consul's office at Ghent. She brushed up on her German and read through books on international law. She memorized the contents of the Consular Manual and then submitted an application to President Andrew Johnson and his secretary of state, William H. Seward. To her "chagrin and disappointment," the application was not acknowledged. She let the matter drop but later criticized herself for having been "weak-kneed."[7] But Belva was harsh in this judgment. She had acted fearlessly, taking aim at the federal government, defying custom, and risking ridicule. Her application represented direct action, something that would become the signature of her politics. With a few pieces of paper, she had challenged the hiring practices of the United States government.

A year after settling in Washington, 37-year-old Belva McNall met Ezekiel Lockwood, a dentist and lay minister in his mid-sixties. On March 11, 1868, the couple married in an evening ceremony at their new home. Ezekiel was a temperance man who cultivated opportunity. His advertisements promised, "Teeth extracted without pain."[8] In addition to dentistry, he worked as a rental agent and a veterans'pension claim agent, and had just won a commission as notary public. Although modest, this was the kind of striving that Belva expected and admired.

Belva had been reading law books before she and Ezekiel married. She confided her dream of becoming an attorney to her groom and continued to study. Like Lavinia Goodell, she spent a good deal of time learning William Blackstone's *Commentaries on the Laws of England*. After Jessie Lockwood was born in late January 1869, Belva reported that marriage and motherhood had not cured her "mania for the law."[9] That winter the new mother read James Kent's commentaries on American law when not caring for her small daughter.

Several months after Jessie's birth, her parents received an invitation to attend a lecture by the Reverend George Samson, president of Washington's Columbian Law School. Samson, Ezekiel's fellow parishioner, had attended the Lockwood's wedding but presumably knew nothing about Belva's "mania for the law." Still, his summons, innocent as it undoubtedly was, marked the beginning of Belva's public struggle to become an attorney.

Columbian College had been founded by Baptists in 1821. The Law Department, abandoned in 1828, had been revived and in 1869 was offering lectures in the late afternoon and evening in order to encourage the enrollment of government clerks. Samson's efforts at Columbian were part of a national movement to institutionalize legal training by moving apprentice education out of law offices and into college classrooms. On the day that Lockwood went to hear Samson, she was nearly thirty-nine, the mother of two daughters, one barely a toddler.

Belva was already helping Ezekiel with his claims work, and told people that she had "wearied" of teaching. She believed that law "offered more diversity, more facilities for improvement, better pay, and a chance to rise in the world."[10] However, any efforts she had made to become a law apprentice had not succeeded.

Lockwood knew women who had risen in status. Her suffrage, temperance, and peace reform work brought her into close contact with an unconventional vanguard, women with public and professional lives. Josephine Griffing, among the first of Belva's women acquaintances in Washington, was an established figure in the National Freedmen's Relief Association and an accomplished lobbyist. Julia Archibald Holmes joined their circle and became the first president of the Universal Franchise Association (UFA), an organization launched by Lockwood and others. Holmes and her husband operated a printing office that, against custom, employed women as typesetters. UFA meetings also gave Lockwood the opportunity to befriend Sara Spencer, who ran the woman's department of the Spencerian Business College, as well as doctors Susan Edson and Caroline Winslow. Elsewhere, she met journalists, including Emily Briggs (who wrote under the pen name Olivia), Mary Clemmer Ames, and Dr. Mary Walker, writer and physician.

Women's rights activism commanded a good part of Lockwood's time. In 1870, working with Tennessee congressman Samuel M. Arnell, she had lobbied for the first major employment legislation addressing sex discrimination in the federal government.[11] As a member, and later president of Washington's Universal Franchise, as well as at the National Woman Suffrage Association, she poured endless hours into the fight for woman suffrage—speaking, writing, and marching. In April 1871 she led a vanguard of local women to City Hall in an attempt to be permitted to sign the book of registered voters.[12] Locally, she was the face of women's struggle for professional advancement. In 1874 Lockwood emulated Myra Bradwell's and Alta Hulett's earlier action in Illinois and petitioned Congress for legislation barring discrimination toward women attorneys. In the same period, Lockwood joined with eight other Washington women who together incorporated a school, called the Women's National University, to provide women "a thorough knowledge of Science, law, Divinity, and Medicine."[13] The venture did not succeed.

The women Lockwood worked with in the women's rights movement had a profound effect on her. They were tough, assured, and
accomplished. In them, Lockwood found a circle of friends and as-
sociates who would encourage her, educate her, and, critically, respect her. When, after attending Samson's lecture, Lockwood presented herself for matriculation, ready to pay the entrance fee, they
supported her, even after Samson said no. In a brief note, the president had written, "Madam,—after due consultation [the faculty]
have considered that such admission would not be expedient, as it
would be likely to distract the attention of the young men."[14] Lockwood viewed the decision as a slap in the face but, after granting a
few newspaper interviews, let the talk and hard feelings die down.
Months later Jessie died, with symptoms of typhoid fever. While
grieving, Lockwood resumed her public activities, intent upon being resilient. To protect other people's children, she lobbied for a local anti-liquor law.[15]

Despite Jessie's death, determination and news from within the
women's rights community also fed Lockwood's resolve to find a law
school that would admit her. She knew Ada Kepley had been attending law classes at Union College in Illinois, while Belle Mansfield
apprenticed with Henry Ambler, and Lemma Barkaloo and Phoebe
Couzins matriculated at Washington University in St. Louis. She had
met Couzins at the 1870 National Woman Suffrage Association convention and, of course, followed Myra Bradwell's effort to upend the
Illinois Supreme Court's ruling against her.

Sometime in 1870, Lockwood thought that she had a found a way to
join this small band of rebels. Officials at Washington's new National
University Law School invited Lockwood and several other women to
attend classes, presumably to increase enrollment (and tuition). She
later insisted that the offer was "part of [their] plan to admit women
to membership on the same terms as men," and that the program
would be coeducational.[16] In the winter of 1871 fifteen women, including Lockwood and twenty-year-old Lura, enrolled in the law program.
Most of the women matriculated as a novelty without an adequate
idea of the work involved.

The students came to the school believing that the administrators sympathized with the idea of equal opportunity, but once there they discovered that they were wrong. They would be permitted to attend certain lectures with the male students, but their regular recitations would be sex-segregated. Lockwood called this a compromise between prejudice and progress that the group accepted.[17] Even this compromise, however, caused the male scholars to "growl" and the administration to capitulate, pushing the women into a completely segregated program.[18] The resulting rancor, and the work, prompted most of the women to resign. Only Lockwood and Lydia Hall, a government clerk, completed the year-and-a-half course of study. Just before graduation day, when they expected to sit with the men, receive their diplomas, and, through the District's "diploma privilege," gain automatic admission to the D.C. bar, school officials told the two women that they had not studied sufficiently long, and could not graduate.[19]

Not surprisingly, Hall and Lockwood fought back. Belva spoke about the situation wherever she could. In May 1872 Bradwell invited her to Chicago. In the Windy City Lockwood delivered her talk, "Woman and Her Relations to the Law."[20] Bradwell and Lockwood liked one another, in subsequent years visiting when possible and exchanging professional news. Lockwood recognized the importance of the *Chicago Legal News* as a public relations venue for professional women. She fed Bradwell items about Washington women that the newspaper owner presented with tremendous sympathy to her male and female readership—just as she did news about all women lawyers.

Like Lavinia Goodell, Hall and Lockwood enlisted the aid of male attorney friends who supported women's rights. Francis Miller arranged for the two women to stand an oral bar examination. They were tested by local practitioners and pronounced proficient in the law. Anonymous lawyers, however, blocked their admission by privately speaking against them.[21] Hall gave up, married, and left the city. Lockwood waited three months, prevailed upon Miller again to nominate her, and was reluctantly administered yet another (three-day) examination. Several weeks passed without word from the committee. Full of fury, Lockwood called the men of Washington's bar old-time conservatives, culprits "opposed to innovation," lawyers who had created a protectionist league.[22]

Temporarily beaten, Lockwood, just before the 1872 presidential
election, accepted an offer from New York newspaper editor Theodore
Tilton to make a three-month tour of the South as a canvassing agent
and correspondent for his paper, *The Golden Age.* She wrote travel accounts and commentary on Reconstruction policy but avoided the
issue of women's rights until arriving back in Washington, when she
sent Tilton a column devoted to the accomplishments of the professional woman of the nation's capital. In "Women of Washington," she
identified and praised women who dared to think and act on their
convictions, an "advance guard" in public opinion.[23] She did not mention suffrage but, by implication, made the point that Washington was
full of sensible, educated, independent women deserving the ballot.

And then, after the election of Ulysses S. Grant, Lockwood once
more attempted to obtain her law school diploma. This time she did
not petition the faculty, or the university's chancellor. Rather, she
wrote directly to Grant, who, by virtue of his political office, was president, ex officio, of National University. In this January 3, 1873, letter
Lockwood documented the facts of her case and the "manifest injustice" experienced by the fifteen women matriculates. Her text observed the rules of decorum while the tone of the letter reflected a sober and patient, if disappointed, supplicant. She wrote about studying
through the "long hot days of Summer" and having been "deprived
of an honest means of livelihood, without any assignable cause."[24] No
record of a response exists.

Lockwood then tried unsuccessfully to matriculate in the law program at Georgetown College. She did receive permission to attend
law lectures at Howard University but apparently did not go. Friends
and family asked for legal advice, which she gave. Well-liked by several men of the bench, Lockwood was recognized, in the winter of
1873, as counsel by the justices of the peace, Judge William B. Snell
of the police court and Judge Abram B. Olin of the probate court.[25]
By the end of the summer she was fed up, and convinced that her
contest with officials of the National University must be renewed.

She again approached President Grant with a short and alarmingly rude note:

> September 3, 1873
>
> Sir,—You are, or you are not, President of the National University Law School. If you are its President, I desire to say to you that I have passed through the curriculum of study in this school, and am entitled to, and demand my diploma. If you are not its President, then I ask that you take your name from its papers, and not hold out to the world to be what you are not.[26]

President Grant did not send a reply but two weeks later the chancellor of National University presented Lockwood with her long-denied law diploma. The "culprits" previously opposed to her stepped aside and on September 24, 1873, Belva Lockwood was admitted to the District of Columbia bar. She became the second woman in the capital to be licensed to practice law. The first woman admitted to the District bar, Charlotte E. Ray, had enrolled at Howard Law School in 1870, completed the course of study, and won admission to the District bar in March 1872, when the names of her entire class were forwarded to the bar committee. Debate continues, however, as to whether Ray used her initials and was thought to be a man, or employed the influence of her father, the nationally prominent African American minister Charles B. Ray. She practiced in the District for a few years but then moved to New York City, where she taught school.

Lockwood was not at all apprehensive about her place in the vanguard of women lawyers, and while she was a very active member of the National Woman Suffrage Association, she did not enter law specifically to become a women's rights lawyer. Rather, she expressed a love for reading law and desired the greater professional status and financial security offered by legal work. She liked the fact that law was a man's game and that it could be "a stepping stone to greatness."[27] She always smarted, however, at the way some of Washington's men had treated her. Years after Lockwood had been kept from her law school graduation, she retold, with unvarnished sarcasm, the story of her first months as a woman attorney. "I had," she wrote, "already booked a large number of government claims, in which I had been recognized by the heads of the different Departments as attorney: so that I was not compelled, like my young brothers of the bar who did not wish to graduate with a woman, to sit in my office and wait for cases."[28]

* * *

Any snoop has the ability to find out a great deal about Belva Lockwood's law practice. Thanks to the now-dusty docket books and court case files kept at the National Archives, and the fact that Lockwood was a publicity hound who loved to give newspaper interviews, the records of her professional life are abundant. At first, the new attorney worked out of the family's apartment in downtown Washington. She did not search out law partners, but until his death in 1877, Ezekiel maintained a desk in his wife's office space, putting his signature and notary seal on many of her work documents. Lura joined her mother's business as clerk and office manager and, later still, a young niece became a member of the office staff.[29]

Lockwood had lived in Washington for seven years when she opened her practice. She and Ezekiel were well known in their circle of middle-class strivers. Belva printed business cards, placed occasional ads in the local trade paper, the *Washington Law Reporter*, and benefited from newspaper publicity about her struggle to obtain a legal education and admission to the bar. Belva said, "The attention that had been called to me in the novel contest I had made not only gave me a wide advertising, but drew towards me a great deal of substantial sympathy in the way of work."[30] She attracted a multiracial clientele of laborers, maids, tradesmen, small property owners, representatives of at least two Indian nations, an occasional lady in distress and, aided initially by Ezekiel, veterans with pension claims. The working-class background of her clients helped in Lockwood's success. As a woman, despite the boldness of her personality, she would not have been able, in the words of a female colleague, to make "an extensive acquaintance among business men in an easy, off-hand way, as men attorneys make it in clubs and business and public places."[31]

Her office, eventually on the first floor of a house that she purchased in 1877 at 619 F Street, NW, was similar to those of local male attorneys with small practices. Early on, with Ezekiel and Lura helping, she needed no apprentices, and had none. Within a few years, news of her practice brought women to her door who wanted advice, and mentoring, which she was delighted to give.

Lockwood's goal was a competitive Washington-based legal practice. Initially, after her September 1873 admission to the District bar, she accepted cases that brought her before the Supreme Court of the District of Columbia. Created by Congress (under its constitutional power "to exercise exclusive legislation" over the District), this court was "an unusual hybrid" that had been given most of the trial and appeals authority of other federal courts, but that also heard criminal and civil cases that elsewhere in the United States came before state and local courts.[32]

In her first year of licensed practice, Lockwood appeared primarily as plaintiff's attorney in the Law Division or the Equity Division of this court, a pattern that maintained itself to a lesser degree from 1874 to 1885. She argued cases in which damages were sought following allegations of seduction and breach of marriage contract. Like local male attorneys, she also had her share of debt and repossession proceedings as well as cases involving injunctions, probate proceedings, and trustee appointments. Half of her courtroom equity work, however, centered upon divorce actions. She attracted female clients, and represented wives as complainants against defendant-husbands. After divorce actions, Lockwood's most frequent equity work involved injunction proceedings, lunacy commitments, and actions requesting the partition of land. Much of her civil law work did not bring her to court and is not recorded in docket books, but it is likely that, along with the other storefront lawyers of her day, she worked up bills of sale, deeds, and wills in order to stay busy and make money. Ezekiel Lockwood introduced his wife to guardianship work and to the business of veterans' pension claims. Just as a few early women attorneys living in the West pursued work in natural resources law, Belva's residence in the nation's capital encouraged her specialization in claims against the government and patent filings. Claims works, along with divorce and probate filings, constituted the bread and butter of her practice.[33]

For many people, including U.S. Supreme Court justice Joseph Bradley and Wisconsin chief justice Edward Ryan, the post-bellum emphasis on gentility made the thought of women working in the criminal courts egregious, even loathsome. Society's morally repugnant dramas played out in criminal court—a place, therefore, off-bounds to *ladies*. Lockwood could have refused criminal cases. Yet, despite her religious rectitude and middle-class aspirations, she, like Lavinia Goodell, did not turn away from criminal cases and criminal court argument. Lockwood began with minor offense cases in police court in a room teeming with people, many down on their luck, charged with drunkenness or simple assault. By 1875 she had begun to attract clients charged with more serious crimes, representation that brought her before the judges of the criminal division of the D.C. Supreme Court.

For the next decade she represented dozens of criminal defendants in this court. They were charged with virtually every category of crime, from mail fraud and forgery to burglary and murder. She won "not guilty" decisions in fifteen jury trials and submitted guilty pleas in nine. Thirty-one of her clients were found guilty, while five others were judged to be guilty of a lesser charge. An entry of *nolle prosequi* ended four cases. She won retrials for several others. She handled most of these cases on her own with only an occasional male co-counsel.[34] Before the all-male juries of her day Lockwood showed neither the natural female timidity, nor the delicacy, described by Justice Bradley in his *Bradwell* opinion.

Bradley and Ryan sought to keep Bradwell and Goodell from practicing law. In Washington, the men of the bar continued to be a problem for Lockwood even after she had been admitted to the D.C. bar and had begun to practice in the local courts. In order to serve clients with cases in the federal courts, Lockwood needed to obtain bar privileges, in particular with the U.S. Court of Claims and the U.S. Supreme Court. She had hoped, since she had prevailed with the District bar, that admission would be a simple matter. But it was not. In the end the struggle required five years and became the crusade of a novice attorney who wanted the full opportunities of her profession, for herself and all qualified women lawyers.

This new contest began when Charlotte Van Cort engaged Lockwood to file a claim against the U.S. Navy for the use and infringement of a patent, an action that led client and attorney to the U.S. Court of Claims. Early in April 1874 Lockwood asked A. A. Hosmer, a D.C. attorney, to sponsor her for admission to the claims court bar. They appeared in a room in the Capitol Building where the court held its sessions, and presented themselves. They were met with stunned silence as the five judges looked at Lockwood. Then court of claims chief justice Charles Drake announced the obvious: "Mistress Lockwood, you are a woman."[35] He cited the court's Rule 13, which specifically referred to the admission of *men*, refused to act on Hosmer's motion, and announced a one-week continuance. When she returned with Ezekiel and local friends, Drake charged her with being a *married* woman, subject to the common-law doctrine of coverture. Lockwood replied that the application was made with her husband's approval but this did not satisfy the court, which, again, ordered a continuance.

Five years before, coverture had stopped Myra Bradwell's initial application to the Illinois Supreme Court. Lockwood, however, believed that Drake's position was easily attacked. The Supreme Court of the District of Columbia had not raised the issue when admitting her to its bar because Congress, in 1869, had enacted a married woman's property act for the District that "exploded" the notion of coverture.[36] Lockwood dismissed the fact of her gender by citing new congressional legislation providing rules for the construction of statutes: "[I]n all acts hereafter passed . . . words importing the masculine gender may be applied to females . . . unless the context shows that such words were intended to be used in a more limited sense."[37]

A unanimous court rejected Lockwood's application. She was forty-three and the very model of a proper and ambitious attorney.

The court's opinion in *Mrs. Lockwood's Case* was written by Charles Nott. A liberal in racial matters, Nott proved to be a conservative jurist when gender was at issue, content to rest his reasoning on tradition-bound common law.[38] Belva called the decision a "squelcher" and went back to work in the courts that would have her. She understood the disadvantage the rejection caused: "My clients lacked the confidence in me that I would have commanded had I stood fairly with the court."[39]

* * *

In July 1877, several months after Ezekiel Lockwood's death, his widow bought the house on F Street that they had been renting. The building, a substantial four-story structure with twenty rooms, was a clear statement of Belva's solid middle-class professional status. Although the house was heavily mortgaged, the purchase made good business sense. F Street would be a home, an office, a boarding house, and a long-term investment. Women came to F Street who hoped to become attorneys.

Marilla Ricker, a well-off widow and suffrage activist from New Hampshire, arrived at the F Street house in 1877, drawn by Lockwood's reputation and because the D.C. bar admitted women. Ricker had attended lectures on criminology and wished to become an attorney in order to reform the criminal justice system. Ricker had a strong sympathy for criminals, whom she believed to be "morally diseased" (a contemporary term used by progressives to suggest victimization).[40] Ricker read law with Lockwood as well as several male attorneys and won admission to the D.C. bar on May 12, 1882. The two women established a lifelong personal relationship. Ricker drew Belva into her campaign on behalf of prisoners' rights, while Lockwood brought her protégée into the struggle against employment discrimination. In the perfect meeting of cause activity, the two worked from 1877 to 1882 to overcome the sex discrimination that prevented Ricker from obtaining an appointment as a notary. After President Chester A. Arthur made the appointment, Ricker, "the prisoner's friend," used her office to take depositions without charge from women and men who could otherwise not afford to make a formal statement.[41]

Over the opposition of her family, Emma Gillett traveled from Wisconsin to Washington in order to read law with Lockwood. She apprenticed for a year, enrolled in Howard University's Law Department, and in June 1883 was admitted to the D.C. bar. Gillett took Lockwood as her inspiration but followed her own star as an attorney. She was less outgoing than her mentor and chose the back office, where she thrived. She refused all jury cases. She became a chancery examiner and won a notary appointment from President Arthur following Ricker's successful campaign to open this office to women. Gillett joined a small D.C. firm headed by Watson J. Newton, where she stayed for the rest of her career, making partner in the late 1890s.

Lavinia Dundore was another woman often seen with Lockwood. They began working together on pension claim cases after encountering one another at either a Universal Peace Union or a suffrage meeting. For a short time, Dundore boarded at F Street and helped Lockwood with correspondence and accounts. Dundore, who was not a lawyer, shared Lockwood's and Ricker's feelings about workplace discrimination. She joined their fair employment campaign. While Lockwood was lobbying Congress for legislation to help women lawyers, and Ricker was challenging the government to license her as a notary, Dundore went up before the judges of the District Supreme Court with an application to become Washington's first woman constable and bill collector.[42] Unlike her friends, she did not succeed.

Lockwood's own success did not come quickly, but when it happened she became a national figure. In 1879, five years after the Drake court refused to admit her to the court of claims bar, she was sworn in as the first woman member of the Supreme Court of the United States bar. The contest, according to Lockwood, was a bruising one that called for an "unconscionable" deal of lobbying in which nothing was "too daring."[43]

First, she attempted to convince members of Congress that they should enact a law that no qualified woman attorney should be barred from the practice of law before any United States court because of sex or coverture. She petitioned members of the Senate Judiciary Committee, without success, leaving her no choice but to try another strategy.

Lockwood knew that the Rules of Practice of the United States Supreme Court permitted an attorney to apply to its bar after practicing for three years before the highest-level state or territorial court, a requirement she met in the autumn of 1876. She reasoned that success at the high court would end resistance to her candidacy in the other federal courts. Her friend Albert Gallatin Riddle, a former congressman and D.C. district attorney, moved her admission. On November 6, 1876, Chief Justice Morrison R. Waite announced that a majority of justices had voted against the motion, noting that they did not "feel called upon to make a change until such a change is required by statute."[44] The vote was six to three, with Waite voting to admit Lockwood despite the fact that he often backed away from judicial intervention in favor of legislative action.

Lockwood responded by giving a brilliant speech at the January 1877 convention of the National Woman Suffrage Association (NWSA) and encouraging journalists, including her daughter Lura, who wrote a column for the *Lockport Daily News*, to cover the story. She persuaded Missouri congressman John Montgomery Glover to introduce anti-discrimination legislation. Titled "An act to relieve the legal disabilities of women," H.R. 4435 (later renumbered 1077 and renamed "An act to relieve certain legal disabilities of women") started a two-year process of debate, delay, and backroom negotiation to end this particular discrimination against women attorneys. With numerous supporters, the bill passed fairly easily in the House of Representatives. In the more conservative Senate, however, members told Lockwood they feared the legislation would be "an entering wedge for woman suffrage."[45]

Lockwood had a powerful supporter in Aaron A. Sargent, California's senator and a women's rights supporter. On the floor of the Senate he argued,

> [M]en have not the right, in contradiction to the intentions, the wishes, the ambition, of women, to say that their sphere shall be circumscribed. . . . It

In 1879, attorney and former congressman Albert G. Riddle (1816-1902) motioned to admit Belva Lockwood to the U.S. Supreme Court bar. (Reprinted by permission of the Ohio Historical Society.)

is mere oppression to say to the bread-seeking woman, you shall labor only in certain narrow ways for your living, we will hedge you out by law from profitable employments, and monopolize them for ourselves.[46]

Staunch supporter Joseph McDonald of Indiana extended Sargent's point by insisting that female attorneys, like their male counterparts, should have the opportunity to follow their cases through the appeals process, thus enabling "evenhanded justice" for the client and for the attorney.[47]

Equally powerful senators, including George Edmunds and Roscoe Conkling, opposed her. In her newspaper column, Lura, often her mother's naughty alter ego, described Conkling as "haughty" while dismissing Edmunds as "the fussiest old fossil in the Senate," a man who believed that departure from the practices of yesterday was "diabolical wickedness."[48] Two adverse reports on the bill spoke to the likelihood of defeat, but on February 7, 1879, Senators McDonald,

Sargent, and George Hoar pulled the bill from oblivion in open debate on the Senate floor. Belva had been notified to come quickly and was sitting in the visitors' gallery when it passed on a voice vote of thirty-nine to twenty. On February 15 President Rutherford B. Hayes signed the bill into law.

The victory was enormous. Lockwood and her stalwart male allies, emphasizing the reasonable nature of the legislation, had pushed a reluctant Congress to enact one of the very first federal measures in support of women's rights. The statute reflected the beginnings of society's recognition of women's rights, however limited. Lockwood's effort, encouraged by the women of the suffrage movement, occurred at a time when reformers in several states had succeeded in drawing attention to the unequal nature of married women's right to control their wages and property. The state bar admission campaigns launched by Bradwell and Goodell in the Midwest, and by Clara Foltz and Laura Gordon in California, also signaled members of Congress that Lockwood was not alone in the belief that it was time to lift the legal disabilities that burdened women's employment opportunities.

After the Senate vote, Lockwood held court and sent flowers to the men who had made it possible.[49] Bradwell, who, as Lockwood had written, "started the contest," congratulated her friend in a lengthy editorial: "Ten years ago the passage of such a law would have been impossible. . . . Great credit is due Mrs. Lockwood."[50] And now that the deed was done, Bradwell felt free to link her support for equality of professional opportunity and woman suffrage: "If women are allowed to be physicians, clergymen, and last, but not least, lawyers . . . why should they not be allowed to vote?"[51]

Lockwood waited to make her triumphal appearance at the Supreme Court. The justices were recessed and not scheduled to reconvene until March 3. On that day, at noon, she took a seat near the front of the courtroom in the place reserved for members of the bar and candidates for admission. She was dressed in a plain black velvet dress with satin vest and blue cloth coat, cut *"a l'homme."* Lura, Lavinia Dundore, and friend Mary Walker accompanied her. Jeremiah Wilson and Samuel Shellabarger, prominent members of the District bar, sat at her side. An unusual number of journalists, including the well-known Emily Briggs, were present.

Finally, signaled by the clerk, Lockwood rose and, accompanied by Riddle, moved to the inner rail immediately before Chief Justice Waite. When she stood, there was "a bating of breath and craning of necks."[52] Three years earlier, Riddle had presented her to the Court without success. Speaking in a clear voice, Riddle again said, "I move to admit to the bar of the court Mrs. Belva A. Lockwood, a member of the bar of the Supreme Court of the District, in good standing and having an extensive practice in all branches." He referred the Court to the law under which he made the application and offered "eulogistic" remarks about his "protege."[53] Chief Justice Waite asked with a smile if Riddle would vouch for her character and respectability. Riddle assured the Court that he would. Waite directed Lockwood to step to the clerk's desk to take the oath. She gave a graceful bow and stepped to the side, standing behind the other newly admitted male lawyers who were busy with the clerk. At her turn, she took the oath, kissed the Bible, and signed the name of the first woman to be admitted to practice law before the Supreme Court of the United States. Family and members of the government pressed around her, cheering loudly as the Court's marshal called for order.[54]

* * *

Lockwood's road trip in 1872 was the last of her extended absences from Washington until late in 1884 when she decided to run for the office of U.S. president and added paid lecturing to her resumé. The decade from late 1873 until 1884 presented her with rich professional opportunities, both in court and as a reform cause lobbyist. Several of her cases reveal particular aspects of the politics, changing law, and culture of the last quarter of the nineteenth century.

The veterans' claims clients who came to the office on F Street— the wounded and the widows—expressed the lasting, dreadful effects of the Civil War. There were hundreds of these clients, but the story of veteran James Kelly was particularly heartbreaking. Kelly came to

Bar admission certificate given by the Supreme Court of the United States to Belva A. Lockwood, March 3, 1879. (Courtesy of the New York State Historical Association Library, Cooperstown.)

Lockwood in 1877 near nervous collapse and, since the death of his wife, responsible for two young teenaged daughters. When he was committed to the Soldiers Home, Belva took in the girls and supported them with his pension. Eventually, she became their guardian.[55]

Lockwood also represented several ladies in distress. Mary Jane Nichols became her client in 1875. Nichols had cared for the children of John Barber until, she alleged, he forcibly entered her room, raped her (several times), and made her pregnant. No criminal charges were brought although Mary Jane may well have told her story to the police. Despite this, Lockwood filed a civil lawsuit asking for ten thousand dollars in damages. The civil law of seduction was in flux. In the absence of a criminal trial, Lockwood invoked a recent decision "that under the common law a person whose rights have been violated, is not obligated to stand helplessly by and see his private rights merged in the crime against the public."[56] Historically, in Anglo-American law, the cause of action for seduction had been the privilege of fathers and masters. Only in the middle of the nineteenth century did some states extend this common-law right to women so that they might sue their abusers for damages. Only two years a member of the local bar, Lockwood showed that she was an aggressive and innovative lawyer ready to question received law in an effort to fashion an alternative legal remedy for her client. There is no record, but after eighteen months of pleas, demurrers, and oral argument, it appears that an out-of-court settlement was arranged.

The case of Louisa Wallace, a former slave, provided a different set of circumstances. At the age of forty-seven Wallace was indicted for infanticide several days after the death of her newborn son. Lockwood handled Wallace's defense with co-counsel James Redington. Like Lavinia Goodell, they may have been asked by the court to take the case, or they may have been brought in by the Freedmen's Bureau, which provided legal aid to former slaves.

The all-male jury deliberated less than two hours, rejecting the defense contention that the child had been stillborn. They found Wallace guilty but urged executive commutation of the stipulated sentence, death by hanging.[57] Lockwood immediately filed motions both to have the verdict set aside and for a new trial, citing technical irregularities and lack of "sufficient and satisfying evidence."[58] A new trial was granted, with Lockwood and two male attorneys now defending Wallace. Lockwood called Susan A. Edson, a physician friend, as part of the defense strategy to challenge the prosecution's assertion of death by willful and intentional neglect—to no avail. Again, an all-male jury found Wallace guilty, again recommending a ten-year sentence. Randall Hagner, the presiding judge, rejected the jurors' recommendation of executive clemency and berated the women of the District for not attending the trial and acknowledging what he called the "rudest barbarism" of infanticide.[59] Four days before her sentence of death was to be carried out, President Hayes granted Wallace a conditional pardon, reducing her sentence to ten years.

Mary Jane Nichols claimed to have been raped but could not produce the needed witnesses. The paternity of Louisa Wallace's child
was never established. In the late nineteenth century the law posed
difficult, often impossible, hurdles for women seeking justice who had
been wronged in sexual relations with men. Women's character bore
close scrutiny: was she "loose," designing, given to lying? Victimized
women could choose to do nothing—to take their sullied names, lost
dreams, and out-of-wedlock children, and go on with life. Or they
could seek satisfaction, as Nichols had, through the use of civil law,
public notice, and shaming. A civil action for seduction became popular among women after the Civil War. So did lawsuits for breach of
promise of marriage. They were small but important legal weapons
used to equalize the bargaining power of women, and Lockwood, en-
meshed in women's rights, undoubtedly saw them as an instrument to
be used in unraveling patriarchy.[60]

Lockwood handled several cases claiming breach of marriage
promise. These cases posed evidentiary problems, but Lockwood continued to accept them, and soon after Mary Jane's action she agreed to
represent Lucy Walton Rhett Horton.

Lucy was a belle from Alabama with a long name and a small purse.
In January 1880 she asked Lockwood to bring a civil suit for twenty
thousand dollars on her behalf against John H. Morgan, for seduction and breach of promise of marriage. Lucy claimed that John had
seduced her one warm Selma evening. That was April 1877. Her beau
was attractive, and the son of John T. Morgan, one of Alabama's U.S.
senators. Lucy attempted to hold her beau to his word while still living
in Selma. She told Lockwood that "an indictment" had been brought in
Alabama but that the judge was related to the senior Morgan's wife, and
had recused himself. No other judge stepped forward to hear the case.
Lucy claimed no one wanted to anger the powerful Morgan family.

John H. fled to the protection of his father in Washington. Lucy
followed him on at least two occasions. She wanted John to marry
her, though she no longer wished to live with him. If he refused, she
wanted money and the opportunity to give the world "full notice"
of the base nature of his character.[61] Lucy first hired a series of male

attorneys to attempt a negotiation on her behalf and, if that failed, a lawsuit. Dissatisfied with the preliminary results, she took after John H. with a pistol. Shots were fired but no one was hurt. Senator Morgan sent his son to Harper's Ferry, West Virginia, for safety while Lucy was indicted on the charge of assault with intent to kill.[62]

The criminal prosecution proceeded slowly. Meanwhile, Lockwood was hired, early in 1880, to continue the civil suit, which was now two years old. Lucy insisted that she should not have to live with the burden of a dishonored life, while Senator Morgan, himself accused of "ruining" several young women, was adamant that his son's affair was nothing more than a youthful indiscretion and opposed both marriage and a settlement.[63] The two sides kept the case before the court for two more years. Then, in November 1881, perhaps after private negotiations, Lockwood filed for dismissal.

Jessie Raymond came to Lockwood, in 1879 or early 1880, for the purpose of bringing a lawsuit. She named Benjamin Harvey Hill, a married U.S. senator from Georgia, as the defendant. He was, according to his biographer, the outstanding southern figure in the Congress.[64] According to Jessie Raymond, he was a sexual predator and the father of her child, Thomas Benjamin, born August 1, 1878. Jessie apparently attempted legal action in Georgia without success, a fact teased out in a press interview with Hill in which he acknowledged knowing Raymond, having "seen her once in a law office in Atlanta."[65]

Lockwood was well acquainted with Benjamin Hill. He had been dismissive of her efforts to open the federal bar to women attorneys and had voted against her bill, and she relished the opportunity of bringing this powerful man to justice. She first pursued quiet negotiation. These private discussions were not fruitful, and on February 27, 1880, Lockwood filed a "Notice to Plead" in which her client swore that Hill had "debauched and carnally knew [her]; taking advantage of the fact that she was friendless and alone."[66] On March 2 Raymond petitioned the court to waive the docket fee because she was "poor, having no property or means wherewith to pay [the fee] in advance."[67]

Gossip-hungry Washington read eagerly as front-page news articles described the David versus Goliath battle. Lockwood set out to win ten thousand dollars in damages for seduction and child support, while Hill and his prominent attorney, R. Y. Merrick, sought to bribe Jessie to drop her lawsuit and to discredit Lockwood. It was Gilded Age drama at its best. In a public letter Lockwood challenged Hill to cease his denunciations of her "in the corridors and ante-rooms of the Senate," while threatening to name the Capitol Hill family whose sixteen-year-old daughter Hill had debauched and to whose members Hill was now dispensing jobs.[68] Jessie, according to reporters, made a daily practice of going to the Capitol or to the senator's residence, where she "contents herself with attracting a crowd and talking loudly to them."[69] In the end, shaming Hill may have been all the payment that Lockwood received. Two separate press accounts, one in late March, another at the end of April, allude to a private settlement and the sight of Raymond, sporting a large roll of bills, boarding a train for Richmond.[70] It was a messy lawsuit. Raymond was not an easy client, Hill was a powerful man, and there is no record that Lockwood earned a fee.

As a Washington insider, Lockwood also attracted women who sought her help lobbying Congress. After winning her release from the Illinois Hospital for the Insane and escaping the grip of Theophilus Packard, his wife, Elizabeth, became a reformer working for the rights of mental patients. She came to Lockwood intent on promoting a "mailbox law" that would guarantee incarcerated patients a way to send and receive mail, uncensored by hospital staff. In January 1875 Lockwood and Packard secured a hearing before the postal affairs committee, but the bill that Packard proposed stalled and died in committee.

Marietta Stow, later Belva's running mate in the 1884 presidential campaign, enlisted Lockwood's help late in 1879. A California widow, Stow had become a passionate spokeswoman on the question of marital property and estate laws after, she asserted, being cheated out of two hundred thousand dollars by the self-interested executors of Joseph Stow's estate. Marietta wanted Lockwood to help her with a radical idea: reforming domestic law in the United States by nationalizing it. She had drafted a six-section bill titled "An Equal Rights Marriage Property Act."[71] In her law practice Lockwood worked with clients who had suffered humiliation and poverty as the result of marital property law that, she said, had the "vestige of heathendom."[72] Stow's bill interested her. She took Stow to the Capitol, where they lobbied for the bill but met opposition from legislators who felt such legislation would antagonize male voters, as well as the local officials who jealously guarded the right to control marital and estate law. A compromise version of the bill found its way to the House Judiciary Committee where Stow, Lockwood, and a handful of supporters testified. The bill died in committee, but Stow and Lockwood had the satisfaction of having prodded legislators to think about an issue they wanted to avoid.

Other reform issues concerning women commanded Lockwood's attention. In 1874 Boston women had won the right to run for election to the city's school board. In Washington, as elsewhere, women argued the importance of their sex in fashioning school policy and the logic of women serving on the boards that administered schools. In 1879 Lockwood petitioned the D.C. board of school commissioners for the appointment of women as school trustees. After a particularly acrimonious exchange between Lockwood and opponents, she let the matter drop, shifting her energies to winning support for the recruitment of women police officers in the District as well as a separate Washington reform school for girls.[73]

Lockwood lobbied for provocative causes that seldom enjoyed popular support. Nothing aroused the people of the United States like the question of Mormon polygamy, and the perceived theocracy of the Church of Jesus Christ of Latter-day Saints (LDS/Mormons). Beginning in 1862 the church faced constant attack from members of Congress. When, in 1870, Utah legislators extended the franchise to the women of the territory, Congress responded with legislation that would disfranchise plural wives and ban them from serving on juries.

The hostility pouring out of Congress put the women's rights community in the position of having to decide whether to defend the right of polygamous women to enjoy the voting right withheld from most American women. In 1871 the NWSA took the courageous step of endorsing the first of many resolutions supporting the right of all Utah women to vote. Lockwood slowly adopted this position, and by 1876, speaking as an attorney at the NWSA convention, she reminded the delegates that Utah had conferred woman suffrage in a constitutional and lawful manner. The delegates backed her resolution supporting Utah against Congress and appointed her to a three-woman committee to "watch over the rights of the women of Utah."[74] Out of this work came Lockwood's lifelong friendship with many Mormon women, her appreciation of the Mormons as a hard-working people and, perhaps, her paid lobbying for the church.[75]

Even earlier, Lockwood had joined the Universal Peace Union (UPU), the most radical peace organization in the United States. The principles of the UPU combined a belief in living the Christian gospel of love and nonviolence with an emphasis on promoting the prevention of war through concrete policies, including disarmament, arbitration, and public education.[76] It was a young organization, open to the imprint of members and different from other peace societies in the full welcome given to women. Social justice also commanded the attention of the membership.[77] Lockwood joined the UPU's executive committee in 1875, beginning forty years as an officer and the group's Washington lobbyist.

The many strands and interests of Lockwood's life, including her work on behalf of women, came together in her promotion of policies of peace. She was an avid student of foreign affairs and a great enthusiast of arbitration as a tool of dispute resolution. This came from her training in the law and her recognition of the increasingly interconnected nature of the world. She argued that arbitration should be a part of international diplomacy, saying that its use by disputing nations was a "rational and competent substitute for war."[78] Lockwood made the case for an international system of arbitration in many articles, in face-to-face meetings with elected officials, in appearances on the paid lecture circuit, at several world's fairs, and at international conferences. She also included support for arbitration in her presidential campaign platform.

Lockwood made the decision to campaign as a candidate for United States president in August 1884. She was looking for a larger stage after a dozen years of practicing law. She got the nod from her acquaintance, Marietta Stow, who spoke for the newly formed, California-based Equal Rights Party, and from Stow's activist colleague, attorney Clara Foltz. The nomination began as a lighthearted prank, a joke pointing out the absurdity of women having the power to make such a nomination but not the right to vote. Lockwood, however, saw the opportunity to tease something significant out of the prank. She was not a theorist. Rather, she believed in direct action. Marietta Stow argued that women would not be viewed as equals until they were willing to "share and invite scrutiny."[79] She believed that women's engagement in politics would be empowering. Lockwood took her lead from Stow. Drawing on her strong ego, restless nature, and keen eye for publicity, Belva shaped the ironic act into a serious piece of political theater intended to further the cause of woman suffrage. Newspapers, magazines, cartoonists, and, critically, lecture managers paid attention. Victoria Woodhull had initiated the idea of a female candidacy in 1872; in 1884 (and again in 1888) Belva Lockwood became the first woman to run a full campaign for the office of president. She had electors pledged to her in more than a half-dozen states, and polled forty-seven hundred votes.[80]

Lockwood's life changed as a result of the 1884 campaign, but not as much as she would have liked. She hoped that the serious nature of her campaigning, along with her lawyer's credentials, might win her appointment as a public official. Sex discrimination continued to deny her career choices open to her male lawyer friends, several of whom had run successfully for elective office, or had become judges or district attorneys. Rather than remain within the prison created by this prejudice, she launched a career as a paid lecturer, which she combined with her law practice. She gave talks whose subject matter ranged from "Women of To-day" to "Is Marriage a Failure? No Sir!" There were also travelogues and offerings about the Mormons, and arbitration. As she journeyed around the country, Lockwood also circulated flyers advertising for veterans pension claims.

Law, lecturing, and reform activism filled Lockwood's life until the mid-1890s when income from lecturing and law fell off, something the normally proud woman reluctantly revealed to relatives.[81] She lived principally from her rents and a widow's pension. One important case, however, remained.

Lockwood began representing the Eastern Band of Cherokee Indians in 1875. She collaborated with Cherokee James Taylor, who had been sent to Washington to lobby for U.S. recognition of the Eastern Cherokee and, when recognition was granted, to press treaty-based monetary claims against the United States. Taylor hired Lockwood in 1875, and for thirty years until she won at the U.S. Supreme Court, Lockwood argued that the citizens of the Eastern Band, although geographically separated from the Cherokee Nation (West), were equal tribal members of the nation who must be allocated an equal share of disputed fees, as well as proceeds from land sales, past and present.[82]

The case and Lockwood's representation, like most late-nineteenth-century Indian litigation in U.S. courts, were tied to tribal politics, acts of Congress, and the vagaries of leadership at the U.S. Bureau of Indian Affairs. For two decades events moved in an agonizing dance of promise and uncertainty. When, in 1901, Congress authorized the Cherokee to bring a finding-of-fact case at the U.S. Court of Claims, Lockwood and Taylor decided that this was the opening they had long sought, and Lockwood filed a motion to intervene in the case already underway—a motion that the Claims Court allowed.[83]

Again, there was stalling, but, finally, on January 16, 1906, Lockwood, who had first argued before the U.S. Supreme Court in the 1880 execution-of-deed case of *Kaiser v. Stickney* (making her the first woman to argue before the high court), presented the appeal of the Eastern Cherokee.[84] She was seventy-five years old. Three months later, in a unanimous decision, the Court ruled for her clients, affirming a one-million-dollar award plus interest, five million dollars in all. Lockwood was ecstatic. Anticipating victory, she had written to her good friend, journalist Clara Colby, "[The judgment] gives me a great reputation as a lawyer, which will help all women, and will give me eventually money enough . . . to make my old age comfortable."[85] It did not entirely work out that way, as attorneys in the multi-party case brawled and bickered over the division of the three-quarters of a million dollars in fees and expenses.[86] Lockwood received a cut but not the sum that she had expected to make her last years comfortable.

A quiet life had no appeal for Belva Lockwood despite her advancing age. She worked with her Cherokee clients on the distribution of the court award, pulled in a few more court cases, and made several trips to Europe to attend international peace meetings. In 1913, when she was eighty-three, Lockwood led a group from the American Woman's Republic on a tour of central Europe where, at conferences, the women hoped to argue for the end of war-making.[87] A year later, she took on her last legal client, Mary E. Gage, a wealthy Washingtonian charged with threatening to kill a well-known local banker.[88] Lockwood marched for suffrage and international peace until her final illness.

Belva Lockwood died in Washington on May 19, 1917, at the age of eighty-six. Like Goodell, as a teenager she had dreamed of a life in law, and as with Goodell, the road that Lockwood traveled was infused with ambition and ego. Lockwood had what, today, we would describe as feminist goals. She spent considerable time pushing public officials to open professional positions to women. She sought to build a successful legal practice and lobbied extensively for the use of arbitration as a tool to prevent war. More often than not, she was a fee-for-service attorney with little interest in pro bono work. Senator Conkling saw Lockwood as a troublemaker who wanted to force changes in traditional practices. There is no question that she used her long life to alter the opportunities available to women lawyers. In many ways, she was similar to West Coast rebel Clara Foltz, who also committed herself to challenging discrimination toward women and, in the face of significant barriers, forged a viable legal practice while authoring the idea of an office of public defender.

❖ 6 ❖

Clara Foltz's Story

Breaking Barriers in the West

Let the criminal courts be reorganized upon a basis of exact, equal and free justice; let our country be broad and generous enough to make the law a shield as well as a sword.

—Clara Shortridge Foltz, 1893

IF BELVA LOCKWOOD was restless and ambitious, persistently seeking opportunities and trying new things, Clara Shortridge Foltz was even more so. Ardent in all that she pursued, Foltz led a life that reads like the nomadic road map of a woman in search of work, status, and a more equitable society. Like Lockwood, Foltz fought her way into the profession of law only to spend decades frustrated by the norms and prejudices that made it impossible for her to win appointment as a judge, election to public office, or selection as a corporate law partner.

Courtrooms suited Clara Foltz. Like Goodell and Lockwood, she relished the intellectual challenge and public notice of trial work. And as much as or more than those women, she shone at shaping legal strategies for her clients and speaking to all-male juries. She also excelled as a public thinker, a lecturer and writer particularly original in her contributions to the reform of the criminal justice system.

Clara Shortridge was born in Indiana in 1849 to Talitha and Elias Shortridge. Shortly after "Carrie's" birth her family moved to Iowa, where she spent a number of her early years in the socially and

Clara Shortridge Foltz (1849-1934)(Reprinted from *A Woman of the Century*, ed. Frances E. Willard and Mary A. Livermore [Buffalo, NY: C. W. Moulton, 1893].)

politically progressive town of Mount Pleasant, the community where Belle Mansfield found acceptance as a young lawyer.

Clara was the Shortridges' bright daughter, their lone girl sandwiched between two older and two younger brothers. Her father, Elias, trained as an attorney with Oliver Morton, one of the great civil rights leaders of the period and future governor of Indiana. Shortridge dinner conversation followed Republican talk as well as the theology of the Campbellite (today Disciples of Christ) Church, in which both her parents were raised.[1] Presaging, perhaps, the twists and turns of Clara's later professional life, in middle age Elias Shortridge abruptly quit lawyering and became an itinerant preacher. By the time his daughter was ten or twelve, he headed a Campbellite congregation in Mount Pleasant. Later, Elias would return briefly to the law, and then spend many years mining for silver and dealing in Arizona real estate.

A foundation of racial and gender equality shaped the philosophy of Howe's Academy, the school Carrie attended for several years before the Civil War. She was a good student. Indeed, Elias observed that Carrie had the makings of a lawyer, including a talent for "abstruse thinking," which, as a girl, she could not really use.[2] Though she dreamed of "oratory, politics, and fame," Carrie was sidetracked by romance.[3] In 1864, at age fifteen, she eloped with 25-year-old Jeremiah Foltz, a Union Army soldier, and set up housekeeping as a farm wife. In 1866, their daughter Trella was born. By 1871 Clara had four children and a husband with a restless soul, and perhaps also, a wandering eye. Jeremiah headed west in 1871 to Portland, Oregon. If he intended to desert his young family, he misjudged Clara, who had no intention of being chaff in some man's life.

The Shortridge family was a close one. When Jeremiah left, Clara gathered together her parents and brothers, and they made the decision to join her in a move to Oregon with her four young children. The family hunted down Jeremiah, and shortly thereafter the Shortridge and Foltz families moved to Salem, a farming hub and the state's capital. Jeremiah worked at a farm store while Clara sewed and took in boarders, including members of the legislature.[4] In the decade since Elias Shortridge had lamented Clara's gender, attitudes had loosened enough that one of her more progressive boarders gave her James Kent's four-volume *Commentaries on American Law,* with the advice that she become a lawyer. Over the next several years, in the mid-1870s, Clara learned what her father knew: law was power. She taught herself enough about local codes and statutes to reclaim a sewing machine seized to pay her husband's debts and to fight a neighbor successfully over a cow that was a public health nuisance.

Around 1874 the two families were again on the move, this time to San Jose, California. In 1876, Virginia Foltz, Clara and Jeremiah's fifth child, was born. The event did nothing to bring the couple closer, and by the next year it appeared that Jeremiah, the man with a wandering eye, was about to desert his family. In 1878, he left his family for a woman in Oregon. The next year Clara divorced him. She was twenty-eight. Blessed with curiosity and intellect, she began paying more and more attention to politics despite the demands of raising her children. Her dire economic situation as a single mother with five children to feed intensified Clara's long-standing interest in woman suffrage. It also drew her to the labor philosophy of the Workingmen's Party of California (WPC), which opposed the rapacious rich, as well as the effects of Chinese immigration on employment and wages.

Shortly after Virginia's birth, Clara had concluded that neither teaching nor sewing nor boarding strangers—all forms of "women's work"—would feed her large family. The reality of her situation helped Clara to decide to use her near-photographic memory and the family gift for oratory as a paid public lecturer.[5] A number of suffrage women had taken to the platform. Laura DeForce Gordon, with whom Foltz would soon join forces to lobby for employment and suffrage legislation, began years earlier on the Spiritualist circuit in the East. Moving west in 1865, Gordon shifted to the cause of woman suffrage, and in 1868 she delivered the first public lecture in California on women's rights.[6] In some years, she delivered more than one hundred talks.[7]

At the same time, Elias Shortridge, who had resumed the practice of law and liberalized his views about women becoming lawyers, took his daughter on as a student. Critically, Clara's mother, who relieved her daughter of many child-care and housekeeping duties, and had "uniform faith" and "ready soothing words" for her, joined Elias in supporting Clara's new ambitions.[8]

Beside intellect, Clara Foltz benefited from youthful, fair good looks, graceful mannerisms, and a pleasing voice. She made woman suffrage the subject of her first lecture, which she titled "Impartial Suffrage." Word-of-mouth, and good newspaper reviews, brought bookings and reasonable receipts. Lecturing would become part of her lifetime repertoire of employment.

Foltz studied law with Elias because, like Goodell, she was refused as a student by the town's best lawyer, Francis Spencer. Spencer declined with a stinging letter, calling her desire to be a law student a "foolish pursuit" and her practice of law something that would bring "ridicule if not contempt."[9] Her place, he wrote, was at home. Foltz zinged back with a lecture titled "Equality of Sex," in which she argued that "woman must be either man's equal or his slave. There is no middle ground."[10]

California did not make it difficult for white men to become lawyers. The state code required six months' residence and said nothing about the length, or nature, of an applicant's course of study. The lack of standards made the state a reasonable butt of criticism to eastern lawyers like George Templeton Strong who, nevertheless, would have praised the code's prerequisite that any applicant wishing to join the bar be a "white male citizen." Nellie Tator, temporarily living in Santa Cruz, had passed the bar examination in 1872, only to be refused admission because of her sex. Tator had drafted legislation to defeat this discriminatory requirement, but the bill died in the California Senate.[11]

Obviously, for Foltz, there was no middle ground on the issue of bar admission. The law had to be amended if she was going to have the opportunity to earn a living in California as an attorney. Tator had failed in 1872, and in the same year a highly orchestrated right-to-vote case had resulted in an adverse ruling.[12] Foltz knew, however, that California had an active and expanding women's rights community that encouraged reform policies. Indeed, she was very much a part of this community, having befriended Sarah Knox, president of the San Jose woman suffrage society. Susan B. Anthony and Elizabeth Cady Stanton had toured the state in July 1871 on behalf of woman suffrage, and in the same year Congressman Aaron Sargent, subsequently Belva Lockwood's ally, spoke in favor of women's right to vote as he began his campaign for a U.S. Senate seat. A statewide woman suffrage society was incorporated in 1873, its success resting on the active involvement of numerous women, including Lockwood's eventual 1884 running mate, Marietta Stow. Foltz was also heartened by reform bills in the 1873-74 legislative session. Sarah Knox and other activists had successfully lobbied for a bill making California women eligible to hold school offices, along with another law that provided for women employed in the public schools to receive the same pay as men with the identical credentials.[13]

Foltz judged that approaching the legislature made more sense than challenging the "white males" law in court. She knew the defeat that Bradwell, Goodell, and Lockwood had each encountered with their judicial appeals. Early in January 1878, Foltz drafted a "Woman Lawyer's Bill," simply replacing the words "any white male citizen" with "any citizen or person."[14] Despite negative racial attitudes, the removal of "white" caused no discussion, perhaps because of the ten-year-old Fourteenth Amendment. Rather, the debate, in committee, on the floor of the legislature, and back at boarding houses, centered upon the question of women in public life—women as professionals *and* women as voters. Foltz's bill had nothing to say on the issue of enfranchisement. Yet, in these years, it was the harsh truth that any women's rights legislation was viewed by legislators—in California and elsewhere—as nothing more than a slippery slope leading to woman suffrage. The fact that Sarah Knox, and other noted suffrage women, had joined Foltz in Sacramento only exacerbated this view.

As the new session opened, a record number of bills were introduced and, while Foltz's bill was controversial, she had to fight to get attention for it. The "Woman Lawyer's Bill" was introduced in the Senate by former San Jose mayor Barney Murphy, who had worked with Foltz on professionalizing the town fire department. After successfully lobbying Congress for *her* women lawyers bill, Belva Lockwood told reporters, "[N]othing was too daring for me to attempt."[15] Persuading the California legislature required the same boldness from Foltz, who reported, "I coaxed, I entreated, I almost went down on my knees before them asking for the pitiful privilege of an equal chance to earn an honest living in a noble profession. . . . I would have reasoned. . . . [B]ut I had to beg."[16] Getting by on next to nothing, she spent two weeks living in Sacramento arguing against doomsayers who said such change was against woman's true nature, that it would "unsex" them and would be unhealthful for domestic life. Other opponents contended that women lawyers would work their wiles on male jurors, who would then acquit the guilty. Still others joined Wisconsin's Judge Edward Ryan in thinking that exposing a woman lawyer to all the nastiness of a courtroom was "revolting."

Despite this opposition, Foltz's entreaties and Murphy's support resulted in Senate approval. Needing money, Foltz went off to Oregon, accompanied by her oldest daughter, to lecture. Foltz had lobbied members of the state assembly before leaving, and had assurances from representative Grove L. Johnson that, in her absence, the "Woman Lawyer's Bill" would pass. She left her new friend Laura Gordon to monitor assembly debate. Gordon had significant interest in the outcome, both as a women's rights leader and as a new student of law. Despite Assemblyman Johnson's support, on an initial vote, the bill's opponents prevailed. Only persistent lobbying and a successful motion by Johnson to have the bill reconsidered resulted in the ultimate legislative victory, by a slim vote of thirty-seven to thirty-five. Now, one hurdle remained: Foltz and Gordon had to win Governor William Irwin's signature before the end of the legislative session. By Foltz's telling, some Lockwood-like "daring" was required as she (recently returned from Oregon) virtually flung herself at the governor, called out the number of the bill, and held her breath until he signed it into law.[17] At last, California, like Illinois, Wisconsin and Washington, D.C., forbade the exclusion of qualified women from the bar.

Foltz hurried to study for the bar examination that would occur at the next term of the court at San Jose. The customary panel of men met with her on September 4, 1878, administering, as had also become the custom in the matter of women, an extra-long exam of three hours. She passed, subsequently receiving "highly colored compliments."[18] Foltz became the first woman lawyer on the Pacific Coast when Judge David Belden administered the oath to her. The public called her "Portia of the Pacific." Like Lavinia Goodell, she rented a "jewel" of an office in San Jose, ordered office stationery, and made the space feminine with flowers rather than spittoons. Unlike the childless Goodell, Foltz personalized the space with photographs of her five children.

Goodell's practice began with her saloon cases; Foltz's earliest clients sought to reclaim personal property seized for the payment of alleged debts. A month after going into practice she confidently faced

Cartoons lampooning female lawyers became more common as women continued to join the profession. In this 1909 spoof, part of a postcard series, Walter Wellman suggests that if women gain power, men will be, quite literally, diminished. (Private collection of Jill Norgren and Wendy Chmielewski.)

Francis Spencer, the grand old man of San Jose, in "proceedings to set aside a fraudulent survey."[19] Women and the poor commanded much of her time. Divorce cases were entered in her logbook. Foltz's biographer, Barbara Babcock, later concluded, "[I]f Foltz had continued with small cases like these first ones, she would never have become famous, though she eventually might have established a modestly viable local law business."[20]

Political interests (primarily issues of justice), ambition, and the need for a better income quickly drew Foltz to a life larger than one defined by local practice. In the autumn of 1878 Foltz, along with Laura Gordon, threw herself into two battles. At the newly convened state constitutional convention, she joined the interesting mix of supporters submitting resolutions and petitions for woman suffrage.[21] Arguments ranged from the simple justice of the proposal to a nativist theme of white women voters canceling out the impact of potential Chinese voters. Debate continued through the winter months, but ultimately none of the proposals for woman suffrage prevailed.

In January 1879, Foltz moved to San Francisco with her two boys and eldest daughter. The younger children stayed in San Jose with Talitha Shortridge. Foltz set up a new law office, but the *raison d'être* for the change lay in the opportunity to become a university law student. Months earlier the state legislature had established the first law department in the West, to be known as Hastings College of the Law, at the University of California. Foltz, California's first woman lawyer, hoped to earn the honor of becoming the state's first female law school graduate. She wished to be "learned in the law . . . to master its sources and its theoretical underpinnings, to argue great constitutional cases and to be a famous trial advocate."[22] Wealthy activist Sarah Knox, along with a few other suffrage women friends, helped to make the enterprise possible with a private grant.

Foltz sought to register at a pivotal moment in the history of legal education. While many eastern law schools were years from accepting female students, in the Midwest, in particular, a spirit of equal treatment was finding its way into law school admissions policies. Foltz obviously hoped that Hastings would prove progressive and welcoming. In fact, Foltz's experience mirrored that of Belva Lockwood at the National University Law School. Hastings' board of directors and male students felt that the presence of female students would undermine the value of the school, and the degrees that it would confer.

Before this happened, Foltz felt good about San Francisco and optimistic about law school admission. On the train from San Jose the conductor had referred her to a fellow traveler in need of an attorney. The client, a "Mr. DeWitt," was headed to the United States Land Office to defend ownership of public property assigned to him as a settler.[23] Foltz negotiated a good fee, made her way to the Land Office for copies of the relevant regulations, pulled an all-nighter, and won her first case in San Francisco.

She did not do as well at Hastings, where, after three days of attending lectures, she was barred from returning. She appealed to Judge Serranus Hastings, founder and first dean, who acquiesced with a note requesting that the lecturer admit her until the board established a policy. Laura Gordon joined Foltz for the third day of classes, but at the end of lectures, the women received a "Dear Madam" letter from the registrar. Formally, no explanation was proffered; informally, officials told the two women that "their presence, particularly their rustling skirts," bothered the male scholars.[24] With resolve, they nevertheless continued to audit, holding fast to the fact that the University of California, by law, was coeducational. Several weeks went by before men from the school physically blocked their entrance.

This left the women two options: retreat or sue. They sued. Foltz attempted to join the San Francisco bar in order to argue the case. The presiding judge refused to honor routine reciprocity. Foltz demanded an examination, which she passed with distinction—and became a local bar member. With the state constitutional convention still in session, she and Gordon also drew up, as added ammunition, an amendment to the constitution stating, "No person shall, on account of sex, be disqualified from entering upon or pursuing any lawful business, vocation or profession."[25] Next, they constructed their legal arguments for the court, asserting that the university, and therefore Hastings, was coeducational by law. They sought, as a remedy, mandamus, a writ ordering the board of directors (public officials) to do their duty and admit the two qualified students.

Both women were running out of the funds required to live in San Francisco. They desperately needed a legal strategy that would minimize the time needed for a judicial decision. Their goal was to be back in class. On February 10, ready to try anything, Foltz brought legal action in the trial court while Gordon went directly to the California Supreme Court.[26] The high court rejected Gordon's suit, but Foltz won a decision from the trial court that the Hastings board had either to admit her or show cause why not. The board's lawyers attempted to delay, but Judge Robert Morrison, initially compliant, eventually set February 24 as the trial date and permitted Gordon to consolidate her petition with Foltz's. Although frustrating, the delay worked to their advantage because in this period the constitutional convention added Foltz and Gordon's women's employment section as well as an education clause to the new state constitution.[27]

Before the court Foltz, the petitioner, made a simple argument, repeating the points she had been insisting upon for weeks: that the state university was coeducational; that she met the school's requirements; and, as the *Daily Alta* had reported, given the recent passage of the Woman Lawyer's Bill, that it would be "an anomaly to enact that women might practice in all the law courts of the state, and yet in the same session [of the legislature] establish a law school from which they are excluded."[28]

Attorney Thomas B. Bishop followed Foltz, arguing for the Board of Directors. He drew on the line of reasoning set out by Justice Joseph Bradley in *Bradwell,* social ideas that had, in turn, inspired Wisconsin's Judge Edward Ryan's opinion in the *Goodell* case. Indeed, Bishop read Ryan's text verbatim, and did not acknowledge that Illinois and Wisconsin had since liberalized their codes and admitted women to practice.[29] Delos Lake continued the argument for the board, and then Foltz and Gordon rebutted.

Judge Morrison handed down his decision in *Foltz v. Hoge* on March 5. He accepted Foltz and Gordon's reasoning, cited the Woman Lawyer's act as well as the constitution's new employment section (awaiting ratification), and ordered that the petitioners be admitted to Hastings. Morrison lived three thousand miles from Washington, D.C., but he knew that only two days before Belva Lockwood had been admitted to the U.S. Supreme Court bar after winning her contest with Congress. Foltz later said that Morrison did not "believe in women lawyers . . . but he did believe I was right in the law."[30]

Serranus Hastings also thought that the law was on Foltz and Gordon's side. He did not wish an appeal, and must have believed that his financial contribution to establish the school gave him some clout, but the school's directors, also prominent and conservative pillars of the community, ignored him and appealed. This permitted Judge Morrison, who had been grudging in support of the Woman Lawyer's Act, to stay his order, again keeping the women out of Hastings. The semester would now be long over before the appeal was argued.

Her grant spent, Foltz returned to San Jose to study for the California Supreme Court bar exam, and to prepare her appellate brief in the Hastings case. In December she passed the difficult state supreme court bar examination, which qualified her to argue her case a few weeks later. The high court quickly issued an opinion favorable to women. Drawing upon the education and employment clauses for which Foltz and Gordon had lobbied, it ordered that the law school be opened to qualified women. Foltz was doubly rewarded: the chief justice later told her, "You are not only a good mother; you are a good lawyer. I have never heard a better argument for a first argument, made by anyone."[31] Nearly broke, however, Foltz gave up her dream of a formal legal education and went back to the practice of law. She had brought about this victory for women but had to watch from the sidelines as the first women students, Mary McHenry Keith and Mrs. Marion Todd among them, reaped the benefit of her persistence and talents.[32]

The Foltz family was reunited in San Jose in 1879 after the Hastings appeal. This was the year when Clara divorced Jeremiah on grounds of desertion, just when critics were attacking California's liberal divorce laws as weakening the family while fattening the pockets of lawyers. Foltz did accept divorce cases, but generally avoided speaking in public on the subject. Early in her career she had said that married partners could never really be divorced, particularly when there were children. After years of practice, however, she no longer found "the sacredness of marriage . . . a sound argument against divorce," saying, "[W]hen love is slain, the civil contract is but the husk and shell of marriage."[33]

Seeking to lift her social and professional status, Foltz never referred to the stigmatizing divorce and always called herself a widow. This did not stop her from having a very good male friend, Charles ("C. E.") Gunn, who was always at her side: "Gossip had it that they were lovers; in any case, they were certainly the closest of friends."[34]

By 1880 Foltz had made a name for herself as a lecturer, a reform lobbyist, and the attorney who argued the Hastings cases. She did not, however, want the considerable success of beating reform legislation out of state representatives, and teasing the doctrine of equal educational opportunity from the courts, to be the capstone of her career. Rather, she intended, at the beginning of this new decade, to reach higher and further, to achieve the status of a great jury lawyer, and to become wealthy. This meant not accepting a lifetime of small cases in San Jose.[35] Belva Lockwood and Lavinia Goodell had settled for local practices. Lockwood drew on her knowledge of Washington bureaucracy to solicit veteran pension and patent cases that she combined with other civil, and criminal, work. Goodell's short career mirrored Lockwood's, with fewer southern belles claiming breach of marriage promise and more court-appointed criminal defense cases. Neither achieved significant financial success; each turned to other serious pursuits, both to earn money and to forward their particular reform agendas.

Whatever Foltz's ambition as a lawyer, whatever heft she brought to any endeavor because of her intelligence, personality, and pluck, she was doomed to fail in her larger ambitions. Foltz would not have admitted this. On the one hand, men had stepped forward with strategic counsel, legislative votes, and personal encouragement. On the other hand, at every turn professional and political men had also opposed her ambitions. As a "first woman" Foltz was in *terra incognito*. She chose to believe that whether her course was one opened by the extraordinary changes occurring in post–Civil War America— including those promoted by the women's movement— or one achieved by her as a unique woman, she would prevail as an outstanding attorney.

Legal professionals judged Foltz to have "superior skill" as a trial lawyer.[36] Her personal and professional handicaps, however, overwhelmed this talent. She lacked a depth of legal training thanks to the Board of Directors of Hastings. No established male law firm would take her on as a partner because of her sex and, perhaps also, because of her outspoken support of woman suffrage. This limited her ability to acquire further mentoring as well as her access to a larger pool of clients. She came from a family of strivers, but they lacked extensive social connections. For many male attorneys in nineteenth-century America this did not matter, but for Foltz, lacking access to the wealthy elite of California was one more disability. In 1892, she ran for the office of San Francisco city attorney as the candidate of the People's Party (having failed four years before in her bid to be appointed a prosecutor in San Jose). The position would have provided a steady income, reputation, and possible steppingstones to other opportunities, but she did not win.

Frustration shadowed Foltz throughout the 1880s and early 1890s. She nearly always had legal work but not the lucrative corporate consulting or well-paying criminal defense that she craved. The men in her circle, men like self-made lawyer James G. Maguire and her brother, Samuel, turned legal training and political loyalty into opportunities beyond her reach. In 1882, at the age of twenty-nine, her friend Maguire became a superior court trial judge in San Francisco, serving for six years. In 1892, as the nominee of the Democratic Party, he won the first of three terms in the U.S. House of Representatives.[37] Clara's baby brother, Sam, twelve years her junior, entered the legal profession after several years spent as a teacher. He became wealthy as the partner of Delphin Delmas, one of the best lawyers on the Pacific Coast.[38] Active in Republican clubhouses, early in the twentieth century he was elected twice to the U.S. Senate, and later served in the Justice Department. Clara helped him to campaign.

The journey of the 1880s and 1890s took Foltz to many cities, including San Jose, San Francisco, San Diego, and New York, in a restless search for a community open to an ambitious woman. Late in 1880 Foltz hired on as special counsel to the San Francisco district attorney—the first woman to serve in this position—in a sensational murder case. George Wheeler, "respectably dressed and middle aged, voluntarily appeared at the police station to confess that he had killed Adelia Tillson and stuffed her body in a steamer trunk."[39] He said that they had been lovers. His lawyers encouraged him to enter a plea of insanity. Foltz, well known as "an uncompromising exponent of the rights of women," was brought in to convince the male jury members of their duty to the female victim.[40] In a dramatic counter-move, the defense hired Laura Gordon, Foltz's friend, who had just won an acquittal in a jury murder trial.[41] In *Wheeler* Foltz and Gordon presented strong summations. Foltz prevailed, with Wheeler sentenced to death.

Foltz did not win all of her cases. In 1880 she failed to win the commutation of a death sentence in an appeal by Charles Colby. His was one of a number of pardon cases she handled in this period. Babcock argues that the attorney's "real gain from her pardon practice . . . was a firsthand look at the injustice of harsh sentencing after a trial without adequate counsel, entered without credit for rehabilitation or hope for mitigation."[42]

Foltz, of course, was not alone in appreciating the significant failings of the criminal justice system. Before her early death, Lavinia Goodell, believing jails were "schools of vice and crime," had been developing a theory—and practice—of prison reform. In Washington,

D.C., lawyer Marilla Ricker drew her friend Belva Lockwood into her campaign on behalf of prisoners' rights. Like Ricker, Foltz became a student of criminal courts. Observing the woefully inadequate counsel available to those who were poor, unpopular, or not savvy, and the difficulties of mounting a defense without funds for proper depositions or expert witnesses, in the early 1880s she began to shape a proposal for an office of public defender, which would be staffed by lawyers paid by the government "for the defense of those charged with a crime, just as it did for the prosecution."[43]

Despite her superb skills as a criminal attorney, Foltz found her law work insufficient to support her family and meet the overhead for her office. Often, she inherited the "hopeless" cases of "those who could not afford a male attorney."[44] She advertised as a probate and divorce lawyer, and in the mid-1890s said that more than three hundred women had been her clients.[45] Juries already knew her to be a gifted speaker. Like many prominent women, including Laura Gordon, she therefore turned to paid platform speaking for additional income. Her public recognition, and family affiliation as a Republican, led to Foltz's recruitment in 1880 by state party leaders to campaign for presidential candidate James Garfield. In a maneuver mirroring the *Wheeler* trial, Laura Gordon, a Democrat, was hired to counter her impact by stumping for Winfield Hancock, the Democratic Party candidate. Both women were successful in bringing out large crowds. Foltz spoke throughout California and for her nearly forty political appearances was paid three thousand dollars.[46] The party brought her back four years later to speak for the candidacy of Republican presidential nominee James G. Blaine. In 1886, however, she moved over to the Democrats, and was paid to campaign for their gubernatorial candidate. Her motives are unclear: possibly a Republican made a slurring remark about women in politics, possibly the Republicans refused to meet the price of her oratory.[47]

Foltz had been keeping her law office open six days a week, trying cases throughout the state.[48] She called it a "laborious practice" and sought relief, and money, in national lecture tours that, in the 1880s, became the core of her financial well-being.[49] Foltz made three tours in the decade of the 1880s. She registered at the best hotels, to "indulge herself and project an image of success."[50] Hers was a world in which railroads had changed the nature of travel. It was also, however, a world without radio, television, or the internet. The public craved education and entertainment, and the women and men who traveled the lecture circuit provided both. Foltz joined with, and competed against, women like Gordon, Lockwood, and Frances Willard, and prominent men like Henry Ward Beecher.

Foltz first rolled out a talk entitled "Lawyers," in which she extolled, and defended, the profession, and the role of women lawyers who would "improve the profession because they would practice at a high humanitarian level, with mother-love and solicitude."[51] Explicitly answering Justice Bradley and Judge Ryan, she declared, "[T]he law *is* woman's sphere."[52] Seeking a topic with broader appeal, she researched the life of Civil War hero, lawyer, and public servant Edward Dickinson Baker, a man she had long admired. She also spoke about women's rights in a lecture called "A Woman and Her Partner."[53]

While touring, Foltz earned money, escaped the daily grind of her practice, and met a number of women pioneers in various professions. In Portland, she encountered attorney Mary Leonard, who, after having been admitted to practice in Washington Territory, had come to Portland seeking reciprocity for her Washington credentials. The state supreme court turned her down, "citing the absence of a statute to overcome the 'generally understood' disqualification of women to practice law."[54] Foltz arrived at the time of this decision, "dashed" off a version of her earlier "Woman Lawyer's Bill," used her old contacts to obtain a hearing, and had the bill on the governor's desk in a matter of hours. Leonard was admitted to practice in Oregon, stayed in Portland, and for twenty years handled a large number of criminal cases.[55] Foltz's time in Portland also afforded her the opportunity to visit with her old friend Abigail Duniway, a well-known suffrage agitator. Early in life, Duniway had earned her living as a milliner and dressmaker.

She now lectured, ran the *New Northwest*, a newspaper well known in women's reform circles, and invested in real estate. Duniway's economic proclivities may have influenced some of Foltz's later business decisions.

Foltz used San Francisco as her home base during her first two lecture tours. In 1887, however, she moved her family to San Diego. The city was experiencing a land boom that Foltz, like Duniway, would have loved to use to her financial betterment. Unhappily, she lacked the capital to buy land. Perhaps inspired by Duniway's *New Northwest*, or the newspapers run by Marietta Stow, Myra Bradwell, or Clara Colby, she thought to make money by starting a suffrage weekly. Instead, however, in May 1887 she took advantage of equipment belonging to friends who were publishing a monthly magazine to inaugurate a daily newspaper, the *San Diego Bee*, of which she became the owner and editor. The venture lasted only six months. Foltz had underestimated the work involved in running a daily paper. She had also antagonized powerful business interests over questions of land claims policy.[56]

The years 1888 and 1889 proved largely unsatisfactory, and Foltz surely saw the possibility of wealth and notice slipping away although she was only in her late thirties. With Laura Gordon, she continued to lobby the state legislature on women's rights bills. Paying clients, however, had been scared off by Foltz's land claims politics, and added disappointment came when she failed to secure a position as a prosecutor (with its safe, regular salary). City officials considered women ineligible, as the law required that prosecutors had to be voters.[57] Perhaps influenced by the acting career of her eldest daughter, Foltz even gave a moment's thought to becoming an actress.[58] Then she settled down and combined her law practice with brokering real estate. This offered her opportunity to search and clear titles and draft sales contracts. The timing, however, was poor as the real estate market had gone into a steep decline. Foltz did some lecturing, returned to San Diego, dug in once again, and attempted to make her law practice pay. She made headlines as the press followed her in a client's messy divorce trial but, in a stinging loss, Foltz could not convince the jury to grant the much-abused wife a divorce and family property.[59]

In 1889, it appeared that Foltz's law practice would fail. In the face of this crisis, however, she was buoyed by her involvement in a movement that, in its short life, swept the country and helped to lift Populism and its political arm, the People's Party, into a position of considerable notice. The year before Edward Bellamy had published his utopian socialist novel, *Looking Backward: 2000-1887*. Bellamy, a Massachusetts lawyer, portrayed a benign American society in which every citizen was an equal partner in a state to which he or she contributed, one that in turn cared for each citizen. Bellamy appealed to Americans tired of Gilded Age inequality and democratic hyperbole that ignored the rights of women, workers, African Americans, and Asian Americans. Suffrage women were drawn to the ideas of "Bellamy Nationalism" and formed Nationalist clubs all over the United States. In San Diego Foltz headed a branch claiming six hundred members. Laura Gordon presided over the Nationalists in Lodi, California.[60] While the sensation of Nationalism waned, its principles and plan of action for a more just society influenced Foltz both in her short-term affiliation with the Populists and in her development as a public thinker.

Foltz presented one of her most important, and impassioned, lectures in Washington, D.C., at the February 1890 meeting of the newly formed Woman's National Liberal Union (WNLU). The WNLU, a progressive women's reform organization led by New York State suffrage leader Matilda Joslyn Gage and philanthropists William and Josephine Aldrich, had its first (and only) convention in 1890. On the second day the focus of the meeting turned to the reform of the legal system, and the need for an office of public defender. William Aldrich and Foltz each addressed the delegates, pleading for publicly supported attorneys who would provide a proper complement to the existing system of free juries, witnesses, and courts.[61] Belva Lockwood was also there. She stepped forward after Foltz and Aldrich spoke. She identified herself as a veteran criminal attorney and told the audience that "perfectly innocent" men and women were often sentenced to time in jail, emphasizing, as Aldrich and Foltz had not, the particular burden experienced by "colored men and women."[62] From the convention, Foltz headed back to the West Coast after being admitted to the U.S. Supreme Court bar. She hoped that the WNLU audience, along with the press, would embrace the idea of public defense as a public policy whose time had come.

In 1890 the peripatetic Foltz abandoned San Diego for San Francisco. She still hoped to break into the city's establishment bar. Instead, she found increased unemployment and other signs of what would become the great national depression of 1893. Her law practice did not flourish but, as consolation, Foltz found the state political branches receptive to a number of her reform proposals. Several decades before the founding of the civil liberties and human rights organizations of the twentieth century, she identified critical issues affecting not just women but also individuals brought before the criminal justice system. After the early contests needed to join the California bar, Foltz's work lobbying reform ideas became her enduring legacy.

In 1891 she revived legislative proposals to allow parole for prisoners. At the time, California had a rather corrupt parole system. Foltz argued for a parole board composed of citizens and prison professionals, rather than political appointees, with the intention of ending the bribery that created scandal after scandal. The new process would permit all inmates, including murderers, to be eligible for parole, and each prisoner to have a right to a parole hearing after serving a minimum sentence.[63] The legislation did not pass until 1893 when Foltz was credited with "pioneer[ing] the movement for the establishment of the prison parole system in California."[64]

With Gordon, Foltz also continued to use her time at the legislature to petition for women's right to vote. They failed year after year. California women had to wait until 1911, when voters adopted Proposition 4, granting woman suffrage. Foltz and Gordon did succeed in influencing the passage of a law enabling married women to be executors of estates. In 1891, Foltz also saw the enactment of legislation to limit a husband's control of property acquired during marriage.[65]

Perhaps taking her cue from Marilla Ricker's successful action in Washington, D.C., Foltz pushed for a bill to allow California women to become notaries public. As the likelihood of success increased, a practical Clara Foltz aggressively lobbied the governor for a patronage appointment. She received it only after an important endorsement from one of the leading newspaper owners in the state. When the governor signed her commission, she became the first woman notary in the state, joining women like Ricker in having what was, in the nineteenth century, an important position.

* * *

A year later, now associated with the People's Party, Foltz ran unsuccessfully for city attorney of San Francisco. The press paid attention to her campaign, which featured a number of issues, including the rights of women. The disfranchisement of women meant that many of Foltz's supporters could not vote for her on Election Day. Her campaign was also dogged by those who reminded voters of a statute that required that government officials, including city attorney, hold suffrage. Had she won, Foltz "probably . . . planned to argue that the 1879 constitutional clause enabling women to pursue any calling or vocation would allow her to serve. . . . [S]he had made [this point] when Marion Todd was running for district attorney on the Greenback-Labor ticket in 1881."[66]

* * *

In 1893 the United States hosted a world's fair in Chicago, a coming-of-age party for the nation. Clara Foltz was there contributing, as a public thinker, two important talks, the first at the Congress of Women Lawyers, followed by a presentation to the international Congress of Jurisprudence and Law Reform.

The Congress of Women Lawyers was the brainchild of Chicago attorney Ellen Martin, who believed that her sisters-in-law, now more than two hundred in number, needed to form an association "to control their representation in the general organizations of women."[67] On August 3, 1893, Martin opened the three-day meeting, speaking with optimism about the place of women attorneys in the profession: "Women lawyers have no wrongs to right so far as the bench and bar are concerned, having been almost uniformly well treated by both everywhere."[68] This was a curious conceit at a time when many government and corporate legal positions were not open to women—as Foltz, Belva Lockwood, and others present well knew. Many women spoke, often reminiscing about their early struggles to enter the profession. Lockwood, however, an active member of the Universal Peace Union, avoided autobiography. She came to the podium next to last, and used her time to present the case for a permanent international court of arbitration. Foltz followed her. She, too, put aside her polished "Lawyers" lecture, with its many opportunities to discuss contesting with recalcitrant men, to deliver a new, esoteric talk titled "Evolution of the Law."[69] For both women, the choice of topics said a great deal about how they defined themselves and wanted others to see them.

"Evolution of the Law" was more abstract and intellectual than Foltz's previous talks.[70] It was a "broad jurisprudential survey, culminating in a concrete proposal for legislative reform of the law's institutional mechanisms . . . anticipating the legal thought of the twentieth-century Progressive movement."[71] Foltz began with an honest appraisal of the profession, moving on to five areas of law where she saw progress. Tellingly, she spoke first about freedom of speech, not women's rights. She outlined the "slow steps" from a "bigoted past" to the present where the right to speech is acknowledged and secured by the Constitution. Next, Foltz pointed to women's legal emancipation; "she was 'no longer man's slave.'" And workers, she said, "had been freed from the more humiliating incidents of the feudal regime of master and servant."

Foltz then shifted to an analysis of reforms in civil procedure, "the statutory replacement of the common-law writs, with their jargon, and fictions, by a 'more rational' system based on 'plain statement' and providing that 'facts' be pleaded." She followed her discussion of the civil system with a consideration of the criminal justice system. While often critical, she stayed with her theme: the progress to be seen from a historical perspective. Foltz spoke of the reduction in capital crimes; brutal punishments and trial by ordeal abolished; and torture of witnesses outlawed. Perhaps most surprising for a lawyer who was shaping a proposal for an office of public defender, she noted that "defendants could testify, call witnesses, and be represented by counsel." She anticipated Progressive policy by insisting that "democratic public opinion [was] the driving force behind change in the law, and the legislature its primary agent." Constrained by "their central duty to apply existing law," courts were not a force for progress—as so many women in the room had learned when trying to become attorneys. Despite this conclusion, Foltz proposed a "regular review of existing laws" that would be led by state supreme courts acting as advisory councils to suggest annual improvements in the statutes.

Myra Bradwell would have rolled her eyes if she had heard Ellen Martin state that women lawyers had been almost uniformly well treated by the bench and the bar. Even as late as 1893, in the planning of the Congress of Jurisprudence and Law Reform, male colleagues had resisted the inclusion of women speakers, saying that "women had not earned a place among the top judges, professors, and lawyers."[72] And so Bradwell, only months before her death, along with several other female Chicago lawyers, battled, successfully, to counter that opinion. At the last moment, too late for travel by the foreign women to whom invitations were extended, Foltz and Mary Greene of Massachusetts were asked to speak.[73] Foltz used the opportunity to present her public defender proposal on a platform filled with male jurists from around the world.

The radical idea behind "Public Defenders" took only half an hour to outline. Foltz portrayed the power of the state arrayed against a defendant: "[A]round and behind [the prosecutor] is an army of police officers and detectives ready to do his bidding and before him sits a plastic judge with a large discretion often affected by newspapers."[74] This defendant contended with what Foltz argued was the tendency of prosecutors and police to "mistakenly believe that 'it is the duty of the State to convict whoever is arrested.'" Drawing upon fifteen years of service defending indigent and disabled clients, and often humanizing her legal abstractions with anonymous descriptions of these defendants, Foltz called upon her audience to recognize the price paid by people against whom all the powers of the government are turned, saying, "even if acquitted he 'comes from the court-house a changed man. . . . Disgrace has crushed his manhood and injustice murdered his patriotism.'" She asked for the reorganization of the criminal courts to shield defendants by balancing the scales of justice, scales that would become exact and equal. Such reform would bring about "[c]onstitutional obligations conscientiously kept and government duties sacredly performed."

The legal arguments behind her proposal for an office of public defender were straightforward: prosecutors, Foltz said, had fallen into partisan advocacy, "making a defender necessary for a fair presentation of the case."[75] She argued further that the state had a duty to the accused to provide a defense. The counsel would be a "skilled adversary to equalize the sides and make the presentation fair."[76] It was an entirely new and original solution. Those eligible included all defendants, as the law presumed every person to be innocent until proven otherwise. Drawing upon John Locke's social contract theories, Foltz posited that "[e]ach citizen surrenders his natural right to defend himself and pays his share for the support of the State, under the implied contract that . . . the government will defend his life and liberty from unlawful invasion."[77] She concluded that when "the rights of a person are assailed it is the duty of the government to provide him defense."[78] Foltz, Barbara Babcock argues, was "many generations ahead of her time" in speaking and writing of a constitutional right to free counsel,[79] and anticipated the landmark 1963 U.S. Supreme case of *Gideon v. Wainwright*, holding that "'lawyers for the defense are not luxuries but necessities in criminal cases' and that the state must provide free counsel for the indigent."[80]

Foltz was very much trying to make a go of San Francisco when she returned from the World's Fair. She pressed ahead with her law practice, did some lecturing, and founded the Portia Club. She aimed, in this enterprise, to bring "together the establishment ladies and the movement women . . . [in] law study . . . to attack the 'poverty and distress' that resulted from women's 'ignorance of the most common legal principles.'"[81] While women's clubs in the later part of the nineteenth century had many objectives, a few women attorneys had specifically taken on the task of empowering women through education in law and civics. In 1876, several Washington women, including Belva Lockwood, incorporated the Women's National University, as noted earlier, but failed to capitalize the institution, which would have had a law department. A decade later, young Boston attorney Lelia Robinson, having virtually no clients, sat in her office and wrote *Law Made Easy: A Book for the People*. In 1896, Lockwood's colleagues Ellen Spencer Mussey and Emma Gillett started the small Women's Law Class, which they built into the Washington College of Law.[82] Later still, Edward Gardner Lewis, a St. Louis publisher with a flair for understanding, and cultivating, women's interest in self-improvement, launched the American Woman's League with its political arm, the American Woman's Republic (AWR). The league drew upon Marietta Stow's decades-old idea for a woman's republic and political party. In the AWR, Lewis offered women a platform from which they could be trained in law and civics and from which, at the moment of universal suffrage, they could organize a political party.[83]

Foltz made a modest start with weekly "Portia" classes at her office. She attracted only wealthy San Francisco women because the classes were not free, and because Foltz wanted to train these "elite" women and have them pass their learning along to other classes of women.[84] She demanded disciplined reading and discussion from her students. Foltz hoped that eventually the Portia Club would morph into a law college for women. Although she had sued to assure coeducation at Hastings, she had no trouble making the argument that "[a]t the previously male schools . . . a woman was 'like a skeleton at a feast,' who 'feels that both professors and students wish she were not there.'"[85] By its second season, Portia had clubrooms in different parts of San Francisco, with the intention of fitting one of them out as a moot courtroom. Foltz had made a success of the lectures and discussions, which she augmented with regular attendance at court trials. She agreed with earlier suffragists on the need for women to attend court in order to support women litigants, and in her comments sagely underscored the obvious: the woman litigant "faced by a male judge, flanked by a male jury, surrounded by male lawyers . . . with a male clerk and bailiff and a mob of male bipeds in the lobby. . . . A woman, especially if she is a timid one, is at a terrible disadvantage in such a place."[86]

Courtrooms, civil and criminal, were the setting of many of Foltz's great moments. Anticipating acclaim and hoping for success and a "handsome" contingency fee, in February 1895 she invited the Portias to the Alfred Von Schmidt trial.[87] Von Schmidt had appeared in Foltz's office, badly beaten, eyes bloodshot, front teeth missing. He was an escapee from the Home for Inebriates.[88] On his behalf, Foltz filed a civil suit against the home for false imprisonment, asking one hundred thousand dollars in damages. Alfred claimed that a poor relationship with his father had led to the commitment, one the hospital extended after learning about the father's wealth and, therefore, ability to pay the bills for his son's "care." Alfred testified to the administration of barbarous restraints, beatings, and brain-deadening drugs. He said he did not drink alcohol, but had experienced "a few malarial episodes." Foltz was commanding, and in closing arguments she was sensational, with the courtroom under her spell and heavy applause after her last words. After four hours of deliberation, the jury returned a verdict for Von Schmidt, but with damages of only one dollar, leaving Foltz without her lawyer's fee. The jury apparently had not understood the rules governing awards in the superior court. Jurors returned to the court the following day to try to correct the verdict, but there was nothing to be done.[89]

With ash in her mouth, willing, at least for the time being, to abandon "Portia," late in 1895 Foltz decided to "start over" in New York City. She moved thinking that the New York City legal community would welcome her in ways that San Francisco had not. By January 1896 Foltz had established a general practice in Manhattan. Reporters were attracted to her, and liked her, but the male bar, men who followed in the footsteps of George Templeton Strong, while making no objection to her bar admission, refused to refer clients, or to collaborate.

Gotham held Foltz for barely four years despite the opportunity to spend time with her eldest daughter, Trella, an actress living in the city. She had an insufficient number of clients. With time on her hands she turned to writing more extensively about public defense. Foltz published two law journal articles on the topic, drafted a model statute, and campaigned for its introduction in a number of state legislatures, including personal visits to the state capital in Albany.[90] By the end of the century, having denounced the "ill-concealed, often rude opposition of the legal fraternity," Foltz had moved on—first to Denver and then back to San Francisco, where she tried, and failed, to "create a western version of the New York corporate practice," while also promoting oil and oil fields.[91] In December 1906, after the great San Francisco earthquake and fire, Foltz decamped for Los Angeles, where she spent the last thirty years of her life. Her mother and grandson, William, came with her, and other members of the family followed.

Her years in Los Angeles brought Foltz some, if not all, of the professional and political rewards that she had sought. She found young women who openly admired her accomplishments and joined her in lobbying for suffrage. In 1910, James Gillett, the Republican governor, appointed Foltz to the State Board of Charities and Corrections. She was the first woman appointed to the seven-year-old board. Several months later she was appointed to be a deputy district attorney, again the first woman in California to hold the position. Both appointments came as the result of lobbying by organized clubwomen.[92] In 1912, she received another appointment as district attorney, but shortly thereafter Los Angeles prosecutors became full-time employees subject to civil service rules and she lost the position.[93]

In 1911 Foltz was in Sacramento promoting woman's statutory right to vote. Revealing a split in the movement, other suffrage activists had come to the capital proposing a state constitutional amendment, scorning Foltz's statutory strategy. The legislature approved the constitutional approach, setting the stage for a ratification campaign, the second in California since the mid-1890s. Despite their initial strategic differences, Foltz joined the pro-amendment suffragists and stormed the state, saying that California women were "too busy to sit on . . . pedestals."[94] The suffrage amendment passed, barely, by two percent of votes cast.[95] In the 1912 election, for the first time, Foltz joined the queue of voters.

The appointments that Foltz won from Governor Gillett also gave her a new platform from which to renew her argument that the state should provide a defense for the individuals it accuses.[96] She continued to insist upon the importance of individual advocacy, that the public defender be a "capable jury lawyer, the equal of the public prosecutor in resources and respect," and available to all.[97] As the idea was debated, she resisted an alternative proposal of an appointed counsel system to serve (only) the indigent. She acknowledged that occasionally good lawyers agreed to defend, but "[i]n practice appointees come from the loafers in court and from the young, the untried and inexperienced in the profession."[98] The state, she said, should not be in the business of furnishing victims to young lawyers.[99]

Foltz lobbied for public defense from her criminal justice positions and in her campaigning for suffrage. With women's votes, the first office of public defender was established in 1913 in Los Angeles as part of a new city charter. Around the country the idea was debated and offices, or appointed counsel, became accepted. Babcock argues,

The Progressive-era public defender was, however, quite different from Foltz's original conception of the office. Instead of equal adversaries putting on the best case for the defense, they were officers of the court protecting the factually innocent and pleading the rest guilty. At trial, they would present the evidence in a balanced and fair way—their interest not solely that of clients, but of truth and justice. Foltz's adversarial defender had no place in the Progressive vision.[100]

Foltz, however, remained silent on these differences and enjoyed the growth of the important movement that she had started.

Like Lockwood, Foltz found no appeal in the quiet life she had earned as she advanced in age. From February 1916 to July 1918 she published *The New American Woman,* a monthly magazine that took up issues of politics and culture, and provided Foltz with a venue for autobiographical columns. She was mentioned for various elective offices and judgeships, including, in 1920, assistant attorney general of the United States. She considered running for the U.S. Senate in 1920 since Jeannette Rankin of Montana had been elected to the U.S. House of Representatives in 1916, Anne Martin of Nevada had run—unsuccessfully—as an independent candidate for U.S. Senate in 1918, and numerous women in nearby western states recently had won election to their state legislatures. Foltz, however, deferred to her brother Sam Shortridge, who ran successfully in 1920 for the U.S. Senate. In 1930, at the age of eighty-one, she ran for governor of California in the Republican primary, receiving eight thousand votes. She advocated various reforms, including equal pay for equal work, fewer jails, and sabbaticals for teachers.[101]

In 1934, Foltz died of heart failure. She stood out among the early women lawyers not least because of her intensely restless nature. She used this energy to forge a path for women at the state bar and state law school. She demonstrated that a single mother could build a law practice, one that included trial work before all-male juries, yet she resisted settling in long enough to make her several law offices all that they might become. Like a number of women lawyers, she wrote articles about law and reform issues and took to the lecture circuit to earn money and to garner a larger reputation. Like Goodell, Foltz insisted that changes in the criminal justice system were essential. Among this first generation of women attorneys, a few deserved to be called public intellectuals. Foltz's colleague in the East, Mary Greene, was one, and so, because of the manner in which she argued for an office of public defender, was Clara Foltz.

❖ 7 ❖

Not Everyone Is Bold

Mary Hall and Catharine Waugh McCulloch
in Conversation

Petticoats instead of breeches. . . . Brains and mentality are [often] measured by the formation of the wearing apparel. This will not do for an en-
lightened and a leading state like our own. We must admit feminine lawyers if they apply for admission.
                        —"The Advance of Women," *Chicago Legal News,* 1879

THE COURTROOM SUITED Foltz, Lockwood, and Goodell, but not
every female, or male, lawyer sought the light and fight of trial work.
The back office appealed to many attorneys, including Mary Hall, who
believed that public opinion would be against a woman trying cases in
court.

Hall, the first woman attorney in Connecticut, was one of seven
children born to Louisa and Gustavus Hall of Marlborough, a town
less than twenty miles from the state capital of Hartford. Her birth, on
August 16, 1843, occurred at the beginning of the dramatic transformation in women's civic life. The public agitation for women's rights at
Seneca Falls in 1848, and other conventions, included demands for access to education and to the professions. Hall benefited from that agitation by receiving an education that included a rigorous seminary degree. From there, her professional aspirations led to a landmark state

Mary Hall (1843-1927). (Courtesy of Richmond, Connecticut, Memorial Library.)

Catharine Waugh McCulloch (1862-1945). (Courtesy of the Evanston, Illinois, History Center.)

judicial decision holding that qualified women lawyers were entitled to equal opportunity under the laws of Connecticut.

Hall's wealthy father owned several mills on the Black Ledge River and was both able and willing to educate his daughter, a young woman who wrote and published poetry.[1] After local schooling, she attended Wesleyan Academy in Wilbraham, Massachusetts, graduating in 1866. The school, like several of the earliest Methodist educational institutions, was coeducational and appealed to Hall because it had a strong mathematics and chemistry curriculum. The academy provided her with a good education and, later, a network of "notable" alumni friends who proved important allies in Hall's bid to break into the Connecticut bar.[2]

As a prized student, Hall had no difficulty staying on at Wesleyan to teach mathematics until she was lured away by Lasell Seminary for Women, some eighty miles to the east, near Boston. Eleven years into this teaching career, thirty-four years old and chair of her department, Hall made the decision to study law. She kept her reasons private, but it is possible that news of Lockwood and Goodell had reached her, or even closer, reports on the two women who had started the law program at Boston University. Living near Boston, she may have met Lelia Robinson, who was about to matriculate in the Boston University law program.[3]

Although the Boston University program was open to women, for financial or personal reasons Hall chose to pursue her legal education in the more traditional manner, apprenticing with a family member. In July 1877 she approached her brother Ezra, a lawyer and Connecticut state senator. He did not encourage her, but she persevered, and he made her a gift of James Kent's *Commentaries on American Law*, the same treatise that started Clara Foltz on her quest to become an attorney. Believing the gift signaled that Ezra had warmed to the idea of having her as an apprentice, Hall began reading the *Commentaries*, intending to enter Ezra's office in the autumn. His sudden death in November 1877 frustrated that plan.[4]

The tragedy of Ezra Hall's death might have aborted his sister's bid to join Connecticut's legal fraternity. As Goodell had discovered, few male attorneys were inclined to take on female apprentices who were not family members. Even Ezra had not been wholly enthusiastic. Unlike Goodell, however, Mary Hall was blessed by an acquaintance with John Hooker, a prominent Hartford lawyer. The colony of Connecticut had been founded by a forebear of Hooker's, a man whose liberal theological and civic views had caused him to differ with the leaders of the theocratic Massachusetts colony. John Hooker inherited this progressive and questioning mind. He married Isabella Beecher, daughter of Lyman Beecher, the famous Congregational minister. She was a woman similarly ready to question established laws and mores. The Hookers were active members of the women's rights community, lobbying for suffrage and reform of the state's married women's property laws. Ezra Hall's death gave John Hooker a very personal and concrete opportunity to demonstrate his commitment to equality.

In April 1878, after an appropriate period of mourning had passed, Hooker, then state reporter for the Supreme Court of Errors, invited Hall to apprentice with him. While reading law, Hall worked with her mentor copying and preparing the opinions of the justices.[5] She stayed with him for three years. After a year in his office, Hooker backed Hall for an appointment as a commissioner of the superior court. He endorsed her papers, as did the current and previous governor. She was the first woman in Connecticut to be given this commission, which authorized her, by law, to "sign writs and subpoenas, take recognizances, administer oaths and take depositions and the acknowledgment of deeds."[6] The appointment paralleled gains by women legal professionals across the country. Lockwood had been sworn in as a member of the Supreme Court of the United States only weeks before Hall received her commission, while in the same year Foltz and Gordon won their case against Hastings Law School. The number of women lawyers crawled forward; a few women won appointments as notaries.

Elsewhere, however, government discrimination continued. In 1881, Lelia Robinson's application to become the first female member of the Massachusetts bar was denied, as had become all too common, by the judiciary—in this case the Massachusetts Supreme Judicial Court.

Like most of her sisters-in-law whose aspirations were pinioned by a court, Robinson was forced to turn to the state legislature to open the bar to women by statute.

Mary Hall shunned publicity and had no desire to cast herself as a rebel. She was prepared to take the bar examination in 1881 but wrote Lelia Robinson—some years later—that she "thought seriously of going to some State where women were admitted to the bar, dreading the noise and criticism to which a pioneer in such a matter is always subject."[7] People in the community, however, "induced" Hall to make an application in her home state of Connecticut, which she did in March 1882. John Hooker certified her readiness and good character. He and his wife were among those who had wanted Hall to apply in Connecticut. As Hall had feared, there was "noise." In *A Woman of the Century*, Frances Willard and Mary Livermore reported, "[T]he affair made a sensation. . . . She took her examination in an open court-room, and not under the most favorable circumstances, but went through the ordeal with credit."[8] The examiners included the local U.S. district attorney and three prominent lawyers from the Hartford County bar.

Members of the county bar met after Hall's successful examination and voted to admit her "subject to the advice of the [state] Supreme Court on its legality."[9] Many Connecticut newspapers had supported Hall, with editors at the *Hartford Daily Courant* writing that it would be "a confession of fear on the part of the men" not to admit her.[10] The *Waterbury Republican*, with no mention of suffrage, opined that the question of women's rights "is a bug-bear which men can most easily rid themselves of by throwing open all avenues of employment. Women's natural limitations will quickly decide how far she can go with safety and self-respect, and for our part we would give her ample liberty to exhibit her ability, and do what she can for herself."[11]

Legislative action opened the opportunity of bar membership to qualified women in many places. State and federal courts, however, as Bradwell, Lockwood, Goodell, and Robinson knew, clung to conservative jurisprudence in the matter of women's employment opportunities. Changes in state law or, in Lockwood's case, congressional action reversed the decisions handed down to these four applicants.

Mary Hall had better than average chances of obtaining a favorable ruling from the Connecticut Supreme Court of Errors, although that did not calm her nerves. She could not do much better than John Hooker as a sponsor. The men who had certified her on the bar examination were similarly well known and much respected. Thomas McManus, a former judge, submitted the brief in support of Hooker's protégée. He reminded the justices that the language of the state law regulating attorneys "neither expressly or [sic] impliedly excludes women . . . that the word 'attorney' was always defined as a 'person.'"[12] He pointed to the tendency in state laws and judicial rulings "to give women equal right, scope and opportunity whenever possible." Critically, he dismissed the U.S. Supreme Court's 1873 ruling in *Bradwell v. Illinois* by observing that "Connecticut's legal tradition was far older than the relatively young federal system" and that both the federal Fourteenth Amendment and relevant Connecticut constitutional law "were construed broadly, not restrictively."

The Hartford bar gave local attorney Goodwin Collier the unenviable task of submitting points in opposition, although the bar association was recommending Hall's admission. Collier's short brief identified the attorney licensing law as nearly "identical to the one in effect in 1708, and at that time the statute, and the common-law world, excluded women from the Bar."[13] The legislature had not expressly changed the statute to include women applicants, leaving Collier to reason that it still intended to exclude them. He cited judicial rulings in the *Bradwell, Goodell,* and *Lockwood* cases although each had been superseded by legislative action. It appears that Collier, knowing of these legislative endorsements, thought it appropriate for the Connecticut legislature, not the high court, to settle the matter of Mary Hall's professional rights.

The publicity-shy applicant found herself the subject of articles printed in newspapers around the country. Writers shook their heads at the idea of ancient laws commanding respect and suggested that Connecticut had too many "fogies." There was a time in Connecticut, one particular Florida journalist ribbed, "when a young woman would probably be burned as a witch had she asked to be recognized as a lawyer. It is rather different now, although there are people still living who regularly get excited over a matter like that."[14] Oral argument was held on May 5, 1882, and ten weeks later the state supreme court issued a ruling that favored Hall.[15]

Chief Justice John D. Park wrote for the majority.[16] He opened by noting that it was not contended that the language of the statute regulating admission of attorneys by the superior court was not sufficiently comprehensive to include women. Rather, opponents' claim centered on the fact that women had never been admitted as attorneys, and that a common-law disability had been established in Connecticut that could only be removed by explicit statutory language. Park answered by asserting that the state statute in question, revised in 1875, "is ample for removing that disability."[17] He added that "progress in social matters is gradual. We pass almost imperceptibly from a state of public opinion that utterly condemns some course of action to one that strongly approves it."[18] It was the case, he felt, that when revising the statute in 1875, state legislators left in the words "such persons . . . with full knowledge that they were sufficient to include women, and that women were already following the profession of law in different parts of the country."[19] Without naming Hall, Park also noted that a woman had served as a commissioner of the superior court under a similar statute. Critically, he asserted, "[W]e are not to forget that all statutes are to be construed, as far as possible, in favor of equality of rights. All restrictions upon human liberty, all claims for special privileges, are to be regarded as having the presumption of law against them . . . and can be sustained, if at all . . . by the clear expression or clear implication of the law."[20]

Writing in dissent, Justice W. Pardee stayed close to the points in Collier's brief. He argued, in a mere two sentences, that women were not admitted to the bar at common law, and that it was the duty of the court to "follow rather than precede the legislature in declaring that it has changed its mind."[21]

The *Hall* decision was pathbreaking as the first judicial decision in the United States to hold that qualified women could not be barred from practicing law, that what was due to men was also due to women.

Hall broke new ground by reasoning that "the laws of equal protection applied to all citizens, women included.[22] Chief Justice Park did not assert that the Fourteenth Amendment to the federal Constitution gave women equal rights. Rather, he teased his ruling from the *existence* of the Fourteenth Amendment, and the transformation of women's civic and social lives.

Not surprisingly, Lelia Robinson, in Boston, sent her congratulations and asked Hall for a copy of the decision.[23] Equally predictably, newspapers praised but also questioned the decision. Clara Foltz had once observed that only the poor and desperate come to women trial lawyers. With some irony, the *New York Times* agreed with her, questioning the likelihood that women attorneys would draw a strong client list:

> Litigants are commonly guided in the choice of counsel by hard practical reasons. They employ lawyers who can win their suits. . . . [I]n delicate and difficult cases comparatively few parties to a suit would trust their property or their liberty into the hands of a female attorney for the same reason that a man about to shave himself would not employ the convex mirror.[24]

Hall took her attorney's oath on October 3, 1882. Soon after, she was appointed Connecticut's first woman notary. For eight years she was the only woman lawyer in the state. Hall practiced out of John Hooker's office for many years before establishing an office of her own. She continued to assist him in the preparation of the *Connecticut Reports* while carving out probate work as her specialty. Her clients were generally women with property issues, or in need of a will.

Illinois attorney Catharine Waugh McCulloch described Hall in a letter to members of the Equity Club. The club was a women lawyers correspondence group (letters were circulated) founded in 1886 by women trained in law at the University of Michigan, and so named because "equity [law] has been the savior of woman."[25]

McCulloch wrote that Hall "wears her hair in long curls. . . . She says she confines herself strictly to office work, as public sentiment would be much against a woman's speaking in court."[26] Hall also avoided almost all cases involving divorce. Mid-career, she made a rare appearance in superior court on behalf of a male client, Jacob Lipp, but withdrew once Lipp secured other counsel.[27] Lelia Robinson reported in her 1890 survey of American women lawyers that Hall had been in constant practice since her admission to the bar, "supporting herself comfortably. . . . [and doing] little court work, usually turning that over to her brothers of the profession."[28] In short, Hall had a quiet, rewarding local practice that suited her personality and the demands of her other interests. Her story could not have been more different from that of Clara Foltz.

In the matter of suffrage, however, Hall's attitudes did mirror those of most of the "rebels." She threw herself into the struggle, in 1885 helping to found the Hartford Woman Suffrage Club, and serving as its vice president. McManus and Park had emphasized the "tendency" in Connecticut to give women equal rights and opportunity. In reality, the state's record was mixed. The Hookers had successfully lobbied for an 1877 married women's property rights bill, but year after year the legislature defeated bills to grant woman suffrage. In 1886 Connecticut women became eligible to be school trustees; three years later the legislature permitted women to become assistant town clerks. In 1893, years after similar reform in other states, a school suffrage law passed permitting women to vote in school board elections.[29] The state never enacted a full woman suffrage statute, or constitutional amendment, and women could not vote in Connecticut until passage of the federal suffrage amendment in 1920.

Hall had strong views about women lawyers in court. She had equally strong opinions about the organization and ideology of suffrage. Early in the history of the Hartford Suffrage Club she opposed an attempt to join the work of the club to that of the Woman's Christian Temperance Union.[30] In the same months Hall, a churchgoer, took the lead in a spirited written exchange between suffrage club members and Elizabeth Cady Stanton over the relationship between women's rights and Christianity. Stanton wished to interrogate religious creeds, and to emancipate women "from their religious terrors" by showing how "they all alike degrade the sex, and make us slave and subjects, Pariahs and outcasts."[31] Hall suggested that suffrage women "dig into the past" and believed, unlike Stanton, that early Christian writings had value with respect to the question of women and their rights.[32]

Mary Hall had a second identity as a philanthropist. In the winter of 1880, while reading law, she founded the Good Will Club, a charity for poor boys, in particular, newsboys. Willard and Livermore wrote that Hall "gathered a few boys from the streets and read them stories, played games," or talked about natural history, geology, and other topics "calculated to arouse interest and inspire observation and investigation."[33] The boys promised not to swear, smoke, or drink. In the early years of the club, in warm weather, the boys camped on Hall's property in Marlborough, Connecticut. Hall told Willard and Livermore that her plan was neither that of a day school nor that of a Sunday school but simply an arrangement to afford these children entertainment that would draw them away from "the bad life of the streets."[34] Hall began with nine boys. By 1890 more than eight hundred children were involved in the club, which eventually grew to have nearly three thousand members. The club grew out of post–Civil War reform concerns but also fit easily into ideas of rehabilitation associated with the turn-of-the-century Progressive movement.

Hall practiced law until the early 1920s but, from 1900 on, she spent an increasing amount of time ensuring the success of the Good Will Club and lobbying issues related to making children's lives safer or less severe. As a member of the State Board of Charities, she investigated state charitable institutions. She scrutinized prison and juvenile facilities in other states and countries. She supported the right of girls to sell newspapers as a way of preventing delinquency (presumably, prostitution), a position she argued in 1905 before a hearing of the state judiciary committee.[35] Her personal work for the Good Will Club helped to encourage many young men onto a path of education and upward mobility.

Hall died at the age of eighty-four on November 15, 1927. The Hartford County Bar Association sent a committee of ten to her funeral.

The group included the bar president and the recently graduated woman lawyer, J. Agnes Burns.[36]

In re Mary Hall was a landmark decision in Connecticut. The ruling represented progress in the state's support of equal rights. It opened the way for Hall to practice. Based on the reasoning in the opinion, in 1889 the state also opened the profession of druggist to women. A year later, Lelia Robinson represented Marilla Ricker in her successful bid to give women lawyers the opportunity to become members of the New Hampshire bar. In deciding *Ricker's Petition,* Chief Justice Charles Doe rejected the opinion of the Massachusetts court in Robinson's case, and relied on important aspects of the *Hall* decision.[37] Later still, the New Mexico Supreme Court cited *Hall* when holding that women might be appointed to the office of state librarian even though they lacked the right to vote.[38]

The *Hall* decision was celebrated as a progressive marker in the fight for women's rights. Ironically, however, Hall was criticized. Certain women in the legal community found Hall insufficiently bold for confining herself to office work and believing that "public sentiment would be much against a woman's speaking in court." Her stance was much debated, and not infrequently deplored, by other women lawyers. The dispute centered on the propriety of public speaking and whether it would "unsex" a woman.

The purely professional issue was weighty: would women attorneys have an unfair advantage with all-male juries, thus putting in peril the very foundation of the American judicial system? One male opposing counsel, who held nothing back in stating this fear, said, "Lady lawyers [are] dangerous to justice inasmuch as an impartial jury would be impossible when a lovely woman pleaded the case of the criminal."[39] Women lawyers would "produce the wrong results" by clouding the reasoning abilities of witnesses, juries, and even judges.[40]

Catharine Waugh was one of the attorneys who found Hall's decision to leave court appearances to the men deeply disturbing. Waugh used her membership in the Equity Club to circulate a letter in 1888 in which she essentially invited Hall into a conversation: "Some bristling aggressive woman lawyer ought to stir up those slow going people or

Miss Hall had better come to Illinois, where it is just as honorable for a woman to talk to men publicly as in private."[41] Hall, dignified to a fault, maintained silence and continued to stay out of court.

Catharine Waugh, the oldest child of farmers, was born in 1862 in New York State. Her parents, Susan and Abraham Waugh, brought the family to New Milford, Illinois, five years later. Known to her family as Kittie, she read voraciously and, like Mary Hall, was encouraged to get an education. Her father supported the spunk and independence exhibited by his oldest child, a feisty girl who was not intimidated by the neighbor boys who teased her.[42]

Waugh entered the nearby Rockford Seminary in 1878. The all-girls school was "an evangelical Christian institution." The principal, Anna Sill, was committed "to encouraging her 'unsaved' students to convert while under her care."[43] Waugh was a year behind Jane Addams at Rockford, and took at least one advanced math course with her. Later, when they were adults in Chicago, their paths crossed with some frequency. In 1909 they organized the "Women's Special," a chartered train carrying women to the state capital to lobby for suffrage. Despite several interests in common, the two women did not develop a deep friendship, at school or as adults.[44]

Waugh left Rockford in 1882 after graduating first in her class. Whether she had a conversion experience is unclear, but she was certain about her commitment to temperance, and after leaving school spent more than a year as a temperance speaker in northwestern Illinois. In 1884, the Rockford law firm of Marshall and Taggart hired Waugh, possibly as a copyist.

Many elite law schools maintained their misogynistic admission policies well into the twentieth century; other legal education institutions, however, opened their classes to women in the 1870s and 1880s. Waugh encountered no problem entering Union College of Law in Chicago (later Northwestern Law School) in 1885. She was admitted with one other woman, Catharine Van Valkenburg Waite. Waite had already read law with her husband while he served as a judge in the Utah Territory, and was an established writer. She was in her mid-fifties and became both a friend and a steadying influence on Waugh during their year of law school, particularly in the early weeks of the program when the male students tested the women's resolve. The curriculum included lectures in medical juris-prudence, what Waugh described as "abortion, infanticide and kin-dred topics."[45] Waite was not in this class and her friend was reluc-tant to "hear these delicate subjects discussed before young men." Colleagues in the temperance movement, however, encouraged her to attend, with Dr. Mary Weeks Burnett, a physician friend, saying, "If I was Dean of your Faculty I would not let you graduate if you skipped some lectures just because of your squeamishness." To back up her opinion Dr. Burnett joined Waugh in class each week for the duration of these lectures, a kindness Waugh publicly acknowledged in a *Woman's Tribune* article.

Waugh graduated from law school in May 1886 at the age of twenty-four and was admitted to the Illinois bar on November 9. Getting an education posed few difficulties; finding a job with a law firm was an entirely different matter. After passing the bar, Waugh set out to find a legal position in Chicago. Myra Bradwell, who never stinted with *CLN* articles that might help women attorneys, drew notice to Waugh with a short biography that concluded, "[S]he would like a place in some good law office of this city."[46]

Despite Bradwell's help, Waugh's experience was not a happy one, and she did not find a job. Full of grit, Waugh was not reluctant to publish a tell-all account of what she encountered, an account she and Clara Foltz might easily have shared during an evening of talk about the unwillingness of their legal brethren to hire women:

> Many friends advised me to settle in Chicago and capture my share of the large fees floating about. So I decided to get a clerkship in some first class law firm. . . . Other classmates were doing the same already and why not I? [X] gave me a list of good men and firms and wrote me personal letters to several. Armed with these and letters and recommendations from two Judges friends of mine and the College Professors I sallied forth to seek my fortune. I sailed out inflated with enthusiasm and confidence in my own abilities. I dragged myself back collapsed with chagrin and failure.

Mr F. whose sister was a friend . . . had more clerks than he knew what to do with.

Mr W. was glad to make my acquaintance but . . . [it] was the wrong season of the year to look for such a place.

Mr J. preferred the help of his two sons and must also confess he disapproved of women stepping out of their true sphere, the home. This of course led to some discussion the nature of which you can no doubt imagine.

Pompous Judge J. never knew of anyone who needed a clerk . . . [and spoke] with his eyes still clinging to his newspaper.

Bristly, bullet headed little Mr. B. exclaimed vehemently "I don't approve of women at the bar, they cant [sic] stand the racket. I would prefer to find a place for my daughter in someone's kitchen and I advise you to . . . go home and take in sewing." . . . I assured him it was not in default of having opportunities to enter kitchens that I wished to do law work. . . . inwardly reflecting that only when I had defeated that pettifogger in some illustrious lawsuit would he be fully answered. Take in sewing at 60 cents a dozen for fine shirts? No thank you. He can make shirts himself.[47]

Waugh's experience, like that of Foltz, suggests that large cities were neither more progressive nor more receptive in the matter of women attorneys. Waugh retreated to Rockford, Illinois, which had become her hometown. She rented a modest office, boarded with her parents until her marriage in 1890, and had some paying clients whose fees, she wrote, "kept her from debt."[48] When Lelia Robinson conducted a survey of women attorneys in 1890, Waugh reported that she did "all varieties of work, foreclosing mortgages, obtaining divorces, drafting wills, collecting claims, settling estates, and occasionally appearing in probate and juvenile courts, but seldom doing anything in criminal law."[49]

The local male attorneys and court officials in Rockford were friendly and helpful to her. Still, Waugh had spare time and used it to take classes at Rockford Seminary, earning, in 1888, a B.A. and an M.A. degree with a thesis titled "Woman's Wages."[50] The thesis examined the "manifold excuses for inequality of [women's] wages" and then gave the reasons for this inequality along with the remedies that Waugh argued would end it: "[O]pen the doors to all schools supported by public money as well as technical training, making women eligible for all occupations, and giving them equal political rights."[51] She made the fifty-plus-page study into a book, sent review copies out to newspapers and journals, and printed up an ad offering it for sale at twenty-five cents each.[52]

In 1888 Waugh also accepted nomination as the Prohibition candidate for state's attorney and, although unsuccessful, ran two hundred votes ahead of the party ticket. With the humor that was increasingly evident in her writing, Waugh sent a letter about the experience to the Equity Club. She had fun as a candidate, and thought having men around the county see a woman speak helped on the "woman question," but found campaigning "hard work, [with] no pay, little glory, and a second time, people would call one a chronic office seeker."[53] In these early years of law practice Waugh also began a lifelong custom of assisting poor women who needed legal services. In the same 1889 Equity Club letter she said, "When the client is a poor woman who cannot afford to pay anything I call that a free dispensary case and rejoice that I had an opportunity to learn some new point there."[54]

Suffrage politics also claimed a significant amount of Waugh's time. In the summer of 1889 she published a long essay in *The Farmer's Voice* on the growing debate about Christian theology in relation to women's rights. The target of Waugh's pen was not, as Mary Hall's had been, Elizabeth Cady Stanton. Waugh wrote in response to a male contributor who was "straining hard to prove that the Scripture is opposed to woman's voting and places her subject to man."[55] Waugh opened by reminding her readers that "the subject of balloting for one's legal representatives is not directly under discussion in the Bible and so we can find no direct commandment to men even to vote any more than to women . . . [W]e must study the general trend of its teachings." She fell back into the now familiar discussion of pronouns: Genesis says "let *them* have dominion." She noted that Adam and Eve were both punished, and then "Christ's coming lifted the curse for all." With sarcasm, she continued that "the opposers of woman enfranchisement make little of Christ, the master, and much of Paul, the servant." The whole of her essay shaped an interpretation of scripture that argued, "Bible teaching is for liberty and equality. It is not Christianity which opposes woman's progress but the lack of it and the bigotry and self-ishness which would debar women from a conference or legislature because her admission might keep out some male."

Writing was only one aspect of her suffrage advocacy. In 1890, she joined her legal and political interests and became legislative super-intendent of the Illinois Equal Suffrage Association (IESA). As the association's legislative watchdog and lobbyist, she tried to appeal to all factions interested in women's rights, including clergymen and la-bor unions. She was hard driving and sometimes dogmatic. She drew up a bill that provided for woman suffrage in presidential and certain local elections not limited by the Illinois constitution to male voters. The bill was introduced in 1893, regularly re-introduced, but enacted only in 1913.[56] As superintendent she was successful in winning pas-sage of other legislation important to women, including an Illinois joint guardianship bill. She later became legal advisor to the National American Woman Suffrage Association, serving the organization from 1904 through 1911.[57]

Catharine Waugh had already done a great deal when, at the age of twenty-eight, she married local attorney Frank Hathorn McCulloch, a former Union College of Law classmate. The May 30, 1890, ceremony was performed by the Reverend Anna Howard Shaw, a well-known suffrage and temperance leader. Waugh sent a written announcement to her Equity Club colleagues, saying that she was following the mari-tal example set by Jessie Wright and Lelia Robinson, each of whom had recently wed. Waugh wrote that she had "doubled my joys and halved my sorrows."[58] The bride had previously promised to speak at a suffrage campaign in South Dakota, and so the couple journeyed north on their honeymoon rather than to some fashionable watering spot.

Frank McCulloch was, according to his new wife, a brilliant man who was doing well in his Chicago practice. She told the Equity ladies,

"[S]o you see I won't leave the profession but will really step into a wider field of work."[59] She made this step by giving up her solo practice in Rockford and joining with Frank in McCulloch & McCulloch, a firm that they created. Five months after the wedding she described their life in Chicago: "We reach the office at 9 A.M. and leave at 6 P.M. We are keeping house with my brother and his wife only married recently, and divide between us the responsibility. . . . [B]etween the successful administration of there [home] and our prosperity here at the office, I am more contented and yet more ambitious than ever before."[60]

McCulloch revealed that, as a professional woman, she had been wary of marrying but Frank, bright, affectionate, and respectful, had been a good choice of husband. She confessed to her Equity Club sisters,

> I believe now that instead of crippling my ability to be a lawyer that my prospects are much improved. I believed differently a year ago, but it makes all the difference in the world who one married, and I should never again oppose a woman lawyer marrying, if she devotedly loved her husband and he was clean and brilliant and honorable and progressive enough to be proud that his wife was a lawyer.[61]

Equally forthright, she said that

> as yet I have had very little Chicago business of my own, being generally at work on matters belonging to Mr. McCulloch, but within the last month I had a genuine client and she had sent her friends to me with abstracts to examine and altogether we did $55 worth of work for them. It pleased me that something was coming to me.

In fact, while she built up a clientele, Frank's client list was larger, and he was busier.

Two years out of law school Catharine Waugh had scolded Mary Hall and urged her to summon up some professional gumption, advising her to come to Illinois, "where it is just as honorable for a woman to talk to men publicly as in private." Before, and after marriage, Catharine McCulloch certainly did not hold back. She was outspoken, caring more about shaping public opinion than, as was the case for Hall, responding to it.

Waugh was well known for her unequivocal views about women's rights when she became Catharine Waugh McCulloch. She spoke publicly, and before men. A year after their marriage, the first of the McCullochs' children arrived. The three boys and one girl were well spaced, with birth dates in 1891, 1899, 1901, and 1905. This created less pressure than Clara Foltz experienced with her tightly spaced brood. At a time when middle-class women retired to their homes upon marrying, maintaining a professional identity with even one child presented an indisputable statement of an independent identity. McCulloch sought work-family balance but wrote with real honesty in a memoir, "Necessary attention to children and home duties never wholly diverted Mrs. McCulloch from the family law office."[62]

Participating in a family law practice undoubtedly gave McCulloch a cushion. She may not have sought one, but as her children were born, the flexibility must have been helpful. She wrote very little about the joint practice. It was a given, a backdrop to everyday life. Scraps of her legal work seep out, here and there, of her various autobiographical accounts. In 1897 she collaborated in the representation of a retail dealer in meats, but increasingly McCulloch, not unlike a number of early women lawyers, combined legal case work with other forms of advocacy. Still, in February 1898, she successfully sought admission to the U.S. Supreme Court bar.[63]

Holding down the IESA legislative superintendent's position was one expression of McCulloch's commitment to the suffrage movement. Representing (with Frank) clients advocating for women's municipal suffrage was another. They wrote briefs in support of woman suffrage for consideration by the Chicago Charter Convention as well as the Elections Commission of Chicago.[64] Catharine McCulloch, a talented author, expanded the scope of her pro-suffrage political writing by publishing *Mr. Lex* (1899) and *Bridget's Daughters* (1911), fiction that dissected the case for women's rights. The degree to which she may have diversified her work as a response to a small client list is not something McCulloch talked about.

Three years after her marriage, Chicago hosted the 1893 World's Columbian Exposition. While the nation celebrated its achievements, women's organizations highlighted their history and accomplishments and spelled out an agenda for the coming years. A break-away faction of women formed the Queen Isabella Association, believing that the fair's glorification of Columbus slighted the queen who funded his expedition. The Isabellas, as they were known, vied with the Board of Lady Managers, and others, to be the exposition's voice of women. This feisty group sponsored exhibits and talks, and the first congress of women lawyers. At least fourteen women gave papers, Lockwood, Foltz, and Kepley among them, but not McCulloch. The *Chicago Legal News* reporter did not mention whether she attended. It is curious that McCulloch, an able and frequent speaker, the woman who urged Mary Hall forward, did not speak at this first formal meeting of women lawyers.

In 1894, their fortunes much improved from the early days of boarding with in-laws, the McCullochs moved to the Chicago suburb of Evanston. Catharine spent part of that year leading a political campaign to elect Lucy Coues Flower, a seasoned activist, as the first woman member of the University of Illinois Board of Trustees. Flower's success made her the first woman elected to a state office in Illinois. Through this campaign, McCulloch increased her own reputation as a woman who knew how to expand opportunities for women.

American women began contesting for elective office in the late 1860s.[65] They ran when the law permitted them to be candidates, and sometimes when it did not. In the last decades of the nineteenth century partial, or limited, suffrage opened the door to women campaigning for the position of school board member, county school superintendent, mayor, and later, state representative. In 1894 three women won election to the Colorado state legislature. Two years later, Dr. Martha Hughes Cannon ran successfully as the Democratic candidate for Utah state senator.

In 1907 Catharine McCulloch took the plunge and ran for justice of the peace in Evanston when a mid-term vacancy occurred. Unlike her 1888 campaign for state's attorney, which she undertook when she was single, McCulloch was now married with four children, ranging in age from two to sixteen. This bid for elective office expressed her pro-suffrage belief that women should have the right to participate in all aspects of politics and governance. It was not, however, a symbolic campaign. Smart and competitive, she wanted to win.

The contest was between McCulloch and a plumber named Billie Moore. Municipal suffrage for Illinois women was six years in the future. If McCulloch was to be successful, she had to win election from an all-male voting pool. Aside from her sex, Catharine held all the cards. Newspapers spoke highly of her character and professional training. Rather than let anti-suffrage hecklers confront her, or accuse her of not being at home with her family, McCulloch made the savvy decision to conduct a mail campaign rather than to give public speeches. She laid out her qualifications, her belief that women were eligible to hold office, and her desire to work near her children.[66] She defeated Moore by more than thirteen hundred votes. Moore and his supporters struck back by attempting to block the appointment on the grounds that women were not eligible for office. McCulloch's old law school classmate and friend, Governor Charles Densen, settled the matter by signing her commission.[67]

With the governor's approval of the voters' choice, McCulloch became the first woman in Illinois to hold the office of justice of the peace. The work was less challenging than client demands at McCulloch & McCulloch. She heard cases in a large hall with the jury nearby and often deposed of cases quickly, suggesting that much of her time was occupied with default judgments.[68] And, of course, she had the pleasure of marrying people.

The *Chicago Legal News*, which had survived Myra Bradwell's death, ran an article about McCulloch's victory as well as an article by the new justice of the peace arguing women that could, and should, hold elective office.[69] McCulloch was re-elected in 1909, serving until 1913. Later in life, she wrote her daughter that Florence E. Allen, confirmed in 1934 as the first woman to serve as a federal appeals judge, said that McCulloch's election as justice of the peace encouraged her successful campaign in 1920 for judge of the Cuyahoga County (Ohio) Court of Common Pleas.[70]

McCulloch brought intelligence, savvy, energy, and humor to everything she did. Some people found her feisty and prickly—she had a long organizational feud with Chicago suffrage leader Grace Wilbur Trout—but her accomplishments considerably outweighed any limits of personality. She continued to lobby relentlessly for suffrage, writing informational tracts as well as humorous pieces. While justice of the peace, she invented a women's rights educational game. Questions included "Does a married woman own her clothing?" and "Has any State Superintendent of Public Instruction been a woman?"[71] In this period she also wrote a delightfully satiric essay, "Shall Men Vote?" In it, the fictional Hon. Mrs. Libertas et Justitia, Chairman of the Elections Committee in the Oligarchy-of-Women State, carries on an interlocution with men arguing for male suffrage. The Hon. Mrs. reviews the impediments, saying, "[A] really great obstacle to men voting is that they are too emotional. I have observed it at football games and political conventions. Men of otherwise good character . . . howled like demons."[72] The Hon. Mrs. considers the arguments against male enfranchisement and decides that they are "bosh." Men "should not be governed without [their] consent . . . should have a jury of [their] peers. . . . [W]hen men can vote as well as we women, we will have a government 'of the people, for the people and by the people.'"[73]

Critical of the eastern orientation of the national woman suffrage organizations, in 1912 McCulloch helped to create the Mississippi Valley Conference, which held annual conventions of midwestern suffrage leaders.[74] In 1916, the Illinois Democratic Convention selected McCulloch as one of the presidential electors supporting Woodrow Wilson. A year later she was appointed master in chancery of the Cook County Superior Court, serving several terms.[75] McCulloch also increased the time she was giving to her practice with Frank while serving the Woman's Christian Temperance Union and, from 1916 to 1920, presiding over the Women's Bar Association of Illinois. After the founding of the League of Women Voters, she served as a legal advisor.

In her later years McCulloch sought to improve her understanding of the law, as well as to help legal professionals. In 1929 she and Frank jointly published *A Manual of the Law of Will Contests in Illinois*. In the 1930s the couple traveled widely, "studying progressive social legislation in other countries."[76] Catharine was said to have been particularly impressed with the Soviet Union's legal system, "in which women took an important part."[77]

Women's public role and rights were an abiding concern of McCulloch's. At the time of her death in 1945 she had come a very long way from that day in Chicago when "bullet headed little Mr. B." told her, "I don't approve of women at the bar. . . . I advise you to . . . go home and take in sewing." Unlike Mary Hall, she would not step back because some of the public did not accept the propriety of women in court, or thought that speaking in public would "unsex" them. Yet McCulloch *and* Hall both were women of singular accomplishment whose lives were a conversation in rebellion in the service of community. Each subverted contemporary mores and changed laws, using differing strategies and voices. Each benefited from the status and money of family, teasing from their advantaged lives the opportunity to use their legal knowledge outside of law offices or courtrooms—Hall as a philanthropist, McCulloch as a suffrage organizer and political candidate. Each, like Myra Bradwell, had firm ties to their communities that stood in marked contrast to their West Coast sister, Clara Foltz, whose wanderlust was unique among women who generally counted on local ties and status to build practices and win town and county elections.

❖ 8 ❖

Lelia Robinson and Mary Greene

Two Women from Boston University School of Law

Do not take sex into the practice. Don't be "lady lawyers." Simply be *lawyers,* and recognize no distinction. . . . Let no one regard you as a curiosity or a rara avis. Compel recognition of your ability.

—Lelia J. Robinson, 1887

THEY GAVE COMFORT to one another, Lelia Robinson and Mary Greene, in 1888 the only two women practicing law in Boston. Greene said of their friendship, "I think it is helpful to both of us to feel that neither is 'the only woman lawyer in Massachusetts.'"[1] Robinson agreed that more women lawyers meant each could "march on with a firmer and stronger tread."[2] Women of great intellect, they also had in common New England backgrounds, diplomas from Boston University School of Law, a love of writing, and a talent for the law. They welcomed praise but eschewed flash.

Robinson, born in 1850, was senior in age and had launched her legal career six years before Greene began law school. Boston born and educated, at the age of twenty-one Robinson began writing for several Boston newspapers, including the *Globe,* the *Post,* and the *Times.* While the precise chronology is not clear, she also married in this period and spent time in Berlin as a foreign correspondent. Rupert Chute, the bridegroom, was exposed as a philanderer and so, despite the considerable social and religious stigma of divorce, Robinson took

Lelia Robinson (1850-1891). (Reprinted from *The Green Bag*, 1890.)

Mary A. Greene (1857-1936). (Reprinted from *A Woman of the Century*, ed. Frances E. Willard and Mary A. Livermore [Buffalo, NY: C. W. Moulton, 1893].)

her wandering husband to court in 1878, ended the marriage, and at the age of twenty-eight resumed the use of her maiden name.[3] In the same year, she entered Boston University School of Law. Mary Greene later wrote that Robinson did not enter with the "idea of becoming an apostle of woman's rights, for at that time her views were extremely conservative."[4] Rather, Robinson was said to like to study and "felt that a woman could find a place for the successful practice of law."[5] Robinson's acceptance of divorce and belief in society's ability to embrace women as lawyers suggest that she was not quite as conservative as Greene portrayed her.

Boston University's law school opened in 1872 when Belva Lockwood was still fighting to join the Washington, D.C., bar and Myra Bradwell's case awaited a decision from the U.S. Supreme Court. Pleasing some, and shocking others, the school declared itself a coeducational institution. According to tuition receipts, Robinson matriculated in October 1879. Two women had attended before her for a year and dropped out, making her the lone woman student among 150 men. She paid thirty-five dollars in tuition for her first term.[6]

The law school used the traditional lecture method of teaching. To help to distinguish its program from Harvard's, the Boston University curriculum encouraged the practical application of legal concepts. The school's location at Ashburton Place, then the heart of Boston, placed students close to the local and federal courthouses where they were expected to "observe the organization and working of courts, the actual progress of the most notable cases, the arguments of eminent counsel, the ruling of judges, the processes of decision, exception, appeal, etc."[7]

Robinson arrived at Ashburton Place with the sort of practical questions common to tainted newcomers few wish to help. She introduced herself to the dean, but he introduced her neither to the faculty nor to the students.[8] She was told to "sit anywhere" in the lecture hall when, in fact, seating was alphabetical. An "R," she sat in the place of a "C," a student too gentlemanly to oust her. Yet, unlike in Lockwood's experience, her presence did not cause a rancorous environment in which the male scholars "growled," although the faculty was "puzzled to understand why a woman should want to study law."[9]

Lockwood started law school with a group and a cause; Robinson walked the halls alone and was not identified with woman suffrage. Social and intuitive by nature, she thought it "absurd not to speak to these men whom I was to meet daily, for lack of an introduction," so Robinson began "to bow and speak to all whose faces I could remember, wherever I met them, in school or out." By behaving as though she belonged, Robinson did not feel out of place and the male students complimented her as a "good fellow." Belong she did, in June 1881 graduating fourth in her class.

Robinson's parents and sister lived in Boston. She wished to practice law in the city in order to be close to them. Her experience, however, mirrored that of Goodell and McCulloch before her marriage. Boston's male attorneys did not wish to bring a lady practitioner into their office. After "utterly failing" to obtain any sort of position at a law firm, she opened a tiny workplace of her own in a building used by lawyers, hung her diploma, sent out cards, and, with other members of her graduating class, applied for admission to the Massachusetts bar, the first woman to do so.[10] Unlike the applications of the male graduates, hers was sent to Massachusetts' supreme judicial court. Like any male lawyer without a license, Robinson could not take cases to trial without bar admission, a situation that would affect her reputation and earnings. She was not particularly surprised that the application had been culled from the others, but after two years of law school, and graduation with honors, Robinson was not about to be sidelined. Late in the summer she began writing a petition in defense of her right to take the bar examination.[11]

In 1881 the rules required that an applicant for the bar be at least twenty-one years of age, a citizen of the commonwealth, and of good moral character. The petitioner also had to pass an examination administered by the superior court or supreme judicial court. Robinson's brief argued that the term "citizen" included women, that it was a sex-neutral term, and that she should be examined. She also argued that in withholding the opportunity to take the bar exam, the state was abridging privileges and immunities guaranteed by the U.S. Constitution's Fourteenth Amendment.

Bostonians—Puritans, American revolutionaries, abolitionists—
have seldom shied from strong opinions. After the Civil War, fer-
vor marked the range of viewpoints in the matter of women's rights.
In 1873, nearly a decade before Robinson's bar application, several
women, including Lucia Peabody, created a political tornado by winning election to the Boston School Committee. The women's eligibil-
ity to serve was immediately challenged on the grounds of their sex.
Peabody responded by filing for a writ of mandamus to compel the
school commissioners to permit her to take office. The court refused.
Sympathetic state legislators, seeing the issue differently, stepped in,
supported the women's right to hold this particular office, and enacted
a law providing that women throughout Massachusetts, if elected,
might serve on school committees.[12] The liberalization was hardly
breathtaking, but the legislation illustrated a divide between courts
and legislatures replayed repeatedly, in those years, all over the United
States.

Men and women outside of government also did battle around the
question of women's rights. In 1869 Lucy Stone, Julia Ward Howe, and
Henry Blackwell founded the American Woman Suffrage Association.
Centered in Boston, the organization was dedicated to winning the
vote for women. In 1870 they established the pro-rights *Woman's Journal*, which put reform women all over the country in touch with one
another, and publicized the achievements of pioneers like Robinson.

But in Boston, the "Americans" found themselves on the other side
of the table from equally formidable minds, citizens who opposed
woman suffrage as staunchly as the reformers supported it. Louis D.
Brandeis, rising star in the Boston legal community and future U.S.
Supreme Court justice, in 1884 proudly wrote his brother Al that he
had delivered a speech before a special state legislative committee
against the (municipal) enfranchisement of women.[13] Kate Gannett
Wells, member of a well-known family of Unitarian ministers, joined
him at this session, where she argued that women were politically naïve and emotional.[14] In his 1886 novel *The Bostonians*, Henry James described Boston as "the city of reform."[15] However, in telling the story of
Olive Chancellor, Verena Tarrant, and Basil Ransom, James revealed

considerable discomfort with women's rights. In nineteenth-century Boston, social convention and reform mixed uncomfortably, dating back to differences between the Transcendentalists, who often led unconventional lives, and the Brahmin Unitarians, who promoted many progressive causes but remained conventional about many things, including gender roles.[16]

As Lelia Robinson's case made its way to court, opponents repeated commonplace concerns: the unsexing of women who entered public life; the expected neglect of families; the anticipated link between liberalization of work laws and demands for suffrage, as well as variations on Brandeis's belief that "the franchise was not a right but a privilege, and that the duties involved in exercise of the privilege should be imposed only upon men."[17] The Boston Bar Association, like the local bar in Mary Hall's case, arranged for briefs in opposition. Two Boston attorneys also submitted *amici curiae* (friend of the court) briefs opposed to her admission.[18] Robinson responded with a supplemental brief attacking these prejudices and stereotypes: "In the many states where women have been for years practicing as attorneys . . . [they] have proved that the 'sweeping revolution of social order' . . . has not followed as the result, natural or otherwise, of the admission of women to the bar."[19]

Lelia J. Robinson's Case was argued before the full bench of the Massachusetts Supreme Judicial Court. Vividly demonstrating the bar's division on the question, Robinson was represented in court by former attorney general C. R. Train.

In November the decision came down denying Robinson's petition, with the justices holding that she needed positive affirmation from the state legislature that Massachusetts women had the right to be admitted to the bar. Writing for the court, Chief Justice Horace Gray asserted that, given women's historical exclusion from the practice of law, the word "citizen" in the legislation governing bar admission was not inclusive of the two sexes: "A woman is not, by virtue of her citizenship, vested by the Constitution of the United States, or by the Constitution of the Commonwealth, with any absolute right, independent of legislation, to take part in the government, either as a voter or as an officer, or to be admitted to practice as an attorney."[20] Robinson was seemingly damned, whether the word "male" had or had not been used, as Gray went on to write, "No inference of an intention of the Legislature to include women in the statutes concerning the admission of attorneys can be drawn from the mere omission of the word 'male.'"[21]

Like Belva Lockwood when rebuffed by the U.S. Court of Claims in 1874, Robinson quickly penned language for corrective legislation. The draft specifically authorized qualified women to take the bar examination and to practice in a court of law.[22] At the end of January Massachusetts representative John Hopkins introduced bill number 214, which was assigned to the House Judiciary Committee, hearings to follow on March 15.[23] Charles Train, Thomas Wentworth Higginson, and other prominent men supported the bill. Robinson primed public opinion prior to the hearings by appearing at the Boston Mercantile Library, where she spoke about women's need to earn their living and, strategically, mentioned the need to help "overworked fathers and brothers."[24] She then testified for more than thirty minutes before the legislature.[25] Robinson proceeded with care, insisting that there should be a departure from the "old-established order of things" but acknowledging that such change should be treated as "an experiment." She assured the legislators that passage of the bill would not be a radical act, that fifteen territories and states already permitted women to practice law. Women lawyers would, she believed, limit themselves to appropriate areas of the profession and know their place in society. She argued that women attorneys would not influence juries with "smiles and tears" and, finally, that equal opportunity should guide lawmaking: women lawyers, like men, should be at "liberty to fail or succeed."

The bill passed quickly in both houses and was signed by the governor. It was a small coup in a year when the same legislature failed to vote municipal suffrage for Massachusetts women. In June Robinson became the first woman to take the Massachusetts bar examination— and to pass. She described the moment as crossing "the grand Rubicon which made me a full-fledged attorney."[26]

Robinson had crossed her Rubicon, had made an irrevocable commitment to law. Admission to the bar, however, did not assure her of clients, and she found herself sitting day after day in the small office having "to wait-wait-wearily wait" and "have the funds to endure it."[27] Unlike with Belva Lockwood, who claimed that her contests with the courts won her notice and clients, the attention paid to Robinson's struggle did not bring her cases. Wryly, she commented that women were "more timid and reluctant to trust their affairs to the care of a woman lawyer than are men," with the latter being apt to say, "Give her a chance."[28] Lockwood had her local connections and veteran pension clients, Goodell had her temperance ladies and a local judge, but Robinson reports having no Boston mentors to help her, in a city where people "are reluctant to trust any but gray hairs."[29] Perhaps inspired by Mary Hall's appointment as a commissioner, in 1883 Robinson successfully lobbied for a bill permitting Massachusetts women to become special commissioners who could take depositions and affidavits and administer oaths.[30] She won an appointment from the governor. She welcomed the work but did not find it challenging.

Legal cases came in "very slowly" during her first three years of practice, and consisted mostly "of small and rather hopeless claims for collection."[31] Robinson would engage another lawyer if a case went to court. This meant paying over part of her fees, but like Mary Hall, Robinson had not originally intended to do court business "at all."[32] She later revealed that her friends in the profession in Boston had been contradictory concerning the "advisability of [her] doing court work," perhaps suggesting the influence of peer pressure.[33]

Robinson appreciated that male attorneys also had a difficult time starting out. Still, in 1888, when she read the letter by Kittie Waugh (McCulloch) recounting how she "sallied forth to seek [her] fortune . . . and dragged back collapsed with chagrin and failure," she laughed at the tremendous similarity of their early professional experiences.[34] Kittie Waugh retreated to Rockford. Still unmarried, she used her spare time to earn a master's degree and to write a thesis analyzing the inequality of women's wages. Lelia Robinson initially stayed in Boston and made a rule that she would use her "waiting time" in study.[35] She wanted study with a "specific object," and in casting about discovered "the lack of any reliable treatise giving to the public at large those elementary principles of law which everyone must have in order to conduct the daily affairs of life intelligently." She began the research for a book that, in 1886, became *Law Made Easy: A Book for the People*.

* * *

In the second half of the nineteenth century, the allure of the American West pulled thousands upon thousands of people out of rural towns and crowded cities. Men, women, and children uprooted themselves in search of land, commercial opportunities, work, and, in some cases, new identities. In March 1884 Lelia Robinson joined the ranks of the westward-bound hopefuls, setting out across the continent, alone, for the Washington Territory. She made no secret of her vexation at the limited professional opportunities open to her at home. However, she made the brave, dramatic move chiefly influenced by accounts of the "liberality of western views on the 'woman question.'"[36]

When Robinson entered the Washington Territory in May of 1884, married women's property laws had recently been reformed, and women had just been voted full suffrage rights, and could serve on petit and grand juries.[37] In the view of historian Sandra VanBurkleo, at this moment Washington women "stood at the threshold of political and economic equality. . . . spouses had become co-sovereigns within households."[38] Married women, subject to coverture under the common law, had been *uncovered*. Opponents, however, saw the reforms as "unnatural" or "'womanly' contamination of the body politic."[39] They found the idea of household male-female co-sovereignty, or the smashing of the "unitary household head," vile, and a wrongful interpretation of law.

Robinson hoped to build a large and interesting law practice, ultimately selecting Seattle as the place she would settle. She was probably oblivious when she first entered the city to the degree of the backlash that was developing against these gender reforms.

Life in Seattle drew out talents and inclinations Robinson had previously suppressed. It permitted a very public and outgoing persona to emerge, and to flourish. The networking Robinson pursued in Boston had not paid off professionally. She was sufficiently savvy, however, to obtain at least one letter of introduction. (There may have been more, but if her male supporters —C. R. Train or Thomas Higginson—wrote on her behalf, that paper has been lost.) The letter she presented in Seattle was written by Mrs. Robert Harris, wife of the president of Northern Pacific Railroad, to a prominent member of the city's society, a "Mrs. Weed."[40] It opened doors. Two days after her arrival Robinson was invited to observe a session of the circuit court, sitting for its last week in Seattle. Women were seated in the jury box, ex-governors and ex-judges milled about, mingling, in the way of a still-small city, with most of the town's attorneys. Robinson was delighted, and a bit shocked, by the women jurors. When court ended she was introduced to the presiding judge, Roger Sherman Greene, and well-known territorial jury lawyer John C. Haines. In these men she found professional mentors, relationships that had so persistently eluded her in Boston.

Roger Greene, born into a family of East Coast political bluebloods, practiced law in New York City and Chicago before being appointed by President Ulysses Grant in 1870 as an associate justice on the Supreme Court of Washington Territory. He became a Republican Mugwump, and later a member and candidate of the Prohibition Party. He held Perfectionist Christian beliefs and, by the time Robinson met him, was chief justice of his court.[41] He was a man of very strong opinions. He "believed scoundrels feared women's moral power."[42] In 1884 he told a grand jury that "the opponents of woman suffrage are found allied with a solid phalanx of gamblers, prostitutes, pimps, and drunkard-makers."[43] Some Washingtonians found him eccentric, others said he was "maniacal," still others called him a "fearless ... social reformer."[44] The women's movement had deeply engaged Greene throughout his adult life. It was natural for him to take a hand in building Robinson's Seattle career.

Seattle, despite being a small community, had a remarkable bar.[45] John Haines and Henry G. Struve belonged to that bar, and had a law firm that also included a new partner, 24-year-old Maurice McMicken. Struve, Haines & McMicken was the town's premier firm. Struve had been a judge and would become mayor of Seattle. Haines was later appointed to the federal bench. They might have been "gray hairs" in the mode of Boston, but were not. Indeed, at the time Robinson met him, Haines was only thirty-four years old—about the age of Seattle. The partners demonstrated their liberality by offering Robinson a desk in their office. When she took her place at the firm she met Mary Leonard (later helped by Clara Foltz in Portland), who was reading law with Haines and also had a desk in the office. Leonard was a Swiss immigrant who had worked as a maid and seamstress in Portland. While in Oregon she had also been tried and acquitted of the murder of Daniel Leonard, her husband.[46] Mary Leonard exuded moxie and Foltz liked her. For unstated reasons, Robinson did not. Still, Robinson served on Leonard's bar examination committee and gave her a pass.

Judge Greene rode circuit, making it necessary for Robinson to wait until summer to be admitted to the local bar. When the judge made a quick trip to Seattle, he took up the matter. Greene noted Robinson's Massachusetts experience and her Suffolk County bar membership, and swore her in. With the circuit court in session elsewhere, however, during the summer of 1884 Robinson, new and female, found herself with little work. Refusing to be inactive, she used her free time to learn stenography, most likely from the city's only stenographer, Thomas Purdie.[47] Later, giving practical advice to her Equity Club sisters, Robinson urged "every woman who studies law to study stenography also, for it will be invaluable in getting her clerkship opportunities, and if she practices west, it will give her the chance of filling in empty hours by reporting testimony in court. . . . excellently paying work directly in the line of [our] profession."[48]

Robinson had her first shot at challenging legal research when Henry Struve requested that she work on an appeal brief of considerable interest, and controversy. In May Struve, also riding circuit, had objected to the inclusion of two women being sworn in for a Tacoma grand jury. At first glance, his willingness to take this position, one shared by partner John Haines, appeared at odds with the firm's fair treatment of Leonard and Robinson. It was, of course, a business decision although the firm might have declined the case. Struve's action highlighted a divide in liberal Territorial circles: enthusiasm for certain rights such as woman suffrage or women's employment did not necessarily extend to support for women jurors.[49] Although mixed-sex juries were now the law in the territory, part of the public groused openly and loudly about lady jurors. They spoke about the likely neglect of domestic duties, the rough and tumble of the courtroom, and the anticipation that women jurors would feminize justice, introducing new norms and letting emotion dominate reason.[50]

Whatever his private views, in court Struve contended that the two Tacoma women should not be sworn as jurors because they were married women living with their husbands. He said the jury service statute required that jurors be householders and that under the statute there could be only one householder, the husband. He also argued federal issues. He raised the Fourteenth Amendment and questioned whether Congress, in the 1853 Organic Act establishing the territory, intended to give the territory the power to enfranchise women, or to seat them on juries.[51] Struve was overruled and appealed to the territorial supreme court. Robinson was assigned to research the law buttressing the argument that married women could not be considered householders.

Robinson wrote that the territory's liberality had drawn her across the continent. Once in Washington, however, she began separating her support for woman suffrage from her feelings about women serving on juries. Early in her stay she said, "[W]hatever might be the policy and the desirability of women's voting, it was carrying the matter a little too far to force them to do jury service."[52] However, by the time Struve put Robinson to work on the appeals brief, the women of Washington had won her over. She had observed mixed-sex juries at work and come to admire the comportment and decision-making skills of the female jurors. Researching the legislators' intentions with respect to the term "householders," Robinson understood that her "sympathies were on one side of the question, my work . . . on the other, as sometimes must happen."[53] She wrote a good brief, but in September Judge Greene's court sustained the lower court. Struve appealed to the U.S. Supreme Court on the constitutional issue. (In 1885, with a new member on Greene's court, Struve's position was upheld. Greene wrote a scathing dissent.)

Some attorneys continued to oppose women jurors. However, in her 1886 article "Women Jurors," Robinson delighted in reporting that many male lawyers, initially opposed to the reform, had been "converted" by trying cases before women jurors.[54] They found the women to be "intelligent, clear-headed, quick-witted, and reliable." Attorneys like Struve and Haines sometimes tried to pander to the emotions of female jurors and had to learn that this was a mistake. Haines nearly lost a self-defense case with such a ploy. Robinson wrote that the experience "convinced the astonished lawyer that nothing but straight and square evidence could be made available with women jurors."[55]

Judge Greene was the most consistently helpful of the men Robinson encountered in Seattle. Like the local judges sympathetic to Belva Lockwood and Wisconsin's Judge Conger, who appointed Lavinia Goodell defense counsel in several criminal trials, Greene gave Robinson professional opportunities. As soon as he had developed a sense of her abilities, he appointed her a court referee in divorce cases as well as other civil matters. As a referee she took testimony from witnesses and made recommendations to the judge. The work was, she wrote, "sure pay and good pay."[56]

Greene also believed that Robinson would make a good trial advocate and was not apprehensive that she would bring "gendered justice" into his courtroom. Indeed, as a deeply religious man, he welcomed what he believed were women's unique moral sensibilities. Robinson's other Seattle professional friends agreed that courtroom work was important for a woman, and joined Greene in urging her to do more than back office work.[57] She did not hesitate despite the reserve she had shown in Boston. She did admit, however, to initial "fear and trembling."[58]

Robinson's Seattle debut as a trial advocate came in the October session of Greene's court. At the beginning of the month he had appointed her to defend Ah Mon, who had been indicted for "bringing and aiding and abetting persons to bring in Chinese to the United States from British Columbia."[59] She represented Ah Mon at the arraignment, and prepared her defense in just a week. Robinson argued the case before a mixed-sex jury, making her the first female attorney to bring a case to trial before a jury of men and women. After three hours of deliberation, the jury returned a verdict of not guilty.

Robinson was a true convert. After several trials she concluded that "the public, from whom business must come if at all, judges a woman lawyer as it does a man, largely by his success or non-success in court, and if one is never seen or heard there, one's abilities are a matter of serious doubt."[60] The Ah Mon case established Robinson's reputation. She received other referrals from Greene, and also handled three or four well-paying cases as a member of the Struve, Haines & McMichen firm, including representation of a husband in a high-profile divorce proceeding.[61]

Robinson also gave herself permission to speak in public in support of woman suffrage and women's duty to vote. At a women's meeting sponsored by the Congregational Church she drew upon her knowledge of Boston, where women had the right to vote in school elections but, she said, generally did not do so. She urged Seattle women to do better, and to accept the responsibilities that come with equal legal and political status. Reformer and newspaper publisher Clara Colby, a good friend of Belva Lockwood's, came to Seattle from the Midwest the week of this meeting. The women were introduced and Colby also agreed to speak. She pulled out her best camp meeting voice and argued that "the nation was watching this Northwest corner. If the move is successful here, your actions and words will be mentioned and quoted all over the United States . . . [and] will prove an immense leverage in the hands of woman suffragists all over the land."[62] Robinson and Colby had great success, and at the close of the meeting "the women *en masse* expressed by a rising vote their determination to register and vote at the city election."[63]

Perhaps spending the 1884 Christmas holidays away from her family triggered homesickness, or perhaps Robinson's parents and sister had written to say that they would not, as planned, re-settle in Seattle. Whatever the reason, or reasons, on January 11, 1885, the *Seattle Post-Intelligencer* reported that Robinson would soon leave on a trip to Boston.[64] She attended a farewell party replete with food, music, and poetry, and was off for the East. Although her experience in Seattle had been a very positive one—"I was delighted with the place, climate, people, and the bright new civilization; succeeded well professionally," Robinson wrote her Equity Club friends—she did not return to Seattle because "it proved impracticable for my family to join me," and she had been "exceedingly heart-sick for lack of them."[65] This may have been all for the best as shortly the politics of women's rights, liquor prohibition, illegal gambling, and the Grange tore into the precarious political and legal equality that had been established in the territory, ending the "liberality" that had drawn Lelia Robinson to the West. Judge Greene, who "thought of women as the embodiment of community virtue, and constructed himself as their divinely-ordained custodian, [became] a focus of charges of 'unnatural' feminization and degradation of the polity."[66] By 1888 women suffrage in Washington Territory had been revoked, and women no longer occupied seats in the jury box.[67]

* * *

Robinson returned to Boston in the winter of 1885. Illness of some sort plagued her for months. In the spring, she did not look about for a law office (or if she did, remained mum about it). Instead, Robinson decided to spend several months in Chicago working with the publisher of her manuscript *Law Made Easy*. She had labored on the book since 1882, and now had a lengthy document to refine and edit. A legal practice in Boston would wait. She loved the law but confessed that "the book has taken a deeper hold on my affections and my ambitions than the practice itself, and so it becomes, for a time . . . first in its claims on my time and attention."[68] The "claim" was not a small one.

She followed the six months living in Chicago with a year on the road. One letter to the Equity Club was written from Texas. She was supervising the work of book agents responsible for selling *Law Made Easy*, and did not return to Boston until 1887.[69]

Robinson's book, dedicated to her parents, was a remarkable achievement, both in concept and in substance. The concept was simple, yet daring and revolutionary. She did not write *Law Made Easy* for the "gray hairs," or for law school students, but rather for the lay public. In forty-one chapters she laid out "those elementary principles of law which everyone must have in order to conduct the daily affairs of life intelligently."[70]

In her September 1886 introduction, Robinson wrote that her book would enable the public "to keep clear of the legal pitfalls which yawn before unwary feet in this busy world of ours."[71] It would not be an "every-man-his-own-lawyer kind of book" that caused people to think they knew as much as a lawyer and, therefore, to get into legal scrapes.[72] She avoided the unnecessary use of technical language and made certain to treat all subjects. She trusted that her previous experience in journalism would enable her to understand the public need, and that her legal training would enable her to meet it. She reported, tongue-in-cheek, that "no personal opinions are intruded and no hobby-horses ridden, in any part of this work."[73] This was, of course, untrue. *Law Made Easy* represented her deeply held view that lay people deserved a book through which they could inform themselves about "the every-day business of life."[74]

Robinson told her readers that the text was written "with a view to consecutive reading" and suggested, indeed "beg[ged] all who take up the book at all, to read it through attentively from the first page to the last, at least once. Afterward, it may be used for reference on particular points."[75] The book sold well.

Boston once again became Robinson's permanent home in the autumn of 1887. She had not practiced law in two and a half years and "from my former experience here . . . dreaded the prospect."[76] Insecure about her recall of Massachusetts law, she entered into a general law clerkship—offered to her only because of her knowledge of stenography—in the office of "an old lawyer who [had] a tremendous business . . . that extends from the supreme court to the municipal criminal."[77] Her employer "was entirely unaccustomed to having a woman about the office," and the arrangement ended after only three tiring months.[78]

Again, on her own, in January of 1888 Robinson found a little room in which to start up a solo practice. The space opened from the large offices used by two male attorneys who specialized in trust and conveyancing business (drafting and preparing deeds and leases that transfer an interest in real property). The room pleased her, in part because she had a view of the new courthouse being built across the square. She was given free rent, and in exchange occasionally worked for one or the other of her landlords. The arrangement permitted her to come and go without worrying about losing clients because the office was closed. Her colleagues made their large library available to her, and she learned the practical aspects of abstracting titles. To announce her new circumstances, Robinson sent out business cards and placed an advertisement in the *Woman's Journal*, the publication of the American Woman Suffrage Association for which she often wrote articles.

From a distance, Robinson's professional situation hardly spelled success. It was another beginning. Standing in her shoes, Clara Foltz would have felt stymied. Robinson was nonetheless happy with her practice and, as she saw it, the progress made by women lawyers. In April 1888 she wrote her Equity Club sisters that a great deal had changed for the better: "The Sun do move! . . . Half a dozen years seems to have cleared away the fogs of doubt and hesitation through which I was viewed, and the idea of a woman in the law is no longer an uncomfortable novelty."[79]

Robinson's upbeat appraisal of women lawyers' future was sparked by the positive change in the public's view of her as well as two new alumna of Boston University's law school. After Jessie Wright's 1887 graduation, and Mary Greene's in 1888, Robinson was no longer the sole alumna. She could set aside her feelings of being an oddity. In addition to her practice, Robinson took women as student-apprentices (they studied mostly at home) and began work on a new book, the law of husband and wife, again a primer for the lay public.[80]

And Mary Greene became Lelia Robinson's dear friend. In 1888, with Jessie Wright married and practicing in Topeka, they were Boston's two lady lawyers. They shared many values, contented themselves with small solo practices, and loved to produce legal writing. In published articles and Equity Club letters they seldom passed up an opportunity to refer to one another, or to pass along a compliment.[81]

Greene was born in Warwick, Rhode Island, in 1857. The state had been founded by her ancestors. Greene came to Boston for law school following the death of her father. She was responsible for his widow and in her late twenties entered the program for the practical purpose of understanding the law and, thus, being better able to handle her own and her mother's business affairs.[82] In a letter written to Equity Club members while she was still a law student, Greene described herself as previously "most woefully ignorant of the very first principles of our Common Law."[83] She had also taken to heart the experiences of other widowed women who had been "duped and deceived in money matters by those who should have been their most trust-worthy friends." While in law school Greene had something of an epiphany about business and estate practices. She felt that women with legal problems would prefer a sympathetic female attorney. She said that they would consult women lawyers and talk freely with them, in ways they would not with male attorneys. "Here," she wrote, "was a field for women." The thought pleased her, yet she also spoke gravely of "pioneers . . . [being] narrowly watched and keenly criticized" with a "slight misstep of one bring[ing] suspicion on all."

Law school had been uneventful and pleasant. Greene dealt more easily with the discussion of "delicate" subjects, presumably medical jurisprudence, than Kitty Waugh. She wrote that these discussions were "necessary parts of our legal course, and [must be viewed] in a business light, putting all false modesty aside."[84] She imagined woman's position in medical school with mixed-sex classes as more far unpleasant. In addition to her classes, like Jessie Wright before her Greene spent her last year of school working in the law offices of prominent

Boston attorney Alfred Hemenway. Like Struve and Haines in Seattle, Hemenway had fashioned a mentor's role for himself, leaving Greene to say that not all Boston was conservative.[85] As she prepared to graduate—*magna cum laude*—Greene said she was open to what business came along but wanted to make conveyancing her specialty. Over the course of her thirty-year career in law, she did just this, specializing in conveyancing and estate work.

Judge Walbridge Field swore Greene in as a member of the Suffolk bar on September 28, 1888. Robinson's friendship and example made waiting for clients less painful. Together they drafted legislation on matters of mutual interest. The women successfully wrote and lobbied for an amendment to the overly vague Massachusetts Act of 1883 (ch. 252 permitting women lawyers to be commissioned by the governor to administer oaths, take depositions, and acknowledge deeds). The change clarified their powers as well as giving such women lawyers the powers of a justice of the peace in many matters, such as taking affidavits and issuing summonses for witnesses.[86]

Greene believed that women attorneys ought to go into court. She did not do so with any regularity, in part because of her legal specialty and also because Greene suffered from a lifelong throat ailment that sometimes left her ill for months. (In her sixties she moved to California to improve her health.) She did take charity clients. While some of her Equity sisters-in-law wrote positively of learning from these clients and growing as human beings, Greene did not like the experience: "I, in common with others, have suffered from the ingratitude of that kind of people. I do not mind the ingratitude for favors conferred so much as I do the insinuation . . . that I have not taken the pains in working up his case that I would have done if I had received money for it."[87] She seemed, however, to feel that it was her Christian duty to take such work.

Greene was not alone. Washington, D.C., attorney Emma Gillett wrote that charity and sympathy were wearing. "Charity clients," she said, "should be shunned unless in extreme cases. They have no more right to a lawyer's services for nothing than a washerwoman's, and when one takes charity clients to any extent she lowers her professional tone."[88] Robinson did not agree with Greene and Gillett. She counseled immigrant and working women at Boston's Women's Educational and Industrial Union, and held open hours from two to four o'clock at her office on Saturdays for women too poor to pay her fee.[89]

Like Robinson, Greene had a sharp mind and a talent for writing. In 1889, while trying to attract clients, she became increasingly interested in legal scholarship. In less than four years she would travel to Chicago to deliver a major address in front of the leading jurists of the world.

Greene's first scholarly venture after law school involved the translation from the French of Dr. Louis Frank's pamphlet, *Woman Lawyer*. Frank was a noted Belgian lawyer and reformer who, with lawyer Marie Popelin, co-founded the Ligue belge du droit des femmes (Belgian League for Women's Rights). Lawyer Catharine Waite published the translation in her journal, the *Chicago Law Times*.

Greene next turned to the question of contracts between husband and wife. Greene had started law school with an eye to the problems of widows. She quickly broadened the scope of her interests and, like Robinson, committed herself to the education, protection, and empowerment of all women. In 1889 Greene testified on the issue of husband-wife contracts before the Judiciary Committee of the Massachusetts legislature. She argued in support of a petition for the validity of such contracts. Her concern centered upon the impact of marital privilege interfering with the enforcement of contracts between spouses because they could not testify against one another. After testifying, Greene re-shaped her testimony as a scholarly article and published "Privileged Communications in Suits between Husband and Wife" in the prestigious *American Law Review*.[90] She was the first woman to publish in that journal.

She next wrote a series of articles, "Practical Points of Every-Day Law," for the *Chautauquan*. Updated, her papers on the property rights of woman became a central topic in her 1902 book, *The Woman's Manual of Law*.[91] Business law, prepared and presented to women, also became the centerpiece of her adjunct teaching career. From 1889 to 1906, at Lasell Seminary, the school where Mary Hall taught for many years, Greene offered a well-attended a class titled "Business for Women."[92] Lasell was the first girls' school to give courses in law. Earlier Greene's mentor, Alfred Hemenway, taught Lasell students a class in "Principles of Common Law."

Lelia Robinson had a strong interest in networking with other professional women. Greene joined her in some of these activities. They were both devoted members of the Equity Club. Robinson reported once staying up until midnight to read a packet of club letters.[93] She felt "really acquainted" with the other correspondents—"each one in her own little niche of my thoughts"—and in 1888 made the suggestion that the women come to know each other better through the exchange of photographs. Robinson meant this to have personal value, but she also wrote that there were advantages of a "practical nature to be derived from real familiarity with each other." She made referrals for clients by letter and telegraph to attorneys around the country. It was "especially desirable that we women should be as familiar as possible with each other's professional standing and experience, that we may be able to render mutual aid and support." With men's social clubs closed to women, and many bar associations still engaging in sexual discrimination, Robinson understood the need to build parallel institutions that would serve women.

In 1888 Robinson and Greene founded the Portia Club as just such an organization. Women lawyers and law students from all over Massachusetts, initially a small number, gathered once a month for an informal dinner. The meetings were held on Saturday afternoons in a private dining room of a downtown Boston hotel. The socializing of the Portia Club members was more immediate and intimate than that of the Equity Club members. By 1890 Greene felt free to pronounce the Portia Club "a flourishing institution with its monthly dinners and discussions."[94]

Among attendees at the dinners were eight new women students at Boston University Law School and attorney Alice Parker, a former resident of Lowell who had studied law, and passed the bar, in San Francisco, and had now returned to Massachusetts where she divided her time and professional activities between Lowell and Boston. She was the author of many amendments before the state legislature affecting the property rights of women. In Boston she shared an office with Robinson, whose practice had been steadily increasing, particularly in the probate area, where she had executed "a number of important wills" in most of which she was named executrix or trustee or both.[95] Robinson had also done a little court work, including one criminal case, but seemed happy to be mainly in the office. Parker specialized in probate law and so the match was a good one. Influenced by Robinson and, perhaps, Greene, Parker wrote a series of articles for the *Home Journal* of Boston titled "Law for My Sisters." These essays explored "the law of marriage, widows, breach of promise, wife's necessaries, life insurance on divorce, sham marriages and names."[96]

Robinson's practice was growing at the same time that she was investing considerable energy in two writing projects, one a short treatise and the other a collective biography of women lawyers. In 1889 she published *The Law of Husband and Wife, Comp. for Popular Use.* In contrast to *Law Made Easy* with its forty-one chapters, this new volume—dedicated to "The Portia Club"—covered, in seven short chapters, marriage, property rights, wife's separate estate, wife's support-separate maintenance, custody of children, claims of widows and widowers, and divorce. Like her first book, *The Law of Husband and Wife* also contained a compilation of abstracts of state statutes relevant to the law of husband and wife.

A classic article, still in use, came out of her second project: a survey of the names and achievements of all women lawyers in the United States. The Equity Club as well as the Portias involved only a small number of women lawyers and law students. Robinson loved these groups, but she wanted female and male attorneys to know the full extent of women's achievements in law—the 1890 census listed 208 women lawyers—and she hoped to encourage women lawyers around the country to know one another. She also had business motives, believing that more than one woman lawyer in any community eased the reception of all, and increased the work available to all.[97]

Robinson wanted a national venue and decided upon publication in a new journal, *The Green Bag: A Useless but Entertaining Magazine for Lawyers*. The journal had cachet: Louis Brandeis contributed a history of the Harvard Law School to volume one, which also contained discussions of murder cases and lawyer jokes, news, and gossip. In 1889 Robinson began researching the names and accomplishments of American women lawyers. Through her list of Equity Club members, and correspondence with law school deans across the United States, she established a preliminary list of women graduates, working it into a more comprehensive document using a circular letter.

In January 1890 Robinson brought out the results. Ellen Martin, a Chicago lawyer, had published "Admission of Women to the Bar" in the November 1886 issue of the *Chicago Law Times*. Martin's essay was a start, but Robinson's article was a far more complete and up-to-date biography of America's female lawyers. In thirty pages she laid out crisply written stories of seventy-eight women and made various comments of her own on the state of the law for a woman practitioner. For years, Stanton, Anthony, and Gage had been profiling activist women in the volumes of *The History of Woman Suffrage*. Frances Willard and Mary Livermore would publish *A Woman of the Century*, consisting of biographies of leading American women, but not until 1893. Robinson's article was a singular contribution, a significant step in giving women lawyers recognition and the prod, perhaps, that led Belva Lockwood to produce a far less ambitious article on women lawyers in July of 1890 for *The Illustrated American* in New York.[98]

* * *

In May 1889 Robinson invited her Equity sisters to discuss the pros and cons of whether it was "practicable for a woman to successfully fulfill the duties of wife, mother and lawyer at one and the same time? Especially a young married woman?"[99] Fifteen months later she wrote to tell club correspondents that in April 1890 she had married. She claimed not to have been seriously contemplating marriage for herself when she put her earlier question to the club. Coy or not, she had happily entered into marriage with Eli Sawtelle, a piano dealer who liked to read philosophy, was "proud of [her] professional ambition," and encouraged it.[100] The groom gave Lelia a "fine new roll-top desk" for her office and took her to Washington, D.C., on their honeymoon where, on April 8, the bride was sworn in as a member of the U.S. Supreme Court bar, the sixth woman to take the oath. Pro-suffrage civil-rights activist Senator George Hoar of Massachusetts moved her admission as she stood next to Emma Gillett, who was also sworn to the high court bar on this day.

Members of the Portia Club made the Sawtelle marriage their social event of the year. After the wedding they devoted the monthly meeting to a reception to which gentleman visitors were invited for the first time. Fifteen people sat down to dinner while Alice Parker presided, proposing toasts with comments in rhyme.[101] That year Robinson vacationed for two months at her husband's summer home in New Hampshire, doing some business by letter, going into Boston occasionally, and leaving Alice Parker in charge of work she could not get to.

Lelia Robinson and Eli Sawtelle may have seen one another initially at a meeting of the First Nationalist Club of Boston, developing a romance while becoming club leaders. Like Clara Foltz, Robinson had been attracted to the democratic socialist ideas teased out of *Looking Backward,* Edward Bellamy's best-selling utopian novel.

Robinson attended First National meetings but in 1889 joined several other members in splitting off to form the Second Nationalist Club of Boston, a faction that was less theoretical and more pragmatic in its leanings. Robinson was elected its first chairperson.[102] In keeping with her books, the group emphasized actively working to bring about change in society through lobbying and running for public office. With Eli's support she led the club all through 1890 and talked about running for elective office in 1892 as a Nationalist candidate. While head of the club she brought Clara Foltz to Boston to speak to Second Nationalist members.

In the years 1889 and 1890, Robinson was never plagued with the "waiting around" that had so vexed her in the early 1880s. In addition to her journalism, new marriage, and work for the Nationalists, Robinson kept up her law practice, appearing, for example, with attorney Marilla Ricker in her petition for admission to the New Hampshire bar.[103] She also began to outline her third book, a volume on wills and inheritances. But in February 1891 she fell seriously ill with flu. She stopped her work for the Nationalists and in July, with Eli, left earlier than usual for vacation at his family's home in Amherst, New Hampshire. Troubled with poor sleep, Robinson obtained a prescription for belladonna, took some of the powerful medicine, and on August 10, 1891, died from an accidental overdose. She was forty years old. Her devastated husband ordered a tombstone to read, "The Pioneer Woman Lawyer of Massachusetts, Author, and Journalist. A lover of the true, the good and the beautiful."

Mary Greene found out about her friend's death at her new home in Providence, Rhode Island. She had moved her practice there in 1890 to meet family responsibilities, and with the hope of improving her own health. Alice Parker heard the news in Boston. Robinson's death was reported in many newspapers and journals but Mary Greene waited nearly thirty years to write a remembrance of her friend for the *Women Lawyers' Journal*.[104] The facts she reported were by then well known, but she wished also to write about her friend's deepest strengths. Greene said that Robinson's "strong sense of justice and her independence in expressing her views caused her to be misapprehended at times by those who did not know the warm heartedness that lay beneath."[105] Her disposition, Greene wrote, "was extremely social, and she loved to bring people together for the advancement of their common aims and interests." Her friend stressed that the success of women in the legal profession was "a consuming enthusiasm ... and [Robinson] was always devising means to bring [women] into closer and more social relations with each other, and she was as generously delighted at their successes as she would have been at her own."

In their far longer lives Mary Greene and Alice Parker followed many of the paths laid down by Lelia Robinson. Parker practiced law in Boston for nearly thirty years while also being active in the woman suffrage movement. In 1918, now Alice Parker Hutchins, she moved her practice to New York, where she became editor of the *Women Lawyers' Journal* published by the Women Lawyers' Association (and presumably commissioned Greene's article about their mutual friend). After the formation of the League of Women Voters, Hutchins became an active member and leader.

Mary Greene also kept faith with her friend's ambitions for women. For thirty years she practiced law in Rhode Island. Greene carried forward Robinson's idea of law "for the people" in her Lasell classes, and in her writing for *The Chautauquan* and other publications. She also used her legal training on behalf of the Women's Baptist Foreign Missionary Society, which she served as a vice president and legal counsel for more than a decade. Involvement in the society permitted her to study women's legal status in other societies, and to mentor young women who were going abroad as missionaries.[106]

Lasting fame came to Greene after her speech at the 1893 Chicago World's Fair. On August 7 she addressed the Congress of Jurisprudence and Law Reform, one of the many associations that met during the exposition. This international meeting was special: it was scholarly, and the original list of speakers had included only the names of male jurists. Mary Greene and Clara Foltz had been invited because Myra Bradwell, her lawyer daughter Bessie, and Catharine McCulloch had argued to the male organizers that women *had* earned a place high in law, and deserved to be among eminent jurists speaking about important legal topics.[107]

The paths bringing Foltz and Greene to the congress could not have been more different. Foltz had five children, relied on her parents for help in housekeeping and child care, fought for admission to the bar and to law school, and sought fame and fortune through a court practice. Greene found ready acceptance at law school and at the bar, never married, cared for a widowed mother, achieved recognition as an accomplished legal scholar, and was content with a quiet office practice in her Providence home.[108] Foltz, a fine speaker, came to the congress brimming with reformist passion and presented her radical proposal for an office of public defender. In contrast, Mary Greene offered a lawyerly, measured analysis of married women's property acts in the United States.

Greene was a talented and savvy public speaker. She had written Equity Club members that "[n]ature has blessed me with a rather large amount of self-possession, and I have never in my life known by experience what 'stage-fright' is."[109] Greene excelled as a writer and speaker in part because she modified her rhetoric according to her audience.[110] In her 1893 presentation she argued that while there had been progress in married women's property acts, there were contradictions in these laws as well as areas not yet addressed. Cataloguing the positive changes, she said that in all the states and territories of the Union the property of married women is secured so that it cannot be taken for a husband's debts, and if the wife survives her spouse the property becomes her sole and separate property. A handful of states now had community property laws. But for theoretical, practical, and sociological reasons, reform continued to be needed.

Greene made six recommendations. A wife, she argued, should have control of her own property. and all restrictions should be removed. Women should control and possess the income from real estate. In addition, earnings should be considered part of the personal property of the married woman, and fully owned and controlled by her. Further, contracting statutes should become consistent, all restrictions on a wife's freedom to contract should be removed, and she should hold full power to testify in a contract suit with her husband. To aid women, and society, a married woman should have full power to carry on any trade or business on her own account, and to bind herself as a guarantor or surety. Finally, Greene asked that a married woman enjoy no greater privileges than a husband and that she be made jointly liable with her husband, if she has property, for the support of the family.

These recommendations were, Greene argued, practical, legally logical, and in keeping with new social conditions, namely, the changed nature of the economy. Knowing her male audience, the argument emphasized the protection of commerce rather than justice, or the protection of women: "[W]ith all of the commerce occurring in 1893, the immunity and protection that the common-law gave women 'could . . . be [a] dangerous weapon in the hand of woman . . . , injuring herself and those with whom she deals.'"[111] The talk was a success.

In 1902 Greene cemented her reputation as a scholar, and as a student of Lelia Robinson's, by publishing *A Woman's Manual of Law*. She opened the 300-page treatise by writing that the book's purpose "is to present in a clear, simple, and, if possible, entertaining way, those principles of law governing the business world and domestic life which most men understand in some degree, or think they do, but which most women do not understand, and wish they did."[112] Greene argued that "the entrance of woman into the business and professional world has caused her to realize that ignorance of her legal rights and liabilities entails pecuniary loss."[113] She noted that "women capitalists and a vast army of women wage-earners" were buying and selling, investing, and speculating: "These women are anxious to know the laws that govern the holding and managing of property."[114] Showing her commitment to Robinson's idea of "law for the people," Greene wrote her book guided by a simple principle, that women want to know the law but they do not "wish all the fine-spun details of legal logic; they simply want to know those laws which they are most likely to encounter in dealing with their property."[115] Greene and Robinson, the ladies of Boston University law school, were legal scholars with an admirable philosophy—that the law must be accessible and understood by all if there were to be a level playing field.

Mary Greene lived until August 1936. From the time of her talk in 1893 until her death, she witnessed reform of married women's property statutes in one state after another. She had also predicted broad social and political change, including women legislators, judges, and jurors. Though they were hardly comprehensive, she did see some significant changes: three women elected in 1894 to the Colorado General Assembly; Jeannette Rankin sworn in as a member of the U.S. House of Representatives in 1916; Florence Allen elected to several judicial positions in Ohio beginning in 1920 before being nominated for the U.S. Court of Appeals in 1934 by President Franklin D. Roosevelt; and Hattie Caraway, elected to the U.S. Senate in 1932. In her autobiography Greene accepted her part in bringing this new political and economic power to women.[116]

Lelia Robinson's career provides the same mystery as Lavinia Goodell's: how would she have used her extraordinary talents had she not died at such an early age? She joined Lockwood and Foltz in proving women's ability to shine at trial work. Her books and articles similarly established a model of how lawyers, men and women, might use their training and on-the-job experience. In the spirit of the Progressive era, and Populism, Robinson avoided arcane exposition and endeavored to make an understanding of law something that all literate people could expect. Mary Greene, different from Robinson in certain elements of her philosophy of service, nevertheless used Robinson's example, producing scholarly discourse and a study of "law for the people." Greene's teaching career at Lasell Seminary similarly mirrored the interest that a number of women attorneys had in educating other women. As society's view of women's rights and abilities broadened, the opportunity to teach law to women expanded. Lockwood was before her time in trying to establish an educational institution for women, but Foltz, less formally, and Greene at Lasell, brought a new curriculum to women. Ellen Mussey and Emma Gillett cemented these advances with the establishment of what became the Washington College of Law.

❖ 9 ❖

Law as a Woman's Enterprise

Equality of rights and privileges is but simple justice.
—Belva Lockwood, 1888

FIRST-GENERATION WOMEN ATTORNEYS trained in the law in order to stretch themselves intellectually and to expand what were, otherwise, limited economic opportunities. Women attorneys also valued law as a tool of reform—not all, to be sure, but many. They supported woman suffrage and understood their personal struggles to be part of the larger fight to achieve an equal place in society.

Woman lawyers, like other pioneering female professionals, engaged in endless debate over what they should or should not do, what was good, bad, normal, or eccentric. In 1881 Belva Lockwood saw that male attorneys in the District who had begun using bicycles (adult tricycles) were completing their work more quickly. Practical, and a health enthusiast, she became the first woman in the capital to buy and use a bicycle, a daring and, some felt, immodest act. With resolute determination, she accepted the verbal harassment that came from showing a bit of ankle. She rode about freely and accomplished her work more efficiently. President Grover Cleveland, understanding cycle technology's power of sexual equalization, issued what Lockwood called "an edict," telling the wives of his Cabinet officers that he did not wish them to ride bicycles.[1]

Among themselves, women lawyers puzzled over questions of professional decorum and workplace relations as well as personal issues

This postcard is one in a series, circa 1910, mocking scantily clad women as candidates for public office. (From the suffrage collection of Dr. Kenneth Florey.)

of health and fitness. The best record of their soul searching survives in the letters of the Equity Club, the group to which Lelia Robinson and Mary Greene were so devoted. The original members from Michigan had recruited "sisters-in-law" who, like California attorney Laura de Force Gordon, felt a "want of Professional companionship . . . [and] assurances of that close sympathy born of mutuality of interests, which women alone can extend to a woman."[2] Three dozen women trained in law responded to the invitation of their Ann Arbor colleagues to participate in a discussion of the personal and the professional. The club operated through the simple device of shared letters.

Belva Lockwood sent off her first and only Equity Club letter on April 30, 1887. It typified her spirit in this period, expressing confidence in her professional accomplishments as well as the belief that other women would do well to practice law. Her field was, she said, "far from being a dry study, as many have supposed, but on the contrary, possesses a peculiar and fascinating attractiveness."[3] She also talked about the differences between city and small-town practice. She argued that in large cities an attorney could choose a specialty "and find a practice lucrative enough to fully employ her time."[4] She wrote that "the drafting of Wills, Deeds, Leases and Bills of Sale forms a very pleasant specialty for a woman in a large city where she can draw from a large enough population to secure good custom."[5] In small-town America, however, it was, she felt, necessary to engage in general practice. Many of the male attorneys she had met on the lecture circuit supplemented a general practice with work in real estate.

Lockwood seldom lost an opportunity to speak on behalf of her reform causes, and this letter was no exception. She made two recommendations. She urged the elite Equity Club women to lobby to withdraw from state government the power to legislate domestic law, and to nationalize it instead, so that there would be a unified federal code that applied to all Americans. She also advocated that public schools in the United States establish a new curriculum for girls, one that would educate them in the principles of the state domestic law that she wished to nationalize. "Women," she wrote, "have always been the chief sufferers of bad legislation." Referring to guardianship, property, and divorce law, she contended that if schooled early in these "ground principles, a woman would be better able to protect herself and children."[6] Lockwood, the former schoolteacher, trusted schools to be agents of change, as did Mary Greene.

In a variety of ways, women lawyers struggled with the public perception that they were mentally and physically inferior and required special treatment to do their job. Equity Club women categorically rejected the idea that they had less talent for the law. They acknowledged that their careers might suffer because they were excluded from local fraternal organizations, but club members asserted that society gained from the presence of women in the profession of law. Mary Greene argued that the beneficial influence of her sisters was felt broadly, in particular in the less agreeable moral atmosphere of the courtroom.[7]

Still, the shadow of special treatment, and accusations of inferiority, hung over these women. Happily, then, certain professional questions called forth their sense of humor. Chief among them was women's dress code. Lockwood was an early target. In 1876 a wit styled "E. Quality" wrote to Myra Bradwell's *Chicago Legal News* to ask if women lawyers should not "remove their hats, and address the court with head uncovered, as the gentlemen members of the bar are compelled to do?"[8] Several newspapers were quick to report that, in keeping with a sense of equality, "Mrs. Lockwood always removes her hat."[9] Bradwell observed,

> If a woman lawyer should follow strictly what is known as etiquette, she would not remove her hat in court; but if she should consider the court room as a place where she has to earn her living upon an equality with her brother members of the bar, she would probably remove her hat, for the same reasons that her brethren do their hats, overcoats, and overshoes, when trying a case, because they only serve as incumbrances [sic]; and it is more respectful to the court to remove them.[10]

Lockwood's example, however, did not satisfy all of her Equity Club colleagues. Twelve years after "E. Quality" raised the matter of hats, Lelia Robinson wrote that the issue had not yet been settled "entirely to my satisfaction."[11] She wore a hat in court not wishing "an added sense of unaccustomedness besides that which the place and the business must create."[12] She also believed that women could best "accustom judge, jury, clients and the public to the presence of women attorneys in court" by making few "variations from the usual customs and appearance of women in public places."[13] Robinson, a professional as well traveled and sophisticated as Lockwood, emphasized the need for women to be, well, women, where, in this matter, her Washington colleague followed masculine norms.

In 1889 Chicago attorney Margaret Wilcox put an end to the conversation:

> Allow me to make a suggestion in a matter not requiring a profound knowledge of the law, viz: "The Bonnet" or "Not the Bonnet" in the court-room. . . . If one should choose to lay aside her bonnet in the courtroom, whether on account of a heated atmosphere, or the shabbiness of the bon-net, or because she knows, intuitively, that the jury to be addressed would be prejudiced against her argument by either the extremely fashionable style of her hat, or its lack of style; whether one should plead with bon-net on, feeling confident that its beauty and becoming style lends persua-sion to her tongue, or conscious that her hair needs the friendly conceal-ment of a hat, in either case, I maintain that it is the inalienable right of each lady to follow "her own sweet will." Her keen intuition will guide her aright.[14]

This issue of decorum raised the question of whether, to succeed, women needed to follow the example of men and also pushed the women to interrogate themselves as to whether the "female constitu-tion" permitted women to compete as attorneys. The near-universal answer was "yes." From Iowa City, Emma Haddock wrote, "My health failed in law school. Not, as many thought, from the mental effort, but from the fact that I, like all women who attempt to do anything outside of homework, did really the work of two people, that of a student as well as that of a housekeeper."[15] She rested and went on to post-graduate legal study and a full career in the legal office of her husband. Lettie Burlingame took exception to Ellen Martin speaking of "woman's delicate organization."[16] Using herself as an example, Burlingame wrote of having been "very subject to the peculiar difficulties of my sex," but then said that "I am never in better health or spirits than when put to the spur and excitement of trying cases, nor does any hurtful reaction follow the glow."[17] She pronounced herself "now stronger and able to endure more than at any other period of my life. Indeed, I stand court room work better than many of the men."[18]

Emma Gillett, less swaggering than others, offered a measured assessment of personality and physiology:

> I believe that physically and mentally woman is fitted for the work of the law, and have not myself found my work too hard. I have had to contend all my life with a constitution by no means robust but my health has steadily improved since I began the study and practice of my profession. I have never gone into jury cases and have done very little court work, but I deliberately chose this course at the beginning as I knew by experience that my nervous organism would break under the strain. This lack of nervous endurance I do not count as a feminine failing as I have tested it more especially in caring for the sick or young children, the very place where as a rule, a woman endures beyond a man. Judging from analogy the average woman will endure a prolonged nervous strain better than the average man.[19]

While most of the Equity Club lawyers did not see themselves as prisoners of the female condition, they understood, as Emma Haddock made clear, that doing the work of two people might cause a woman's health to fail. Many practiced regimens for healthful living that included calisthenics and outdoor errands (but, with the exception of Lockwood, not bicycle riding). They were sensible women who, while liking to look smart, had accepted many of the teachings of the dress reform movement, which advocated clothes that gave the wearer greater mobility, as well as the end of the tight lacing of corsets.

Illinois attorney Catharine Waugh was quite specific in the advice she gave while still single. She admonished her Equity sisters to pay more attention to dress, diet, and exercise if they wished to be strong: "My creed includes no corsets, broad, low heeled shoes, reform under garments, dresses in one piece hanging from the shoulders, no tea, little coffee or pork, few pies and cakes, much sleep, a little hoeing in the flower beds and a day in bed when occasion demands instead of sitting and suffering."[20]

* * *

Unlike Mary Greene, who was unsparingly negative in her comments about charity work, a number of first-generation women lawyers combined legal careers with civic contributions or partisan political activity. Even Greene distinguished between the perceived "ingratitude" of her charity clients and the desirability of other forms of community service, such as her lectures on married women's property law and the teaching of young women. Attorney Ada Kepley, slightly older than Greene, testified that her professional training had been of great help in securing enforcement of temperance laws during the ten years she worked for the Woman's Christian Temperance Union (WCTU).[21] From Milwaukee, Margaret Wilcox seconded this testimony, arguing that every branch of the WCTU could benefit from having among its members a woman familiar with technical law. She would have these women lawyers point out "the culpable carelessness of allowing liquor and beer companies to secure the handsomest corner lots for palatial saloons."[22] Wilcox asked her Equity sisters, "Why not try to mould public opinion in this reform by persuasion, as men lawyers have always done in the leading of every great reform. . . ?"[23]

Lettie Burlingame, in Joliet, Illinois, adopted an ambivalent stance. She had participated in the successful 1888 campaign of Republican presidential candidate Benjamin Harrison. She did not regret her political efforts but thought the activity itself a mistake because the neglect of her law office had caused a loss of business. "Still," she wrote,

"I gained a wide acquaintance among business men, as I have in the equal suffrage work."[24] Florence Cronise said that she made it a rule of her professional life "to go quietly on, remaining very closely at my business, and the result I believe to be better than had I answered some of the many calls to appear before the people in behalf of woman's rights."[25] She chastised Kepley and Wilcox: "I cannot agree nor feel any sympathy with our sisters . . . who think woman's mission into the profession is to purify. . . . My mission is to honestly, earnestly, and decently earn my living."[26] Emma Gillett chose not to be lured into "any class of philanthropic . . . work."[27] Cronise and Gillett were joined by a number of other Equity correspondents who avoided reform advocacy because they feared that it would limit their "making headway" in the profession.

Ada Bittenbender had no such fears. She was one of the very few early women attorneys employed to engage in paid advocacy work. Born in 1848, Bittenbender was an easterner who, at the age of thirty, moved to Nebraska with her lawyer husband. They were both fiercely committed to the temperance movement. A year after the move they purchased a local Republican newspaper, the *Osceola Record*, which Ada Bittenbender edited for three years, making it "an able, fearless, moral, family and temperance newspaper."[28] During this period she also read law with her husband and became a leader in the state woman suffrage movement. She was admitted to the Nebraska bar in 1882, the first woman in the state to be licensed. She and her husband, Henry, established the firm of H. C. and Ada M. Bittenbender, and moved to the state capital of Lincoln. In Lincoln, Ada Bittenbender built a reputation as a nearly unbeaten trial lawyer (preferring the courtroom to the office) and a successful lobbyist who worked to influence the policy views of legislators in Lincoln, and Washington, D.C. Her advocacy focused upon the protection of women, and temperance. In 1888 she was elected counsel for the National Woman's Christian Temperance Union, becoming a paid cause lawyer. She used her position to write *The National Prohibitory Amendment Guide* (1889), a plan of action to promote a federal

Ada M. Bittenbender
(1848-1925). (Courtesy
of the Frances E. Willard
Memorial Library and
Archives, Evanston,
Illinois.)

prohibition amendment. Months after her selection as WCTU counsel, Bittenbender acknowledged in an Equity letter that she would make more than her fifteen hundred dollar salary by "sticking closer to the profession . . . [but] [u]sefulness to others I consider the pearl of great price."[29]

Activist Mary Lease, based for many years in Kansas, also presented herself as a woman with no fears. Sometime in the 1880s, in her mid-thirties, she studied law and passed the bar in Wichita.[30] Lease had a family situation not unlike that of Clara Foltz. Financial panics, drought, and a husband who earned too little led Lease to look for solutions to societal problems in reform movement politics. She first joined the Woman's Christian Temperance Union. Temperance permitted her to talk about wives, children, and economic injustice. She spoke with a different passion, and point of reference, than Ada

Bittenbender, who was childless and middle-class. Lease then allied herself with the Farmers' Alliance and Industrial Union, and the
Knights of Labor. A powerful speaker, she could hold the attention of
an audience for hours. She always spoke about toil, privation, danger,
and hardship.[31]

In 1890 the membership of the Kansas Farmers' Alliance acknowledged that more than self-help measures were needed to combat
poverty and unemployment. The Alliance threw itself into electoral
politics and from its grass roots produced one arm of the Populist
movement. Mary Lease was well-positioned to go on the stump as a
Populist Party speaker, arguing the cause of workers against the banking, utility, and railroad money barons. She gave hundreds of speeches
and emerged as one of the party's most effective orators. Her teenage
children stayed in Wichita with their father.

Ada Bittenbender benefited from a fixed salary in her position with
the National Woman's Christian Temperance Union. Lease's financial arrangement was more precarious as her earnings were tied to
her ability to give speeches. And while she was an attorney, and later
practiced part-time in New York City, Lease approached her work for
cause movements strictly as a political partisan. While Bittenbender
sat in a Washington library reading decades of congressional legislation and crafting carefully worded proposals for new legislation, Lease
seemed never to sit down, instead rousing crowds on the campaign
trail with sweeping populist rhetoric. When Kansas Populists won a
number of political offices in 1892, Lease hoped to capitalize on the
votes and national spotlight she had brought to the party by asking
for one of Kansas's U.S. Senate seats (at that time filled by a vote of
the state legislature). She was testing the reach of her fame, and the
sincerity of the party's progressive principles. At a time when American women, at best, could vote for a few local offices and, for the most
part, women candidates ran for local or county offices, Lease, having
nothing to lose, gambled—and lost. Her request was refused. She was
appointed to a position often given to prominent reform women as a
consolation prize, superintendent of charities (in this case overseeing

Kansas's institutions for orphans, the mentally retarded, and elderly veterans).

J. Ellen Foster, like Lease, had a frank interest in partisan politics. A member of the Iowa bar, Foster spent decades raising women's profile within the Republican Party. She argued that a better knowledge of practical politics would help women to lobby more effectively for reform legislation.[32] Like Lavinia Goodell, Foster began her law career juggling anti-saloon damage cases.[33]

In 1874 Foster attended the founding convention of the National Woman's Christian Temperance Union and fell under the spell of its leader, Frances E. Willard. Six years later Foster became the union's legal adviser and superintendent of legislation and petitions. Foster resigned her office, however, when Willard sought to bring the WCTU into the Prohibition Party camp. Foster tried fighting within the organization to block a third-party alliance, fearing it would damage the chances of pro-temperance Republicans, including James G. Blaine, the party's 1884 presidential candidate. Unsuccessful, in 1889 she led Iowa delegates out of the WCTU and founded the Non-Partisan National WCTU. Foster's non-partisan credentials, however, suffered from her close association with the Republican Party. A year before organizing the Non-Partisan WCTU, she created, and led, the Woman's National Republican Association—with the blessing of the Republican National Committee. Hundreds of local Republican women's clubs sprang up through her efforts.[34] By the time of the 1892 Republican Convention, Foster was able to stand before the delegates and shout, "We are here to help you. . . . [A]nd we have come to stay."[35] Contemporary commentators argued that "she had done what few before her had even dreamed of doing. She had made women a recognized factor in party politics and in the party government of a nation."[36]

Foster's party work never ceased but, unlike her husband, she was not rewarded with a permanent patronage job when the Republicans were in office. Like Lease, she had to content herself with consolation work, in her case a number of short-term investigations for the federal government.

Kate Stoneman came to cause lawyering in an entirely different manner. Born in southwestern New York State in 1841, Stoneman moved to Albany as a young woman and matriculated at the New York State Normal School. During her school years Stoneman had her first exposure to a law office when she served as a copyist for Joel Tiffany, the state reporter for the New York Court of Appeals.[37] Stoneman graduated in 1866 and taught for many decades. She also took up the cause of woman suffrage and began working with established women's rights leaders, including Lillie Devereux Blake. Beginning in 1880, they lobbied for the extension of school suffrage to women, along with other property and employment rights issues.

In the early 1880s Stoneman was designated the executrix of a great-aunt's estate, which again exposed her to legal questions. In 1882 she applied for a clerkship in the Albany office of attorney Worthington W. Frothingham. She read law with him for three years and in 1885, urged on by her suffrage friends, passed the New York state bar examination. When Stoneman applied for bar admission, however, she found her way blocked. The New York State Supreme Court denied her application, stating that there was no precedent for her admission and that "there was no call for woman lawyers in New York State."[38] The justices also worried that liberality on the subject of woman lawyers would lead to even stronger demands for woman suffrage.

As an experienced woman suffrage lobbyist Stoneman, like Goodell, Robinson, and others, was ready to take her fight to the state legislature. She was known and respected by a number of representatives. Anticipating the defeat at court, she had begun to circulate a proposal to strike the word "male" from the Code of Civil Procedure that regulated bar admission. Assemblyman John I. Platt of Poughkeepsie took her draft proposal, shaped it into a bill, and in January 1886 introduced the legislation in the state assembly. By May the bill had passed the Assembly and the Senate, and was on Governor David Hill's desk. Stoneman traveled to his office with a coterie of supporters, mostly male, and told Hill that she wished to be admitted to the bar "chiefly to extend the field of women's activity."[39] The governor signed the bill, Stoneman reapplied for admission, and on May

Katherine (Kate)
Stoneman (1841-1924).
(Courtesy of the M. E.
Grenander Department
of Special Collections
and Archives, University
at Albany Libraries.)

20 she was the first woman in New York State to be admitted to the bar. Shortly after, she became the first woman student at Albany Law School. Stoneman maintained a law office in her Albany home but spent most of her time teaching and lobbying for woman suffrage. For Kate Stoneman the very act of becoming a lawyer was her cause. She sought to establish a precedent and to open the profession of law to women. She wanted women to have the opportunity to use law to influence the affairs of government and to choose, if they wished, a new sphere of life by which to earn a living.

Women lawyers quite naturally identified access to legal education as a necessary reform. While some law programs opened to women early—1869 at both the University of Iowa and Washington University in St. Louis—until the turn of the century there were not many programs that welcomed women. Belva Lockwood had wished to work in the profession of her choice and believed that all women should have a similar opportunity. In the 1870s, when professional schools were in their infancy, she grasped their power to determine who would wear the badge of lawyer, or doctor—who would enjoy economic well-being and status. In the autumn of 1873 she sent to President Grant, and members of Congress, a plan for a sexually integrated national university "worthy of the Capital."[40] She described an institution with departments of law, medicine, science, and the arts that would maintain high standards and where "the race" for admission would be "equal."[41]

Lockwood failed to win support for a showcase public university but did not give up on the idea of an institution where women might pursue professional training in an environment less hostile than the one she and Lydia Hall had endured as students. With D.C. colleagues, she tried again in 1876 but failed to attract a sufficient number of shareholders. Her idea was ahead of its time. Clara Foltz explored the idea with her Portia Club, as did a number of well-to-do women in New York City in the late 1880s who started what became the Women's Law Class, a program taken over by New York University.[42]

Twenty years after Lockwood's failure, her friend, D.C. lawyer Ellen Spencer Mussey, revived the notion of a woman's law school and in little more than a decade, with the help of Lockwood's protégée, Emma Gillett, built the Washington College of Law into a nationally known program. Mussey and Gillett had originally planned to tutor students and have them transfer to Columbian College (later George Washington University) for a final, senior year of legal study. In 1898 they sent up the names of six qualified women only to be told that conservative members of the Columbian Board of Trustees would not agree to admit the women. Old, tired arguments were trotted out: women, they said, were incapacitated by the "conditions of their sex" and lacked "the mentality for law."[43] Reluctantly, Mussey and Gillett decided to address this prejudice by expanding their program. On April 9, 1898, they incorporated the law school, establishing a three-year course of study (rather than the more common, less rigorous two years). They founded the program to serve women but accepted men, who were attracted to it because of the low tuition. A whites-only policy prevailed, unsurprising given the open racism of the late nineteenth century but nonetheless paradoxical: Emma Gillett, a Caucasian, had taken her law degree at Howard University, which had been founded to serve African American students. Mussey became the dean of Washington College, the first woman to head an American law school.

Until Ellen Mussey asked her to teach, Emma Gillett had resisted Belva Lockwood's example of the ways law could be used to educate the public and be a force for change. It was Gillett who, in 1888, told the Equity Club women that she would not permit herself to be "lured into any class of philanthropic or other work, knowing the law to be a jealous mistress and believing that I could do no better work than to prove that a woman could by persistent application earn a competency at the law."[44] While Lockwood used lecturing and campaigning as a springboard for reform work and for public notice, Gillett worked the back office of Watson Newton's law firm where, after fifteen years, she made partner. Late in life she became the second dean of the Washington College of Law.

Mary Lease triumphed as an orator but failed to obtain the U.S. Senate office that she coveted. Even when they were stars, accomplished in court, reform advocacy, or women's politics, the first generation of female lawyers experienced significant limits with respect to their ambitions. Of course, not every male lawyer did well practicing law. Many male attorneys did not succeed at making a living in law, and most male lawyers never glimpsed the world of cigars, wealth, and power that came with being a successful late-nineteenth-century railroad or corporate attorney.[45] Most male lawyers of this period had no access to corporate positions, but they could run for all elective offices, and patronage positions were open to men who were party activists. Women lawyers lacked these opportunities.

The life of Vermont teacher and lawyer John Henry Senter epitomized the profound divide in the prospects of male and female lawyers in the last quarter of the nineteenth century.[46] Born in 1848, Senter taught school while studying law in the Montpelier office of Clarence H. Pitkin. He was admitted to the bar in 1879 at the age of thirty. He opened an office in Vermont and, like Lockwood, Foltz,

Robinson, and others, was a joiner, active as a Democrat and in civic affairs. Unlike these women, a decade after starting his law practice Senter, a man of modest means, with no family connections, began a second career as an elected official and office holder. He held many municipal positions, including justice of the peace and mayor. He went on to represent Montpelier in the state legislature. He served as chairman and secretary of the Democratic State Committee. During his first term in office, President Grover Cleveland appointed Senter to be national bank examiner. Later, he was appointed United States district attorney for Vermont, and then United States attorney for the District of Vermont.

Women with, and without, law training understood the limits imposed on them. However, particularly in civic matters they refused to be marginalized. They began with suffrage, and temperance. In fighting "demon liquor" they turned to courts and law when moral suasion and protests failed. Ohio's so-called Adair law allowed any person to sue bar owners, and liquor dealers, to recover damages caused by an intoxicated buyer.[47] In one notable early-1870s case brought by the desperate wife of a drunkard against a rum seller, a sympathetic local newspaper cooperated by running articles urging temperance women to come to court and bear witness. At the end of this trial, Mrs. E. D. Stewart, "Mother Stewart," rose to make a closing argument. Stewart did not hold a law degree, nor had she passed a bar exam. She was, however, a well-known temperance activist who made "a career" of showing up as an advocate in Adair law cases.[48] Judges allowed Stewart to argue with defense attorneys, one of whom cursed her, saying that it was "infamous to bring a female in to influence the court and jury."[49] Numerous saloon closings permitted Stewart to acquire judicial experience. Sober-faced male jurors listened to her appeal to men's God-given obligation to provide for their families. At a time when women like Lockwood and Goodell were still fighting to become attorneys, Stewart, along with the women temperance activists who cheered her from the galleries, successfully manipulated the male-dominated judicial system long enough to introduce anti-liquor messages in court and, in a number of instances, to win damages.

In 1880, there were fewer than one hundred women lawyers in the United States. By this time reformers and union activists had begun to develop an increasingly refined understanding of the problems faced by women. Clearly, however, not all Equity Club lawyers felt an obligation to help sisters-in-need. Individuals like Mother Stewart drew attention to women's problems, but only locally. Issues of poverty, sexual and physical abuse, and economic injustice demanded systematic attention and redress.

In New York, Chicago, and Philadelphia, legal aid organizations for poor women were created in the last quarter of the century to do just this. The aid came from women functioning as lay lawyers, women who created legal aid as a "deeply feminized" sphere.[50] Legal aid dates back to the Civil War and the creation, in New York City, of the Working Women's Protective Union (WWPU), an organization whose mission was to provide legal aid to women in the needle trade whose employers failed to pay their wages. Elite New Yorkers applauded the union as an efficient and praiseworthy organization run by male attorneys. Legal historian Felice Batlan, however, argues that the day-to-day work of the organization, including much of the legal work, was carried out by women. The union's superintendent was always a woman with a female staff. Potential clients met with the superintendent, who evaluated the complaint and offered advice. She sent out demand letters to employers and worked to keep the number of lawsuits low by negotiating settlements. In these years, before Kate Stoneman opened the New York bar to women, Batlan makes the case that the WWPU's superintendent, "who was always a woman," and her staff "were essentially practicing law."[51] Refused admission to the bar, they carved out a self-defined place for themselves in the field of cause lawyering.

In 1886 women activists in Chicago created a similar organization after study led them to understand the number of crimes involving sexual and physical abuse whose victims were women and children. They were determined to make the legal system protect these victims, and convinced several women's clubs and associations in the city to support the work of what became the Protective Agency for Women and Children (PAWC).[52]

The organization's mission was broader than that of New York's WWPU. PAWC gave free legal assistance to women and children who had experienced physical and sexual crimes, as well as non-payment of wages. PAWC staff and volunteers also lobbied for reform of laws that cobbled their clients, and undertook public education campaigns that would help to secure social justice. This ranged from laws affecting repossession of working women's sewing machines to statutes defining seduction, age of consent for sex, and proof of rape. Like Mother Stewart and her allies, these Chicago women went into courtrooms in support of clients, vigilantly watching to make certain that judges followed the law. When PAWC instituted a campaign to replace corrupt justices, particularly ones who systematically dismissed criminal assault cases involving husbands who beat their wives, Caroline Brown, PAWC's chairwoman, spent a year documenting the behavior, and judgments, of local judges.

PAWC activists carved out a mission largely using non-licensed law activists. As legal training and the profession of law became more formal, with more stringent state laws governing the practice of law, the independence and influence of these non-licensed activists diminished.[53] Charlotte Holt was one of the few women involved with PAWC who could, or would, pursue formal legal training in order to become a licensed cause lawyer.[54]

These lay lawyers, along with the first generation of women members of the bar, were a bridge to the next generation of women attorneys who understood what had been involved in the early fight to join the profession, and the varied nature of the first generation's philosophies of how to practice law. The stories of this second generation are as noteworthy and compelling as those of the first generation. Mrs. Mary G. Quackenbos, a wealthy New Yorker, graduated from New York University's law school at the turn of the century. Like Mary Greene, she took up the study of law to manage her property but became interested in the problems of the poor. After law school she joined the Legal Aid Society and in May 1905 used her money to establish the People's Law Firm. The Legal Aid Society, she said, served people with no funds. This left the working poor either without

counsel, or prey for shyster lawyers. At People's Law she gave working men and women quality representation, "at a cost within their
means."[55] Cases came to her by word of mouth, and from judges in the
courts, charitable organizations, and a local settlement house. Quackenbos began alone and within two years had a stenographer and three
lawyers working with her.[56]

Rosalie Loew graduated from New York University several years
before Quackenbos. While law school and the bar presented no hurdles, Loew did not have Quackenbos's wealth, and in addition to being a woman, she was Jewish. In an article published by *Metropolitan
Magazine*, Loew wrote circumspectly that women lawyers must "take
their place in the ranks by their brothers and scale the walls . . . handi-
capped [because of] the energy required overcoming a probable prejudice."[57] She practiced briefly with her father and then became the first
woman lawyer at the New York Legal Aid Society. Her case load was
large, eighteen to twenty-three cases on the docket a day, "scattered
through the eleven divisions of the Boroughs of New York."[58] Many
were wage claim cases.

Florence Kelley had the advantage of being born into a well-es-
tablished Pennsylvania family deeply involved in reform advocacy,
including abolition. Kelley's father was a lawyer, judge, and congressman; his daughter, born in 1859, learned about law and politics at a
young age. While a student at Cornell University, Florence Kelley
began researching the legal status of children. As a graduate student
at Zurich University she was drawn to socialist groups, and trans-
lated into English Friedrich Engel's *Condition of the Working Class in
England*.

After her return to the United States Kelley, "intellectual, socialist, and reformer," devoted herself to fieldwork investigations, writing
articles about bettering labor conditions, and lobbying for protective
labor laws for women and children.[59] While she was at Chicago's Hull
House, the governor of Illinois appointed her to the newly created
position of state factory inspector. To facilitate her work, Kelley took
a degree from Northwestern Law School and by 1893 was enforcing
state regulatory powers through the prosecution of manufacturers

for violations such as employing women to work over eight hours a day. In 1899, Kelley agreed to head the newly created National Consumers League (NCL). She solidified her reputation in this position, continuing, with colleagues such as Josephine Goldmark, to refine the use of social and economic data ("fact-based jurisprudence") to defend protective labor legislation against legal challenges.[60] Even more than Ada Bittenbender, Kelley defined the combined role of cause lawyer and reform advocate, and in the work of the NCL created a model that influenced twentieth-century civil rights and civil liberties organizations.

CONCLUSION

The entrance of women into the profession of law was nothing short of a revolution. In the last quarter of the nineteenth century, the "rebels" of this book succeeded in breaking into one of America's most influential professions. At this time, men controlled the profession's knowledge base, credentialing, client referral system, and networking. In order to end this male monopoly, these women had to challenge patriarchy, law, arrogance, prejudice, and the fear of change. They succeeded in what their opponent, Judge Edward Ryan, called "a sweeping revolution of social order."

Nevertheless, picturing this revolution as a coup would be incorrect. The entrance of women into the legal profession is not served by hagiographic history. Nineteenth-century women did gain admission to a number of law schools, and achieved membership in numerous bar associations. With the exception of Myra Bradwell, the "rebels" committed themselves to the lifelong practice of law. They also wrote, lectured, engaged in political activities, and theorized about critical legal issues ranging from the nationalization of domestic law to reform of the judicial and criminal justice systems. Lay women "lawyers" also augmented contemporary cause work in important ways, innovating services for poor women and children at legal aid societies.

Regardless, by the end of the nineteenth century, while the number of women lawyers in the United States had grown, male attorneys dominated the numbers: in the national census of 1900, one thousand women identified themselves as attorneys, compared with one hundred thousand male attorneys. By 1900, only twenty women lawyers had been admitted to the U.S. Supreme Court bar. Many law schools continued to refuse to admit women. Harvard Law did not open its doors to women until 1950.

Once they passed the bar, nineteenth-century women found that employment opportunities were anything but equal. A critical lesson of the revolution centered on the fact that the federal government, corporations, and the larger, more prominent law firms refused to hire women attorneys. Women often made the federal government a target of protest when they contested this systematic employment discrimination. They intended to hold elected officials accountable, in the most basic manner, for the breech of civic ideals. They demanded that they be shown, through the hiring and appointment of women, that all citizens are created equal—that their civic ideals were not sham notions. They learned, as an additional lesson, that while sweeping away the most basic forms of exclusion required two decades, broad change would take more years than the days of their lives. This larger change would bring parity in the admission of male and female law students, the hiring of women by government and corporations, as well as women on the United States Supreme Court and women lawyers using their credentials to run for public office and to take up high non-elective office. These changes, however, would take another century.

The letters of Equity Club members demonstrate vividly that these first women lawyers varied tremendously in their opinions. By no means did these "rebels" see eye to eye on all personal, political, or professional issues. Nevertheless, the Equity letters are marked by tolerance. There were differences but there was also, critically, sisterhood.

The "rebels" pondered many issues: how to educate themselves in the law, how to practice, where to practice, with whom to practice, what fees to charge (or not charge) and, yes, comportment and the wearing of hats. Yet, even as they barely had a foot in the door, these first women attorneys, unlike the lay women lawyers, appear to have accepted that they would enter a profession defined by men, rather than creating a parallel field of female lawyering.

It is impossible to know whether these women would have tired of the slow pace of change, of their very slow climb into the profession of law. With their sisters in the larger women's rights movement, they faced deeply engrained patriarchal attitudes. These women lawyers, along with women doctors, ministers, professors, and journalists, were the vanguard. They were on a public stage even when they did not wish to be, representing the struggle for equal rights. Some "rebels" delighted in the role; others tried to guard their privacy. Each of them outwitted history by being models of female accomplishment and independence. Each has a place in the history of law and women's advancement.

Epilogue

FOUR WOMEN HAVE now served as an associate justice on the Supreme Court of the United States. Sandra Day O'Connor, the first of these justices, was not appointed until 1981. For a short while after O'Connor retired, Justice Ruth Bader Ginsburg, who joined the court in 1993, was the sole female member. In 2009, U.S. district court judge Sonia Sotomayor joined her. Elena Kagan, the first woman dean of Harvard Law School, was confirmed a year later.

The first generation of women lawyers imagined such success and status for themselves but were barred by custom, prejudice, and, in some instances, law from the most prestigious positions in their profession. Early in 1912, after the death of Justice John M. Harlan, the District of Columbia Woman Suffrage Association forwarded to President William Howard Taft the names of three first-generation women lawyers, Mrs. Ellen Spencer Mussey, Miss Emma M. Gillett, and Mrs. Belva A. Lockwood, as possible candidates to fill the Harlan vacancy. Association president Julia White Leavitt wrote to Taft, "As you seek a suitable lawyer . . . we beg to remind you that we have capable women lawyers in this District, who have been more than a decade practitioners before the United States Supreme Court."[1] Leavitt also reminded the president of women's growing voting power. The position went to New Jersey Supreme Court chancellor Mahlon Pitney.

Women were challenged in their ambitions even when they sought the most local positions. In 1870 Amelia Hobbs was elected justice of the peace in Jersey County, Illinois. Because of her sex, Hobbs's right to take office was contested, and it is unclear whether she ever took office.[2]

Women lawyers sought elective and judicial positions even before they could vote, usually as candidates of third parties. In the 1880s

As of 2012, four women have served as associate justices of the Supreme Court of the United States: *left to right*, Sandra Day O'Connor, Sonia Sotomayor, Ruth Bader Ginsburg, and Elena Kagan. (Courtesy of Steve Petteway, Collection of the Supreme Court of the United States.)

Belva Lockwood ran twice for the presidency. In 1891 and 1893 temperance activist Ada Bittenbender ran for the office of Nebraska Supreme Court judge on the Prohibition ticket, each time winning several thousand votes. Catharine Waugh McCulloch lost her 1888 campaign for state's attorney but in 1907 defeated a male candidate for the office of justice of the peace. She was re-elected and served until 1913. McCulloch's victories inspired lawyer Florence E. Allen to run her successful campaign of 1920 for judge of the Cuyahoga County, Ohio, Court of Common Pleas. Fourteen years later Allen was confirmed as the first woman to serve as a federal appeals judge. She remained at the Sixth Circuit appeals court until her retirement in 1959. Allen was often spoken of as a possible nominee for the U.S. Supreme Court. However, both President Franklin Roosevelt and President Harry Truman passed up opportunities to send her name to the Senate as a nominee. Constance Baker Motley had a distinguished career from 1946 to 1966 as counsel for the National Association for the Advancement of Colored People (NAACP) Legal Defense and Education Fund. In 1966, after nomination by President Lyndon B. Johnson, she became the first African American woman federal judge.

In 1900 twenty women were members of the U.S. Supreme Court bar. The number increased gradually in the new century. The federal government slowly began hiring women attorneys after ratification of the Nineteenth Amendment. This gave women lawyers greater opportunity to argue cases in the federal courts, including the Supreme Court. Annette Abbott Adams served briefly in 1920 as an assistant attorney general in the Justice Department, charged with enforcing the Eighteenth Amendment (prohibiting the manufacture, sale, or transportation of intoxicating liquors) and the National Prohibition (Volstead) Act. During her year in Washington, Adams argued five Supreme Court cases, losing only one.

Mabel Walker Willebrandt followed Adams at the Department of Justice, and from 1921 to 1929 was also responsible for enforcement of the Volstead Act. She made aggressive use of tax laws in the fight against illegal liquor, earning national respect as "Prohibition Portia." Her friend, Judge John Sirica, said, "If Mabel had worn trousers, she could have been President."[3]

In the 1930s and 1940s, at the Internal Revenue Service, the Department of Labor, and, later, the Justice Department, extraordinarily talented women, including Helen R. Carloss, Bessie Margolin, and Beatrice Rosenberg, also earned respect prosecuting Prohibition Act and tax-related cases, as well as participating in fair labor standards, equal pay, and age discrimination cases. From 1943 to 1972, as an attorney in the Justice Department's criminal division, with an expertise in search and seizure law, Rosenberg argued more than thirty cases before the Supreme Court. In the 1970s, the Office of the Solicitor General (OSG) began to hire women lawyers. Harriet Sturtevant Shapiro was brought in, followed shortly by Jewel Lafontant, appointed by President Richard Nixon as deputy solicitor general. She was the first woman, and the first African American, to hold a high position at OSG. In 1993 Janet Reno, from Florida, became the nation's first woman attorney general.

Southern women were not represented in the first generation of attorneys. In the second generation Betty Runnells of Louisiana graduated from Tulane University in 1898 and was admitted to the bar in Louisiana. Several Mississippi women born in the 1890s became influential members of the profession. Helen Carloss was one. Lucy Somerville Howorth was another.[4] Howorth came from a pro-temperance, pro-suffrage family, graduated from Randolph-Macon College, and after being denied admission by Columbia Law School because she was a woman, entered the University of Mississippi law school. Howorth graduated at the top of her class in 1922 but then had the usual struggle in attracting clients and building a reputation as a respected solo practitioner. Eventually, she won two appointments that advanced her career, one as a member of the Mississippi Board of Bar Examiners and a second as the commissioner (magistrate) of a United States district court in Mississippi, where she heard many civil and criminal federal cases. In 1928 she married, and in 1931 Howorth was elected to the Mississippi House of Representatives. A lifelong Democrat, she moved to Washington, D.C., with her husband after Franklin Roosevelt's election, and spent two decades in various federal positions.

Burnita Shelton Matthews grew up visiting the Copiah County, Mississippi, courthouse where her father served as clerk of the chancery court and tax collector.[5] She married in 1917, and with her husband's encouragement entered law school in Washington, D.C., working during the day as a clerk at the Veteran's Administration, taking classes at night, and picketing the White House for woman suffrage on weekends. She passed the bar in 1920 but, unlike Helen Carloss, was unable to secure a lawyer's position at the Veteran's Administration. Believing that she would not be hired for a government position, she opened a law firm with Laura Berrien and Rebekah Greathouse.

Matthews became an advocate for women's inclusion on juries after ratification of the Nineteenth Amendment. In 1934 she became the president of the National Association of Women Lawyers (NAWL), which had grown from a women lawyers club in New York City with, in 1899, eighteen members to a national professional organization.[6] In 1949 thirty new federal district court judgeships were created. Matthews's name was sent to President Truman; confirmed, she became the nation's first woman federal district court judge. Despite the example of Judge Florence Allen, the *Washington Post* chose to discuss how to handle the powder room question rather than Matthews's qualifications.[7]

The powder room question is only one of several new decorum issues. Fussing over whether to wear a hat in court has given way to women judges determining where to robe, or what style of neckpiece to wear, while female attorneys seek to determine an appropriate balance between feminine attire and pinstripes. In the late 1970s Nancy Gertner, then a young criminal attorney in Boston, shaped a courtroom identity complete with red suit—skirt, not pants, lest any juror find her too masculine.[8] Female attorneys on Wall Street, and in the corporate world, always concerned about making partner, ponder these professional dress issues with even greater concern.

In various ways issues of professional decorum raise the question of whether, to succeed, women need to follow the example of men. In March 2011, however, a far more troubling matter was raised by Supreme Court Justice Sonia Sotomayor. Speaking to a group of Northwestern University law students, Sotomayor said that female candidates for the judiciary are treated differently than their male counterparts.[9] Women jurists, she contended, need a thick skin. "There are expectations about how women and men should behave," she said. "I am probably a bit more aggressive, but to hear people describe me as brash, and rude, the language used suggests a difference in expectations about what's OK for people's behavior."[10] The justice also suggested that unmarried female judicial candidates experience a more thorough vetting process, and harsher questioning, with respect to their private lives than is the case with male candidates. Sotomayor, divorced for many years, said that she is very careful in her private life, contending that if she behaved like single male colleagues who date, her morals would be questioned.

The story of women in the profession of law is, then, neither one of complete triumph nor one of Sisyphean failure. The first generation provided the shoulders upon which subsequent generations of American women lawyers have stood as they struggled to expand the place, and contributions, of women attorneys. The struggle is not over: women account for about one-fifth of law firm partners, and even fewer Fortune 500 general counsels.[11] In 2009 male federal judges outnumbered women judges three to one.[12] Imagine, however, what Myra Bradwell, Belva Lockwood, and Lelia Robinson might say about the large number of women graduating from law schools, and about the fact that there are now opportunities in corporate law firms. Other changes are found in the work available to women lawyers in state and federal government, the presence of women associate justices on the Supreme Court of the United States, and the larger number of women arguing cases at the high court.

The first generation of women lawyers fought for equality of opportunity, and knew it would take several generations to realize their dreams of an unfettered place in the profession. Justice Ruth Bader Ginsburg has said that there has been "exhilarating change," even as vigilance is necessary in maintaining the trend.[13]

Notes

ABBREVIATIONS USED IN NOTES

CLN	*Chicago Legal News*
HWS	Elizabeth Cady Stanton, Susan B. Anthony, and Matilda Joslyn Gage, eds., *History of Woman Suffrage* (1881-1922; reprint New York: Arno, 1969 and Project Gutenburg eBook)
LC	Library of Congress
LDJ	*Lockport (New York) Daily Journal*
LGP	Lavinia Goodell Papers, Chapin Library of Rare Books, Williams College
LRS	Lelia Robinson Scrapbook, Chapin Library of Rare Books, Williams College
NA	National Archives
SCPC	Swarthmore College Peace Collection
WGF	Papers of the William Goodell Family, Hutchins Library, Berea College
WL	Virginia G. Drachman, *Women Lawyers and the Origins of Professional Identity in America: The Letters of the Equity Club, 1887-1890* (Ann Arbor: University of Michigan Press, 1993)
WLH	Women's Legal History Biography Project: http://wlh.law.stanford.edu/biography_search/articles

PREFACE

1. *Bradwell v. Illinois*, 83 U.S. 130, 141 (1873).

2. *In the Matter of the Motion to admit Miss Lavinia Goodell*, 39 Wisc. 232, 245-46 (1875).

3. *Bradwell*, 130.

4. Catharine G. Waugh (McCulloch) to Equity Club members, 2 May 1888, *WL*, 136.

5. Ibid., 136.

6. LRS, *Boston Times*, September 11, 1881, quoting the *Globe*.

7. In 1894, African American Ida Platt graduated with honors from the Chicago College of Law and, as a member of the second generation of women lawyers,

helped to establish the Cook County Bar Association, the nation's oldest African American bar association.

CHAPTER 1

1. Barbara Sapinsley, *The Private War of Mrs. Packard.* (New York: Kodansha International, 1991), and the Directory of Jacksonville State Hospital Patients, 1854-1870. Her name was spelled incorrectly with an "s." Elizabeth Packard was discharged on June 18, 1863. http://www.rootsweb.ancestry.com/~ilmaga/morgan2/statehosp/mc-sh_adm-pq.html.

2. Edith B. Gelles, *Abigail and John: Portrait of a Marriage* (New York: Morrow, 2009), 77.

3. Rosemarie Zagarri, *Revolutionary Backlash: Women and Politics in the Early Republic* (Philadelphia: University of Pennsylvania Press, 2007), 1.

4. Linda Kerber, *Women of the Republic* (Chapel Hill: University of North Carolina Press, 1980).

5. Zagarri, *Revolutionary Backlash*, 146, 180; Catherine Allgor, *Parlor Politics: In Which the Ladies of Washington Help Build a City and a Government* (Charlottesville: University Press of Virginia, 2000), 30, 47.

6. Sarah Grimke culled data from twenty thousand newspapers and used this information in her book *American Slavery*, which sold one hundred thousand copies, at least one of which was in the hands of Harriet Beecher Stowe when she wrote *Uncle Tom's Cabin*.

7. Margaret Fuller, *Woman in the Nineteenth Century* (New York: Norton, 1971), 171.

8. "Declaration of Sentiments and Resolutions," available with commentary at http://ecssba.rutgers.edu/docs/seneca.html All subsequent quotations from the Declaration may be found at this site.

9. Elizabeth H. Thomson, "Elizabeth Blackwell," in Edward T. James, ed., *Notable American Women, 1607-1950* (Cambridge, MA: Harvard University Press), 1: 163.

10. Barbara M. Solomon, "Antoinette Louisa Brown Blackwell," in James, *Notable American Women*, 1: 159. See also Rebecca Larson, *Daughters of Light: Quaker Women Preaching and Prophesying in the Colonies and Abroad, 1700-1775* (New York: Knopf, 1999).

11. Kathryn Kish Sklar, *Catharine Beecher: A Study in American Domesticity* (New York: Norton, 1976), 78.

12. Ibid., 97.

13. Ibid., 181.

14. *Our Mothers before Us: Women and Democracy, 1789-1920* (Washington, DC: Center for Legislative Archives, National Archives and Records Administration, 1998), 2: 31.

15. *Evening Herald* (Utica, NY) editorial, reprinted in Geoffrey C. Ward and

Ken Burns, *Not for Ourselves Alone: The Story of Elizabeth Cady Stanton and Susan B. Anthony* (New York: Knopf, 1999), 68.

16. Ibid., 68.

17. Joan Hedrick, *Harriet Beecher Stowe* (New York: Oxford University Press, 1994), 11.

18. Solomon, "Blackwell," 1:159.

19. Andrea Moore Kerr, *Lucy Stone: Speaking Out for Equality* (New Brunswick, NJ: Rutgers University Press, 1992), 60.

20. *HWS*, 1: 228.

21. "American Anti-Slavery Anniversary," *The National Anti-Slavery Standard*, May 13, 1865, 2.

22. Stanton to Phillips, 25 May 1865, reprinted in Theodore Stanton and Harriet Stanton Blatch, eds., *Elizabeth Cady Stanton* (New York: Arno, 1969), 2: 104-5.

23. Helena B. Temple, "Interview, Mrs. Belva A. Lockwood," *Women's Penny Paper*, October 5, 1889, 1.

24. "Woman Suffrage," *Evening Star*, January 19, 1870, 4.

25. Ibid., 4.

CHAPTER 2

1. Jerold S. Auerbach, *Justice without Law? Resolving Disputes without Lawyers* (New York: Oxford University Press, 1983), 3.

2. Ibid., 8; James Willard Hurst, *The Growth of American Law: The Law Makers* (Boston: Little, Brown, 1950), 277.

3. Gerard W. Gawalt, "Sources of Anti-Lawyer Sentiment in Massachusetts, 1740-1840," *American Journal of Legal History* 14 (1970): 284.

4. Ibid., 284. Gawalt writes that the need for lawyers in Massachusetts Bay Colony was first formally recognized in 1701 when the legislature established an oath of office for attorneys, and set maximum fees for court cases that only regularly admitted attorneys could collect. Gawalt, "Sources," 284.

5. J. Hector St. John de Crèvecoeur, *Letters from an American Farmer and Sketches of Eighteenth-Century America* (1782; reprint New York: Penguin Books, 1981), 151-52. Lawyers loyal to England also provoked petitions that they be disbarred. Gerard W. Gawalt, *The Promise of Power: The Legal Profession in Massachusetts, 1760-1840* (Westport, CT: Greenwood Press, 1979), 48-50.

6. Washington Irving, *A History of New York from the Beginning of the World to the End* (London: John Murray, 1820), 261.

7. Gawalt, *Promise of Power*, 51.

8. John Phillip Reid, *Legitimating the Law: The Struggle for Judicial Competency in Early National New Hampshire* (DeKalb: Northern Illinois Press, 2012), 22. Reading Federal as well as Republican New Hampshire papers, Reid observes "how much anti-lawyerism was part of the political culture." Ibid., 23.

9. Philip S. Foner, ed., *The Complete Writings of Thomas Paine* (New York: Citadel Press, 1945), 29.

10. Alexis de Tocqueville, *Democracy in America* (New York: Random House, 1945), 1: 282.

11. Ibid., 283.

12. Ibid., 283. Tocqueville offers a brief caveat: "I do not, then, assert that *all* members of the legal profession are at *all* times the friends of order and the opponents of innovation, but merely that most of them are usually so." 1: 284-85.

13. Ibid., 283.

14. Reid, *Legitimating*, 26.

15. Perry Miller, *The Life of the Mind in America from the Revolution to the Civil War* (New York: Harcourt Brace & World, 1965), 242. Italics in the original. In the 1860s Waterville College was renamed Colby College. Reid, *Legitimating*, 26.

16. Gawalt, "Sources," 291.

17. Susan Dunn, "When America Was Transformed," *New York Review of Books*, March 25, 2010, 29. Banking had become less elitist. One observer noted that by 1820, "wherever there was a church, a tavern, and a blacksmith, one could also find a bank." Ibid., 30.

18. Charles Sellers, *The Market Revolution: Jacksonian America, 1815-1846* (New York: Oxford University Press).

19. Ibid., 51.

20. Ibid., 47, 51.

21. Miller, *The Life*, 109; Morton J. Horwitz, *The Transformation of American Law, 1780-1860* (Cambridge, MA: Harvard University Press, 1977), 140, 154; personal communication from John Phillip Reid, 29 July 2010. In *The Americanization of the Common Law*, William E. Nelsen also explains that contracts were no longer enforced according to community values but according to the purpose intended by the parties to the contract.

22. Horwitz, *Transformation*, 144.

23. Ibid., 226.

24. Miller, *Life*, 237-38.

25. Horwitz, *Transformation*, 253.

26. Reid, *Legitimating*, 26-27.

27. Laura F. Edwards, *The People and Their Peace: Legal Culture and the Transformation of Inequality in the Post-Revolutionary South* (Chapel Hill: University of North Carolina Press, 2009), 4.

28. Ibid., 4.

29. Ibid., 48, quoting historian Lars C. Golumbic. Edwards argues that within the culture of localized law "everyone participated in the identification of offenses, the resolution of conflicts, and the definition of law." This local commitment to "peace" empowered the powerless as even members of the community without rights—wives, children, servants, slaves—as well as free blacks, unmarried free

women, and poor whites had direct access to the process by which neighbors sought to re-establish the all-important social order.

30. Ibid., 80. See also John Phillip Reid's study of the law-mindedness of ordinary people: *Law for the Elephant: Property and Social Behavior on the Overland Trail* (San Marino, CA: Huntington Library, 1980).

31. Edith B. Gelles, *Abigail and John: Portrait of a Marriage* (New York: Morrow, 2009), 206.

32. Sellers, *Market*, 47; Gawalt, *Promise of Power*, 172.

33. Emma (Mrs. E.D.E.N.) Southworth allegedly based her immensely popular nineteenth-century novel *Ishmael* on Wirt's life and career.

34. For a full discussion see G. Edward White, *The Marshall Court and Cultural Change, 1815-1835* (abridged ed.) (New York: Oxford University Press, 1991), 95-117.

35. Walter Theodore Hitchcock, *Timothy Walker: Antebellum Lawyer* (New York: Garland, 1990), 96.

36. Ibid., 101.

37. Steve Sheppard, ed., *The History of Legal Education in the United States: Commentaries and Primary Sources* (Pasadena, CA: Salem Press, 1999), 1: 292.

38. Hurst, *Growth*, 256.

39. Gawalt, *Promise*, 60, 66, 91, 93-118.

40. Robert T. Swaine, *The Cravath Firm and Its Predecessors, 1819-1947* (New York, Ad Press, 1946), 1: 6, quoting to the issue of June 27, 1818.

41. George Shattuck to Walker, 29 March 1831, Walker Papers, reprinted in Hitchcock, *Timothy Walker*, 125-26.

42. Hitchcock, *Timothy Walker*, 25.

43. Ibid., 59.

44. Miller, *Life*, 259.

45. Ibid., 259.

46. Allen Nevins and Milton Halsey Thomas, eds., *The Diary of George Templeton Strong* (New York: Macmillan, 1952), 1: 301.

47. Ibid., 1: xxiii and 165.

48. Ibid., 3: 28; Edwin G. Burrows and Mike Wallace, *Gotham: A History of New York City to 1898* (New York: Oxford, 1999), 967-68.

49. Nevins and Thomas, *Diary*, 1: xxix-xxxi; 2: "1854"; William P. LaPiana, *Logic and Experience: The Origin of Modern American Legal Education* (New York: Macmillan, 1994), 81-87.

50. Hitchcock, *Timothy* Walker, 14-15; White, *The Marshall Court*, 105, citing to William W. Story, ed., *The Life and Letters of Joseph Story* (Boston: Little, Brown, 1851), 2: 1-7.

51. Nevins and Thomas, *Diary*, 2: 388; 3: 25, 29, 31, and 269.

52. For a variety of reasons, state and even county bar associations did not flourish in the first decades of the nineteenth century. Some associations sought to control local admission standards, but many were largely quasi-social clubs.

Bloomfield argues that "it was the judiciary, not the bar, that did most to establish the guidelines for legal practice, with the acquiescence of state legislatures." Maxwell Bloomfield, "Lawyers and Public Criticism: Challenge and Response in Nineteenth-Century America," *American Journal of Legal History* 15 (1971): 272. Some state legislators tried to limit their growth, describing bar associations as undesirable protectionist leagues (e.g., New Hampshire from 1842 until 1872). Robert Steven, *Law School: Legal Education in America from the 1850s to the 1980s* (Chapel Hill: University of North Carolina Press, 1983), 9.

53. 10 U.S. 87 (1810).

54. R. Kent Newmyer, "Joseph Story," in Kermit L. Hall, ed., *The Oxford Companion to the Supreme Court of the United States* (New York: Oxford University Press, 1992), 842.

55. *Cherokee v. Georgia*, 30 U.S. 1 (1831) and *Worcester v. Georgia*, 31 U.S. 515 (1832). See Jill Norgren, *The Cherokee Cases* (Norman: University of Oklahoma Press, 2004).

56. Nevins and Thomas, *Diary*, 1: xxiii.

57. Edwards, *The People*, 49.

58. Nevins and Thomas, *Diary*, 1: xxiv; Deborah S. Gardner, *Cadwalader, Wickersham & Taft: A Bicentennial History, 1792-1992* (New York: Cadwalader, Wickersham & Taft, 1994), 2-3.

59. David Dudley Field, "The Study and Practice of the Law," *Democratic Review* 14 (April 1844): 345.

60. Ibid., 345.

61. Ibid., 346.

62. Ibid., 345.

63. Ibid., 349.

64. Ibid., 349.

65. Ibid., 349.

66. Ibid., 349-50.

67. Mark E. Steiner, *An Honest Calling: The Law Practice of Abraham Lincoln* (DeKalb: Northern Illinois University Press, 2006), 103-4.

68. Ibid., 125-26. U.S. Constitution, Article I, Sections 2 and 9, and Article IV, Section 2.

69. Steiner, *Honest Calling*, 137-59.

70. Gordon Morris Bakken, *Practicing Law in Frontier California* (Lincoln: University of Nebraska Press, 1991), 2; Reid, *Law for the Elephant*, 17.

71. Bakken, *Practicing Law*, 41.

72. Ibid., 83.

73. Ibid., 103.

74. Ibid., 112; C. Robert Haywood, *Cowtown Lawyers: Dodge City and Its Attorneys, 1876-1886* (Norman: University of Oklahoma Press, 1988), 242-43.

75. Bakken, *Practicing Law*, 118.

76. Ibid., 12.

77. Rebecca Edwards, *New Spirits: Americans in the Gilded Age, 1865-1905* (New York: Oxford University Press, 2006), 4.

78. Swaine, *The Cravath*, 91-92.

79. Hurst, *Growth*, 297-98. American writer Winston Churchill warns about the power of railroads and their lawyers in his 1908 reform novel *Mr. Crewe's Career*. He makes a hero of lawyer Austen Vane, who would not take a retainer from the railroads.

80. Hurst, *Growth*, 311. Hurst demonstrates that the top bracket earners, in contrast, did very well. He also describes the competition encountered by local attorneys as title insurance companies and debt collection agencies expanded their reach. Ibid., 319 ff.

CHAPTER 3

1. Jane M. Friedman, *America's First Woman Lawyer: The Biography of Myra Bradwell* (Buffalo, NY: Prometheus Books, 1993), 18, 41.

2. Mary A. Livermore, *The Story of My Life* (Hartford, CT: A.D. Worthington, 1898), 457.

3. Friedman, *America's First Woman Lawyer*, 38-39, quoting the *Chicago Tribune*, May 12, 1889, 26.

4. Ibid., 38.

5. Mary A. Livermore, *My Story of the War: A Woman's Narrative* (1887; reprint New York: Da Capo Press, 1995), 411.

6. Ibid., 455.

7. Ibid., 430. The manuscript, placed by its owner in the archives of the Chicago Historical Society, burned in the Great Chicago Fire.

8. Livermore, *My Story of the War*, 439-40.

9. Livermore, *The Story of My Life*, 479.

10. Ibid., 479.

11. Ibid., 481.

12. Ibid., 482.

13. Morton J. Horwitz, *The Transformation of American Law, 1780-1860* (Cambridge, MA: Harvard University Press, 1977), 141. Founded in 1808, it was the first law journal in the United States.

14. Maxwell Bloomfield, "Lawyers and Public Criticism: Challenge and Response in Nineteenth-Century America," *American Journal of Legal History* 15 (1971): 274.

15. Gordon Morris Bakken, *Practicing Law in Frontier California* (Lincoln: University of Nebraska Press, 1991), 29-30.

16. Editorial, *CLN*, October 3, 1868, 1.

17. Friedman, *America's First Woman Lawyer*, 77.

18. "Laws Relating to Women," *CLN*, October 31, 1868, 37.

19. "Laws Relating to Women: Married Woman's Property," *CLN*, November 14, 1868, 53; "Law Relating to Women, the Property Rights of Married Women. To the Editor of the Legal News," *CLN*, December 12, 1868, 85. The state enacted some of the reforms urged by Bradwell in March 1869. See "An act in relation to the earning of married women," *Illinois Laws* 225 (1869).

20. Friedman, *America's First Woman Lawyer*, 80-81.

21. *CLN*, March 13, 1869, 188, column 1.

22. Friedman, *America's First Woman Lawyer*, 79.

23. *CLN*, September 21, 1878, 5, column 1.

24. Friedman, *America's First Woman Lawyer*, 89-91.

25. Ibid., 84.

26. Ibid., 29.

27. Mary Greene to Equity Club members, 27 April 1887, *WL*, 52.

28. 9 October 1869 entry, Allan Nevins and Milton Halsey Thomas, eds., *The Diary of George Templeton Strong: Post-War Years, 1865-1875* (New York: Macmillan, 1952), 4: 256. Strong followed with the confession that he loathed the ladies who had taken up the cause of women's rights. He postured behind the offer to rescue women. So did his contemporary, Dr. Edward H. Clarke, a Harvard medical school physician, who argued in his book *Sex in Education* that hours of daily study would re-direct energy from a woman's reproductive organs to her brain, causing ill health and potential danger to her unborn offspring.

29. For a discussion of the "confusion and controversy" surrounding Cary's law school career, see Shamina Sneed, "Mary Ann Shadd Cary: A Biographical Sketch of the Rebel," WLH, 17-23.

30. This account draws on the work of Teresa Federer, "Belle A. Mansfield: Opening the Way for Others," WLH, 1-77.

31. Ibid., 35.

32. Ibid., 37-38, citing to the District Court Record, Henry County, Iowa, Book Hat 54-55, June Term, 2nd Day, Tuesday, June 15, 1869.

33. Ibid., 38-39.

34. Bradwell followed Mansfield's story and wrote about her success. Myra Bradwell, "A Married Woman Admitted to the Bar in Iowa," *CLN*, October 16, 1869, 20.

35. It is generally thought that Couzins did not practice although she was admitted to the bar in Missouri and Arkansas in 1871, Utah in 1872, and subsequently in Kansas, the Dakota territories, and the federal courts. Matthew J. Sanders, "An Introduction to Phoebe Wilson Couzins," WLH, 8. Sanders writes that in 1871, "Couzins reportedly established a law office in downtown St. Louis . . . but she handled very few, if any, cases in her lifetime." Ibid., 8-9; Federer, "Belle," 40-41.

36. *CLN*, March 31, 1877, 229, column 1. For reviews of several of these cases,

see Gwen Jordan, "Stepping-Stones to Women's Emancipation: The Origins of a Woman's Law Reform Movement in Illinois, 1855-1875." Paper presented at the Midwest Law & Society Retreat, Madison, Wisconsin, September 15-16, 2006, 54-56.

37. "Chicago Woman Suffrage Convention," *CLN*, February 20, 1869, 164. In 1869 Bradwell was elected corresponding secretary of the newly formed Illinois Woman Suffrage Association.

38. See Jordan, "Stepping-Stones."

39. Ibid., 38; Myra Bradwell, *Additional Brief*, reprinted in "A Married Woman Cannot Practice Law or Hold Any Office in Illinois," *CLN*, February 5, 1870, 145-46.

40. Jordan, "Stepping-Stones," 39.

41. Bradwell, "A Married Woman Cannot Practice," 145.

42. Elizabeth Cady Stanton, "The Sixteenth Amendment," in Ann D. Gordon, ed., *Against an Aristocracy of Sex: The Selected Papers of Elizabeth Cady Stanton and Susan B. Anthony* (New Brunswick, NJ: Rutgers University Press, 2000), 237. The ratified Fifteenth Amendment reads, "The right of citizens of the United States to vote shall not be denied or abridged by the United States or by any State on account of race, color, or previous condition of servitude."

43. *Bradwell v. Illinois*, 83 U.S. 130 (1873).

44. Several thousand copies of her comments, titled *The Memorial of Victoria C. Woodhull*, were mailed out requesting petition signatures from women suffrage supporters. Barbara Goldsmith, *Other Powers: The Age of Suffrage, Spiritualism, and the Scandalous Victoria Woodhull* (New York: Knopf, 1998), 248-57.

45. Ibid., 253, citing to Elizabeth Cady Stanton's letter of 21 June 1871, to Victoria Woodhull. Washington lawyer Albert G. Riddle was also convinced that the Fourteenth Amendment guaranteed women's right to vote, and in 1871 he helped to establish a test court case in the nation's capital. Jill Norgren, *Belva Lockwood* (New York: New York University Press, 2007), 58-66.

46. Susan B. Anthony to Myra Bradwell, 30 July 1873, cited in Friedman, *America's First Woman Lawyer*, 22-23. Carpenter argued Bradwell's case on January 18, 1872. The court waited to render a decision for more than a year, until the results of the election of 1872 had been announced.

47. *The Slaughter-House Cases*, 83 U. S. 36 (1873).

48. *Bradwell*, 139. Without offering an opinion, Chief Justice Salmon P. Chase "dissented from the judgment of the Court and from all opinions." Justice Miller was the father-in-law of attorney George B. Corkhill, who examined Arabella Mansfield for membership in the Iowa bar. "George B. Corkhill Dead," *New York Times*, July 7, 1886. Available at http://query.nytimes.com/mem/archive-free/pdf ?res=F10A10FE3B5410738DDDAE0894DF405B8684F0D3.

49. *Bradwell*, 141.

50. Ibid., 141.

51. Jordan, "Stepping-Stones," 44-45, citing to the *Boston Daily Advertiser,* April 16, 1873.

52. Jordan, "Stepping-Stones," 46-47.

53. *Journal of the Illinois House of Representatives,* March 21, 1872. Bradwell's appeal had been argued in January, before passage of the legislation. The Supreme Court did not declare her case moot.

54. Jordan, "Stepping-Stones, 52-53.

55. "Deep-Rooted Prejudice," *CLN,* June 14, 1873, 453.

56. Lucia M. Peabody entry, http://www.herhatwasinthering.org/Site/default. aspx. In 1875 the Illinois General Assembly opened the office of notary public to women, a reform slowly occurring in many places.

57. For an account of the help that Bradwell and her husband extended to Mrs. Lincoln, see Friedman, *America's First Woman Lawyer,* chapter 3 and 202-8.

58. Lelia J. Robinson, "Women Lawyers in the United States," *The Green Bag,* January 1890, 14. Myra Bradwell's son, Thomas, was also a lawyer.

59. Friedman, *America's First Woman Lawyer,* 40.

CHAPTER 4

1. *In Memorium, William Goodell* (Chicago: Gilbert and Win, 1879), 18, in WGF. Lavinia Goodell wrote this remembrance although her name does not appear on it.

2. Maria Goodell Frost, *The Life of Lavinia Goodell,* 6-7, WGF. Gerrit Smith and the Tappan brothers, for example, were friends and visitors.

3. Ibid., 8.

4. Ibid., 28, 31, and 57.

5. Lavinia Goodell to Maria Goodell Frost, 18 March 1858, quoted in *The Life of Lavinia Goodell,* 39-41, WGF.

6. Ibid., 42.

7. Ibid., 42.

8. Ibid., 43.

9. Frost, *Life,* 68.

10. Goodell to Frost, 18 March 1858, quoted in *Life,* 41.

11. Frost, *Life,* 69.

12. Ibid., 78.

13. Ibid., 82.

14. Ibid., 82.

15. Ibid., 88.

16. Ibid., 95.

17. Ibid., 96. The senior Goodells also repaid Lavinia the money she had given to them over the past several years.

18. Frost, *Life,* 96.

19. Ibid., 96.

20. Lavinia Goodell to Sarah M. Thomas, 2 January 1872, LGP.

21. Ibid., 96.

22. Item, *Woman's Journal,* August 16, 1873, 258.

23. Lavinia Goodell to Sarah M. Thomas, 7 March 1872, LGP.

24. Ibid.

25. Ibid.

26. Ibid.

27. Lavinia Goodell to Maria Goodell Frost, 6 April 1873, quoted in Frost, *Life,* 100. Seven months later she summarized her work to date: "I have read 16 vols of law since I commenced study, which considering how much I have been interrupted, is doing pretty well, I think." Goodell to Frost, 18 November 1873, HC4, Box 15/7, WGF.

28. Catherine B. Cleary, "Lavinia Goodell, First Woman Lawyer in Wisconsin," *Wisconsin Magazine of History* 74 (Summer 1991): 249; Lavinia Goodell to Sarah M. Thomas, 18 August 1873, LGP.

29. Lavinia Goodell to Sarah M. Thomas, 18 August 1873, LGP.

30. Lavinia Goodell to Maria Goodell Frost, 18 November 1873, quoted in Frost, *Life,* 102.

31. Ibid., 102.

32. Ibid., 102.

33. Ibid. 102. She also maintained respectability through her strong commitment to temperance. In the summer of 1873 Goodell joined in the planning of a temperance coffee house to "cut out the saloons." Lavinia Goodell to Sarah M. Thomas, 18 August 1873, LGP.

34. Lavinia Goodell to Sarah M. Thomas, 7 March 1872, LGP.

35. Lavinia Goodell to Maria Goodell Frost, 18 November 1873, quoted in Frost, *Life,* 103. Holland's *Janesville City Directory, 1870,* lists the town's lawyers and law firms.

36. Lavinia Goodell to Maria Goodell Frost, 18 November 1873, quoted in Frost, *Life,* 103.

37. Ibid., 103-4.

38. Ibid., 104.

39. Ibid., 104. The next quotation also cites to this source and page.

40. Lavinia Goodell to Maria Goodell Frost, 22 February 1874, quoted in Frost, *Life,* 106-7.

41. Lavinia Goodell, undated letter, quoted in Frost, *Life,* 112.

42. Lavinia Goodell to Maria Goodell Frost, 8 June 1874, quoted in Frost, *Life,* 113. The following quotations in this and the next three paragraphs cite to this letter.

43. Lavinia Goodell to Sarah Thomas, 18 June 1874, quoted in Frost, *Life,* 115. Maria also received a letter announcing "your little sister is a member of the Wisconsin bar." Goodell to Frost, 18 June 1874, HC, Box 15/9, WGF.

44. Ibid., 116.

45. Cleary, "Lavinia Goodell," 251.

46. Lavinia Goodell to unknown recipient, July 1874, quoted in Frost, *Life*, 121.

47. Walter Theodore Hitchcock, *Timothy Walker: Antebellum Lawyer* (New York: Garland, 1990), 25.

48. Lavinia Goodell to Sarah Thomas, 18 June 1874, quoted in Frost, *Life*, 118.

49. Lavinia Goodell to Maria Goodell Frost, 30 June 1874, quoted in Frost, *Life*, 123.

50. Lavinia Goodell to Maria Goodell Frost, 28 June 1874, quoted in Frost, *Life*, 119. All quotations in this paragraph cite to this letter, 119-22.

51. Lavinia Goodell to Maria Goodell Frost, 14 July 1874, quoted in Frost, *Life*, 124.

52. Ibid.

53. Ibid.

54. Goodell to Frost, 14 July 1874, 125.

55. Lavinia Goodell to Maria Goodell Frost, 6 August 1874, quoted in Frost, *Life*, 126.

56. Ibid., 126-27.

57. Goodell to Frost, 28 September 1874, quoted in Frost, *Life*, 128. All quotations in this paragraph cite to this letter.

58. Lavinia Goodell to Maria Goodell Frost, 8 October 1874, quoted in Frost, *Life*, 131.

59. Ibid., 131; Lavinia Goodell to Maria Goodell Frost, 15 October 1874, quoted in Frost, *Life*, 132. Goodell later learned that the jury was divided in the second liquor case, which she lost. They deliberated for six hours but then "everyone wanted to go home," and they voted for acquittal. Ibid., 134.

60. Goodell to Frost, 8 October 1874, 131-32.

61. Ryan was sent to Clongowes Wood College (later James Joyce's secondary school). As the second son, he could not inherit. The family may have hoped that he would become a priest. My description of Edward Ryan's life and career draws upon Alfons J. Beitzinger, *Edward G. Ryan: Lion of the Law* (Madison: State Historical Society of Wisconsin, 1960), as well as lengthy obituaries that describe his work and temperament. These death notices are singular in all mentioning that Ryan was afflicted by "a bitterness and irascibility," that he exhibited a "petulant temper," and that "the frailties of [his] temper were colossal"—a problem that nearly destroyed all ability to make contributions to his profession. Several writers speak with frankness about his failures as a husband: "His wife was long ago driven from his side by his unkindness." Edward G. Ryan Papers, State Historical Society of Wisconsin, Madison.

62. Beitzinger, *Edward G. Ryan*.

63. Herbert G. May and Bruce M. Metzger, *The Oxford Annotated Bible* (New York: Oxford University Press, 1962), 1227.

64. My discussion of this lecture draws upon Beverly B. Cook's article, "Lecturing on Woman's Place: 'Mrs. Jellyby' in Wisconsin, 1854-1874," *Signs* 9 (1983): 361-76. Cook argues that Ryan "was attempting to prepare Wisconsin citizens to resist" the ideas of the young woman's movement. Ibid., 366. The manuscript of his lecture is found in the Edward G. Ryan Papers, State Historical Society of Wisconsin, Madison.

65. Cook, "Lecturing," 374. Cook excerpts about one-fourth of the lecture at the end of her article.

66. Ibid., 374.

67. Ibid., 374.

68. Ibid., 374.

69. Ryan was elected in 1875 to fill out the rest of Dixon's term, and in 1876 won election to a full six-year term. He wrote well-regarded opinions on government regulation of corporations and railroads, tort liability, and tax law.

70. Cook, "Lecturing," 370, note 41. Ryan was a Jeffersonian Democrat. In addition to his conservative views on sex roles, he supported the Fugitive Slave law.

71. "A Dead Chief Justice," *Sunday Telegraph*, October 24, 1880 (ms. pages 13 and 14) in the Edward G. Ryan Papers, Wisconsin Local History & Biography Articles, Wisconsin Historical Society, Madison.

72. Ibid., 367.

73. Lavinia Goodell to Maria Goodell Frost, 16 February 1875; and Goodell to Frost, 7 June 1875, quoted in Frost, *Life*, 136-37.

74. Lavinia Goodell to Maria Goodell Frost, 2 August 1875, quoted in Frost, *Life*, 139.

75. Lavinia Goodell to Sarah M. Thomas, 4 February 1876, LGP. Subsequent quotations in this paragraph also cite to this letter.

76. Lavinia Goodell to Maria Goodell Frost, 2 August 1875, HC, Box 15/10, WGF. On September 4, 1875, *The Woman's Journal* published an essay by Goodell, "Shall Women Study Law?" It is an excellent, succinct summary of her views and contains sensible professional advice.

77. Lavinia Goodell to Maria Goodell Frost, 20 December 1875, quoted in Frost, *Life*, 150. Emma C. Bascom, wife of the president of the University of Wisconsin, urged Goodell to have the *Wisconsin State Journal* publish her argument. The editors acceded to the request and cast Goodell in a positive light. Cleary, "Lavinia Goodell," 258.

78. Lavinia Goodell to Maria Goodell Frost, 18 November 1875, quoted in Frost, *Life*, 140-41. All quotations in this paragraph cite to this letter. Goodell wrote about meeting these two prisoners in "My Tramp," *The Christian Union*, December 1 and 15, 1875.

79. Lavinia Goodell to Maria Goodell Frost, December 1875 (no day), quoted in Frost, *Life*, 142; and Goodell to Frost, 1 January 1876, quoted in Frost, *Life*, 143.

80. Goodell to Frost, 18 November 1875, quoted in Frost, *Life*, 141.

81. Goodell to Frost, 1 January 1876, quoted in Frost, *Life*, 144.

82. Ibid., 144.

83. Lavinia Goodell to Sarah M. Thomas, 4 February 1876, LGP.

84. Ibid.

85. Lavinia Goodell to Maria Goodell Frost, 17 February 1876, quoted in Frost, *Life*, 144.

86. Lavinia Goodell to Sarah M. Thomas, 24 February 1876, LGP.

87. Ibid.

88. Ibid., 145.

89. Ibid., 145.

90. Beitzinger, *Edward G. Ryan*, 148-58.

91. *In the Matter of the Motion to admit Miss Lavinia Goodell*, 39 Wisc. 232, 239-40 (1875).

92. Ibid., 244.

93. Ibid., 243.

94. Ibid., 245-46.

95. "Should Women Practice Law in Wisconsin! Judge Ryan's Opinion Reviewed," *The Woman's Journal*, April 8 and 22, 1876. All quotations from Goodell's response to Ryan cite to these reproductions of her article.

96. Item, *Wisconsin State Journal*, February 16, 1876, 1. This was a Republican-leaning paper.

97. Lavinia Goodell to Sarah M. Thomas, 22 March 1876, LGP.

98. Cleary, "Lavinia Goodell," 266. She was admitted to the bar at Janesville on September 6, 1878.

99. Lavinia Goodell to Maria Goodell Frost, 5 January 1877, quoted in Frost, *Life*, 166-67. In this letter Goodell also reports "drafting some laws intended to ameliorate the condition of married women, and some for prison reform." She writes nothing more about these proposals.

100. Lavinia Goodell to Maria Goodell Frost, 7 March 1877, quoted in Frost, *Life*, 170.

101. Ibid., 168. At the same time that she learned of the cancer, Goodell underwent a religious conversion and joined Janesville's Congregational Church. Speaking about Goodell and her conversion, her pastor, the Reverend T. P. Sawin, later said, "This step was taken with the utmost deliberation. . . . For years she had entertained deep-seated doubts of the truth of many of the formulas of the Christian faith, but at last the light came." Rev. T. P. Sawin, "Obituary," WGF, 234.

102. Lavinia Goodell to Sarah M. Thomas, 16 November 1876, LGP.

103. Frost, *Life,* 186.

104. Lavinia Goodell to Maria Goodell Frost, November 1877 (no day), quoted in Frost, *Life,* 180. Later, Goodell wrote out her thoughts on penal legislation. Lavinia Goodell to the Rev. G. W. Lawrence, November 17, 1879, HC4, Box 16/15, WGF.

105. Lavinia Goodell to Maria Goodell Frost, 27 June 1877, quoted in Frost, *Life,* 177.

106. Lavinia Goodell to Sarah M. Thomas, 4 January 1878, LGP.

107. Ibid., 177.

108. Frost, *Life,* 198. In the spring of 1876 some of her "boys" gave her "grief and anxiety," and she wrote her cousin Sarah that "[I] shant adopt any more children at present." Her interest in them, however, was keen, and Lavinia soon increased her prison work. Lavinia Goodell to Sarah M. Thomas, 31 May 1876, LGP.

109. Lavinia Goodell to Sarah M. Thomas, 17 January 1879, LGP. Subsequent quotations in this paragraph cite to this letter.

110. Lavinia Goodell to Sarah M. Thomas, 28 October 1879, LGP.

111. Lavinia Goodell to Sarah M. Thomas, 14 March 1879, LGP.

112. Lavinia Goodell to Maria Goodell Frost, 5 April 1879, quoted in Frost, *Life,* 218. Goodell's argument was reprinted in the *CLN* by Myra Bradwell. See Lavinia Goodell, "Women as Lawyers," *CLN,* April 26, 1879, 260-61.

113. Lavinia Goodell to Sarah M. Thomas, 29 March 1879, LGP.

114. *Application of Miss Goodell,* 48 Wis. 693 (1879).

115. Lavinia Goodell, Brief for the Wisconsin State Supreme Court, *The State of Wisconsin against Thomas Ingalls, Defendant, Lavinia Goodell, Attorney for the Defendant.* HC4, Box 16/12, WGF.

116. Diary of Lavinia Goodell, August 22, September 20, October 29, 1879, WGF.

117. Lavinia Goodell to Sarah M. Thomas, 20 November 1879, LGP.

118. Ibid. The room was probably in the offices of attorney J. M. Bowman.

119. Lavinia Goodell to Sarah M. Thomas, 17 December 1879, LGP.

120. Frost, *Life,* 233.

121. In addition to Bradwell's paper, suffrage journals, law periodicals, and various newspapers around the country printed information on Goodell. See, e.g., Item, *LDJ,* April 28, 1879, 2; "The Advance of Women," *Albany Journal,* reprinted in *CLN,* April 26, 1879, 298; and "Wisconsin's Female Lawyer," *San Francisco Chronicle,* March 23, 1879, 6.

122. *Last Will and Testament of Lavinia Goodell of Janesville Wisconsin,* HC4, Box 13/4, WGF. Goodell wrote her will on July 7, 1879.

123. Ibid.

124. Ibid.

125. Ibid.

CHAPTER 5

1. Belva A. Lockwood, "My Efforts to Become a Lawyer," *Lippincott's Magazine*, February 1888, 216.

2. Belva A. Lockwood, "The Women Who Tried to Vote," *LDJ*, May 13, 1871, 1.

3. Lockwood, "My Efforts," 216-17.

4. Belva Ann Lockwood, "Belva A. Lockwood." Autobiographical manuscript sent to Susan B. Anthony for Johnson's *New Universal Cyclopaedia*, 24 July 1876, found in *The Papers of E. C. Stanton and S. B. Anthony*, 18: 938-41, LC.

5. Lockwood, "My Efforts," 219.

6. Ibid., 221.

7. Ibid., 221. Her ambition was not completely misplaced. Willam Dean Howells, born poor and without connections, won an appointment, at the age of twenty-four, as American consul to Venice after writing Abraham Lincoln's campaign biography.

8. "Dentistry, Dr. Lockwood," *Evening Star*, August 11, 1866, 1.

9. Lockwood, "My Efforts," 222. Jessie Belva Lockwood was born on January 28, 1869.

10. Belva Lockwood, "Old Homeweek Speech," in "McEnteer Portrays Belva Lockwood," *Tioga County Courier*, March 10, 1993, 2.

11. The Arnell bill, H.R. 1571, targeted discrimination in hiring, promotion, and salaries. A version favored by conservatives passed. Jill Norgren, *Belva Lockwood* (New York: New York University Press), 35-39.

12. Norgren, *Belva Lockwood*, 58-66.

13. Incorporation Certificate, June 30, 1876, Acts of Incorporation, Liber 2, Folio 105, D.C. Archives and Records Center. The school did not succeed, but two decades later Washington lawyers Ellen Spencer Mussey and Emma Gillett revived the idea of a professional school for women and established the Washington College of Law. The school merged in 1949 with American University.

14. Lockwood, "My Efforts," 222. Samson's note was dated October 7, 1869. Washington's *Morning News* noted that Lockwood had attended the school's opening-term exercises. Elmer Louis Kayser, *Bricks without Straw: The Evolution of George Washington University* (New York: Appleton-Century Crofts, 1970), 165.

15. Lockwood, "Women Who Tried to Vote," 1.

16. Lockwood, "My Efforts," 222. In 1954 National merged with George Washington University (once Columbian College).

17. Lockwood, "My Efforts," 223.

18. Ibid., 223.

19. Diploma privilege negated the requirement of an examination to join the bar. Justice Noah Davis, of the New York Supreme Court, criticized it as "a cheap, easy and *secure* road to the bar." Diploma privilege did not come to an end in New

York State until 1882, following intense lobbying of the state legislature. William P. LaPiana, *Logic and Experience: The Origin of Modern American Legal Education* (New York: Macmillan, 1994), 87.

20. "Mrs. Belva A. Lockwood," *CLN*, May 4, 1872, 236.

21. "Female Lawyers," *Evening Star*, April 23, 1872, 4.

22. *Lockwood*, "My Efforts," 223.

23. Belva A. Lockwood, "Women of Washington," *The Golden Age*, December 21, 1872, 2.

24. Belva A. Lockwood to President Grant, 3 January 1873, Ferdinand Julius Dreer Collection (collection 175), The Historical Society of Pennsylvania. In my biography, *Belva Lockwood: The Woman Who Would Be President*, I incorrectly identified this letter as one written on September 3, 1873. The correct date of this first letter to Grant is January 3, 1873. The second letter was written on September 3, 1873.

25. Lockwood, "My Efforts," 224.

26. Ibid., 224.

27. Ibid., 221.

28. Ibid., 224.

29. Lura McNall married DeForest Payson Ormes on July 3, 1879. The couple spent virtually all of their married life living with Lockwood. Clara Bennett, Belva's niece, married William Harrison, a notary who boarded with Lockwood. After his premature death, Clara and her son stayed on at Lockwood's house for several years.

30. Lockwood, "My Efforts," 224.

31. Ellen A. Martin to "Dear Miss Pearce, Secretary of the Equity Club," *WL*, 113.

32. Jeffrey Brandon Morris, *Calmly to Poise the Scales of Justice: A History of the Courts of the District of Columbia Circuit* (Durham, NC: Carolina Academic Press, 2001), xvii. In the Anglo-American system equity law follows from the principle that no right should be without an adequate remedy.

33. The Lockwood law office handled seven thousand pension cases from the 1870s through the 1890s. "Belva Lockwood Is 86 Years Old," *Evening Star*, October 24, 1916, 10.

34. My survey of the relevant docket books, which is the basis of this reporting of outcomes, revealed that Lockwood was the sole attorney of record in 80 percent of her criminal cases.

35. Lockwood, "My Efforts," 225.

36. *In re Mrs. Belva A. Lockwood, Ex Parte*, 9 Ct. Cl. 346, 347 (1873).

37. "An Act prescribing the Form of enacting and resolving Clauses of Acts and Resolutions of Congress, and Rules for the Construction thereof," February 25, 1871, 16 U.S. Stat. (1871), 431.

38. 9 Ct. Cl. 346, 352.

39. Lockwood, "My Efforts,"226.

40. Lura McNall, "Our Washington Letter," *LDJ*, November 21, 1877, 2.

41. "Women as Notaries," *National Republican*, December 20, 1877, 1. In Wisconsin Goodell had most trouble obtaining an appointment as a notary, while in Illinois in January 1870, Governor John Palmer rejected the petition of sixty members of the Chicago bar, asking that he appoint Myra Bradwell as a notary for Chicago. He cited coverture while commenting that otherwise he would "cheerfully" make the appointment. Jane M. Friedman, *America's First Woman Lawyer: The Biography of Myra Bradwell* (Buffalo, NY: Prometheus Books, 1993), 155-56.

42. Lura McNall, "Our Washington Letter," *LDJ*, January 3, 1878, 2; *HWS* 3: 72.

43. Lockwood, "My Efforts," 229; "The Surprise," *LDJ*, February 17, 1879, 2.

44. Supreme Court of the United States, *Minutes*, November 6, 1876.

45. "Belva Lockwood, 82 Years Young," (NY) *World*, November 3, 1915, N5.

46. *Congressional Record,* Senate, February 7, 1879, 1084.

47. Ibid., 1082-83.

48. Lura McNall, "Our Washington Letter," *LDJ*, May 8, 1878, 2; Lura McNall, "Our Washington Letter," *LDJ*, April 12, 1878, 2.

49. "Woman's Right to Practice before the United States Supreme Court," *LDJ*, February 11, 1879, 2; Lura McNall, "Our Washington Letter," *LDJ*, February 18, 1879, 2.

50. "Admission of Women to the Bar," *CLN*, February 15, 1879, 179.

51. Ibid., 179.

52. "Mrs. Lockwood's Victory," *Woman's Journal*, April 12, 1879, 1.

53. Ibid., 1.

54. Lura McNall, "Our Washington Letter," *LDJ*, March 6, 1879, 2; "Mrs. Lockwood's Victory," 118; and "Mrs. Lockwood's Victory," *Washington Post*, March 5, 1879, 1.

55. Brief of the Committee, 3, RG 21, Equity Case 7177, NA.

56. *Nichols v. Barber*, Original Bill, March 16, 1875, 1, RG 21, Law 13854, NA.

57. *U.S. v. Louisa Wallace*, United States Marshal's Office, Jurors' Recommendation, December 20, 1878, RG 21, Criminal 12529, NA.

58. Motion for a new trial, 1, RG 21, Criminal 12529, NA.

59. "Another Death Sentence," *Evening Star*, April 12, 1879, 4.

60. Reform of the criminal as well as civil law code was debated in Washington in this period. Lura McNall wrote that legislation had been proposed to make rape a capital offense in the District, commenting that "something should be done for the protection of those ladies who are forced to be out at night." *LDJ*, March 9, 1880, 2.

61. *Horton v. Morgan*, Lucy Horton to Mr. Jno. H. Morgan, 17 January 1878, 2, RG 21, Law 20954, NA.

62. *U.S. v. Lucy W. R. Horton*, Docket Book No. 13271, RG 21, NA.

63. *Horton v. Morgan*, Stenographer's transcript, January 31 and February 4, 1880, 33, RG 21, Law 20954, NA.

64. Haywood J. Pearce Jr. *Benjamin H. Hill* (1928; reprint New York: Negro Universities Press, 1969), 308.

65. "Jessie Raymond's Charge against Hon. B. H. Hill," *Evening Star*, March 3, 1880, 1.

66. *Raymond v. Hill*, Notice to Plead, February 27, 1880, 1, RG 21, Law 21680, NA.

67. *Raymond*, Declaration, affidavit & notice to plead, March 2, 1880, RG 21, Law 21680, NA.

68. "A Sharp Letter," *Syracuse Standard*, reprinted in *LDJ*, March 17, 1880, 2.

69. "The Raymond-Hill Scandal," *Evening Star*, March 23, 1880, 1.

70. "Jessie Raymond and Tommy," *Evening Star*, March 26, 1880, 1; "A Denial from Senator Hill," *Evening Star*, April 23, 1880, 1.

71. "Original Bills and a few other items considered, December 12, 1879-January 7, 1880," H.R. 2623, 46th Cong., 2d Sess. Stow's proposal was introduced as "An Act to Regulate Estates in the District of Columbia and in the Territories of the United States."

72. Testimony of Belva A. Lockwood, December 16, 1879, in Behalf of the Widow's and Orphan's Bill, reprinted in the *Woman's Herald of Industry*, December 1884, 2.

73. For a full discussion of these issues, see Norgren, *Belva Lockwood*, chapter 9.

74. *HWS* 3: 5.

75. Norgren, *Belva Lockwood*, 122-23.

76. Charles DeBenedetti, *The Peace Reform in American History* (Bloomington: Indiana University Press, 1980), 60.

77. Wendy E. Chmielewski, "Yours, for Radical Peace: The Universal Peace Union, 1866-1913." Paper presented at the Conference on Social and Political Movements, Indiana Association of Historians, February 1998, 2-3.

78. "Publications," December 12, 1889, Universal Peace Union, Reel 13:3, SCPC; "Petition" from Jacob M. Troth, Daniel Breed, Belva A. Lockwood, and Chalkley Gillingham to Rutherford B. Hayes, January 15, 1879, Misc. Letters of the Department of State, 1784-1906, RG 59, NA.

79. "Stow's Response to 'Please Take It Down,'" *Women's Herald of Industry*, August 1884, 1.

80. A full discussion of Lockwood's two presidential campaigns, and platforms, may be found in Norgren, *Belva Lockwood*, chapters 10 and 12.

81. Belva A. Lockwood to Munsey Bull, 19 November 1899, Bull Family Letters, Bancroft Library, University of California.

82. *Cherokees of North Carolina v. Cherokees of Indian Territory*, Equity 4627, RG 21, NA.

83. Ct. Cl. Cong. Jurisdiction Docketbook, vol. 2 (May 4, 1900-July 1, 1902), 196, RG 205, NA.

84. *Kaiser v. Stickney*, 131 U.S. clxxxvii Appx. (1889: "Cases Omitted"); U.S. Supreme Court, *Minutes*, January 16-18, 1906, RG 267, M215, Roll 24, NA; *United States v. Cherokee Nation*, 202 U.S. 101 (1906).

85. Lockwood to Colby, 18 May 1905, Clara Colby Papers, State Historical Society of Wisconsin.

86. For a full discussion of Lockwood's Eastern Cherokee case see Norgren, *Belva Lockwood*, 204-15.

87. Ibid., 223.

88. Belva A. Lockwood to Lella Gardner, 7 April 1912, Belva A. Lockwood Papers, SCPC; "In the matter of the Mary Gage case," 1912, Belva A. Lockwood Papers, SCPC.

CHAPTER 6

1. Barbara Babcock, *Woman Lawyer: The Trials of Clara Foltz* (Stanford, CA: Stanford University Press, 2011), 4.

2. Ibid., 5.

3. Ella Sterling Cummins, "Clara S. Foltz, History of Her Life, Struggles, and Success," *San Jose Daily Mercury*, October 15, 1884, 3.

4. Babcock, *Woman Lawyer*, 7.

5. Ibid., 14-15.

6. Barbara Allen Babcock, "Clara Shortridge Foltz: Constitution-Maker," *Indiana Law Journal* 66 (1991): 866.

7. *HWS* 3: 752, 755-56.

8. Babcock, *Woman Lawyer*, 14.

9. Ibid., 18.

10. Ibid., 19.

11. The statute that Tator and, later, Foltz and her allies sought to change was 1851 Cal. Stat., ch. 1, Sect. 275, at 64. For background on Tator, see *HWS* 3: 757 and Jennifer A. Drobac, "In Search of Nettie C," a paper submitted to the seminar on Women's Legal History, Stanford Law School, 1998, available at http://wlh-static. law.stanford.edu/papers/LutesN-Drobac98.pdf.

12. *Van Valkenburg v. Brown*, 43 Cal. 43 (January 1872).

13. *HWS* 3: 757.

14. The discussion of the Woman Lawyer's Bill draws upon Babcock, *Woman Lawyer*, 22-30.

15. Belva A. Lockwood, "My Efforts to Become a Lawyer," *Lippincott's Magazine*, February 1888, 229.

16. Babcock, *Woman Lawyer*, 23.

17. 1851 Cal. Stat., ch. 1, Sect. 275, at 64 (old code); 1878 Cal. Stat., ch. 600, Sections 1-3 at 99 (amended).

18. Babcock, *Woman Lawyer*, 31.

19. Ibid., 33.

20. Ibid., 34.

21. Babcock, "Clara Shortridge Foltz," 878-94.

22. Babcock, *Woman Lawyer*, 42.

23. Ibid., 41.

24. Ibid. 44.

25. Cal. Const. art. xx, Section 18 (1879). Foltz and Gordon believed that the amendment might aid their lawsuit, bring practical benefits to women, or, at least, prevent a future session of the legislature from repealing the Woman Lawyer's Act. Babcock, *Woman Lawyer*, 47.

26. Babcock, *Woman Lawyer*, 47-48.

27. Babcock, "Clara Shortridge Foltz," 894-99. The education clause read, "No person shall be debarred admission to any of the collegiate departments of the University on account of sex."

28. Babcock, *Woman Lawyer*, 49.

29. Ibid., 49.

30. Ibid., 55.

31. Ibid., 57.

32. "Mrs. Marion Todd," in Frances E. Willard and Mary A. Livermore, eds., *A Woman of the Century* (Buffalo, NY: C. W. Moulton, 1893), 718-19.

33. Babcock, *Woman Lawyer*, 59, citing to "Woman at the Bar: The First Female Lawyer of the Pacific Coast," *San Francisco Chronicle*, January 30, 1879, 3, and Editorial, *Albany Law Journal* 54 (March 7): 1896.

34. Babcock, *Woman Lawyer*, 63.

35. Ibid., 64.

36. E.g., Comments of the chief justice in the Hastings case; appraisal of law Professor. Barbara Babcock, *Woman Lawyer*, 65.

37. Ibid., 85. Maguire ran for governor in 1898, and lost.

38. Ibid., 65.

39. Ibid., 75.

40. Ibid., 76.

41. *People v. Saldez*. No citation is available.

42. Ibid., 90.

43. Babcock, *Woman Lawyer*, 89.

44. Ibid., 89.

45. Ibid., 161.

46. Ibid., 66.This would be about sixty thousand dollars calculated at today's worth.

47. Ibid., 68.

48. Ibid., 94.

49. Ibid., 94.

50. Ibid., 94.

51. Ibid., 96.

52. Ibid., 97.

53. Ibid., 104, 125-26.

54. Ibid., 100-101.

55. Ibid., 100-101.

56. For the complete story of Maria Ruiz Burton and her claim, see Babcock, *Woman Lawyer,* 110-17.

57. Babcock, *Woman Lawyer,* 117; Editorial, *San Diego Bee,* September 18, 1887.

58. Babcock, *Woman Lawyer,* 118.

59. Ibid., 121-24. This was the Arvilla and Richard White case.

60. Ibid., 129.

61. "Hon. William F. Aldrich," *Peacemaker* 16 (1898): 154-56. The need for public defenders was being discussed in socialist and utopian circles. Aldrich had written about the idea in the January 1890 issue of WNLU's *Liberal Thinker.* Foltz followed her appeal for an office of public defender with an impromptu attack on the suffrage movement, arguing that women's indifference was "the main barrier to success." Babcock, *Woman Lawyer,* 258.

62. Matilda Joslyn Gage, ed., *Woman's National Liberal Union: Report of the Convention for Organization, February 24th and 25th, 1890* (Syracuse, NY: Masters and Stone Publisher, 1890), 78.

63. Babcock, *Woman Lawyer,* 137.

64. Ibid., 137.

65. Ibid., 138.

66. Ibid., 142.

67. "Women Lawyers at the Isabella Club House," *CLN,* August 26, 1893, 451.

68. Ibid., 451.

69. Clara Foltz, "The Evolution of the Law," *Albany Law Journal* 48 (1893): 345.

70. Babcock, *Woman Lawyer,* 226.

71. Ibid., 226. The talk is fully explored on pages 226-31. The subsequent discussion draws on this text.

72. Ibid., 305.

73. "Women in the Law Reform Congress," *CLN* 25 (1893): 435.

74. Babcock, *Woman Lawyer,* 307. Subsequent quotations are from 307-11.

75. Ibid., 309.

76. Ibid., 310.

77. Ibid., 311.

78. Ibid., 311.

79. Ibid., 309.

80. 372 U.S. 335, 341-45 (1963). See also *Powell v. Alabama*, 287 U.S. 45, 71 (1932).

81. Ibid., 152.

82. Grace Hathaway, *Fate Rides a Tortoise: A Biography of Ellen Spencer Mussey* (Chicago: John C. Winston, 1937), 106-7.

83. For a discussion of the American Woman's Republic, see Jill Norgren, *Belva Lockwood* (New York: New York University Press), 219-23.

84. Babcock, *Woman Lawyer*, 152-53. Babcock suggests that "part of the appeal of the Portia Club was its potential for developing new clients from among the society ladies who joined." Ibid., 163.

85. Babcock, *Woman Lawyer*, 153, citing to *HWS* 4: 479, and "Now the Portia Club," *San Francisco Examiner*, January 20, 1894.

86. Babcock, *Woman Lawyer*, 156-57.

87. Ibid., 165.

88. Ibid., 164-65. The account of the trial, and subsequent quotations, are from pages 164-69.

89. Ibid., 168.

90. Babcock, *Woman Lawyer*, 312.

91. Ibid., 203, 205.

92. Ibid., 215, 217.

93. Ibid., 218.

94. Ibid., 283.

95. Ibid., 285.

96. A full discussion of Foltz's conception of public defense appears in Barbara Allen Babcock, "Inventing the Public Defender," *American Criminal Law Review* 43 (Fall 2006): 1267, as well as Babcock, *Woman Lawyer*, chapter 7.

97. Babcock, "Inventing the Public Defender," 1267.

98. Ibid., 1311.

99. Ibid., 1311.

100. Babcock, *Woman Lawyer*, 318.

101. Ibid., 323.

CHAPTER 7

1. Matthew G. Berger, "Mary Hall: The Decision and the Lawyer," *Connecticut Bar Journal* 79 (2005): 36, note 41.

2. Ibid., 36, note 41.

3. Lelia J. Robinson, "Women Lawyers in the United States," *The Green Bag*, January 1890, 29-30.

4. Mary Hall Scrapbook, Connecticut Historical Society manuscript no. 78249, newspaper clipping dated April 12, 1890; "Miss Mary Hall," in Frances E. Willard and Mary A. Livermore, eds., *A Woman of the Century* (Buffalo, NY: C. W. Moulton, 1893), 350-51.

236 NOTES TO CHAPTER 7

5. Berger, "Mary Hall," 37.

6. *In re Mary Hall*, 50 Conn. 131, 136 (1882); Willard and Livermore, *Woman of the Century*, 351. The office of commissioner, in Connecticut, was then independent of the position of attorney at law.

7. Robinson, "Women Lawyers," 29.

8. Willard and Livermore, *A Woman of the Century*, 351.

9. Berger, "Mary Hall," 41.

10. *Hartford Daily Courant*, March 25, 1882, 4.

11. Berger, "Mary Hall," 41.

12. Berger, "Mary Hall," 41-42. Subsequent quotations in this paragraph also cite to these pages. John Hooker is listed with McManus as "for the application." *In re Mary Hall*, 131. Berger gives short biographies of the examining committee, McManus, and Collier, at 40-42, notes 61, 67, and 74.

13. Berger, "Mary Hall," 42-43. Subsequent quotations in this paragraph also cite to these pages.

14. Ibid., 43.

15. *In re Mary Hall*, 131.

16. Park was joined by Justices Carpenter and Loomis. Matthew Berger presents both sides of the argument as to whether Park, or John Hooker, authored the opinion. Berger, "Mary Hall," 44, note 84.

17. *In re Mary Hall*, 132.

18. Ibid., 132.

19. Ibid., 135.

20. Ibid., 137.

21. Ibid., 138-39.

22. Berger, "Mary Hall," 46, and note 93.

23. Mary Hall Scrapbook No. 4 (1882).

24. "Miss Attorney Hall," *New York Times*, September 27, 1882, found in Mary Hall Scrapbook No. 4.

25. Martha A. Pearce, 1888 Equity Club Annual Report, 6, *LRS*.

26. Catharine Waugh McCulloch to Equity Club members, 2 May 1888, *WL*, 136.

27. Berger, "Mary Hall," 53. The appearance occurred in 1897.

28. Robinson, "Woman Lawyers," 29.

29. Berger, "Mary Hall," 48-52.

30. Ibid., 49.

31. Elizabeth Cady Stanton to Sara Francis Underwood, 9 May 1885, and Elizabeth Cady Stanton to F. Ellen Burr and the Hartford Equal Rights Club, 24 April 1885, in Ann D. Gordon, ed., *The Selected Papers of Elizabeth Cady Stanton and Susan B. Anthony: When Clowns Make Laws for Queens, 1880 to 1887*, vol. 4 (New Brunswick, NJ: Rutgers University Press, 2006), 416 and 412.

32. Ibid., 412.

33. Willard and Livermore, "Woman of the Century," 351. Berger, "Mary Hall," 38, note 52, lists the several men of means who later helped to put the organization on a firm financial footing, and purchased space for its activities. Hall was one of the first individuals to organize this kind of charity. The Rev. Willard Parsons of Sherman, PA, founded the Fresh Air Fund in 1877. Elsewhere, single-sex women's retreats were established, such as Fernside in Princeton, Massachusetts.

34. Willard and Livermore, "Woman of the Century, 351.

35. Berger, "Mary Hall," 54 and note 138.

36. Ibid., 57.

37. *Ricker's Petition*, 66 N.H. 207 (1890). Doe used the principle of adequate remedies. The question, he stated, should not be "whether women could lawfully be admitted, but whether they could lawfully be kept out." In the absence of an explicit statute excluding women they were, he wrote, eligible for the New Hampshire bar.

38. Berger, "Mary Hall," 55, citing to *State v. Lola Chaves de Armijo*, 18 N.M. 646, 140 P. 1123, 1128 (1914).

39. Barbara Allen Babcock, "Women Defenders in the West," *Nevada Law Journal* 1 (Spring 2001): 2-3.

40. Babcock, "Women Defenders," 3; Berger, "Mary Hall," 47.

41. Catharine G. Waugh (McCulloch) to Equity Club members, 2 May 1888, WL, 136.

42. Julia Wilson, "Catharine Waugh McCulloch: Attorney, Suffragist, and Justice of the Peace," WLH, 3.

43. Louise W. Knight, *Citizen: Jane Addams and the Struggle for Democracy* (Chicago: University of Chicago Press, 2005), 76.

44. Personal communication from Louise W. Knight, Addams's biographer, to Jill Norgren, 13 June 2011.

45. Catharine G. Waugh, "A Young Girl's Experience in a Law School," *Woman's Tribune*, February 18, 1888, 6. Subsequent quotations in this paragraph also cite to this article.

46. Item, *CLN*, June 5, 1886, n.p.

47. Catharine Waugh, "Women as Law Clerks." Mary Earhart Dillion Collection, 1869-1945, Schlesinger Library, Radcliffe Inst., Series VI. Undated, but written before 1890.

48. Wilson, "Catharine Waugh McCulloch," 6.

49. Robinson, "Women Lawyers," 14.

50. Paul S. Boyer, "Catharine Gouger Waugh McCulloch," in Edward T. James, Janet Wilson James, and Paul S. Boyer, eds., *Notable American Women, 1607-1950* (Cambridge, MA: Harvard University Press, 1971), 459.

51. Review, "A New Book: Woman's Wages," possibly published in *The Farmer's Voice*, n.d. Catharine Waugh file, Mary Earhart Dillion Collection, 1869-1945, Schlesinger Library, Radcliffe Institute, Series VI.

52. Advertisement, "Woman's Wages is for sale by the author." Item found in the Catharine Waugh file, Mary Earhart Dillion Collection, 1869-1945, Schlesinger Library, Radcliffe Institute, Series VI.

53. Catharine G. Waugh to the Equity Club, 26 April 1889, *WL*, 177.

54. Ibid., 174.

55. Catharine G. Waugh, "A Lady Lawyer Makes a Plea," *The Farmer's Voice*, June 22, 1889. n.p. All quotations in this paragraph also cite to this article.

56. Boyer, "McCulloch," in *Notable American Women*, 459.

57. Catharine Waugh McCulloch to Catharine McCulloch Spray, 1 November 1943, McCulloch Papers, 1862-1945, ser. VI, in Women's Suffrage: The Midwest and Far West, Radcliffe College Women's Studies Manuscript Collections (hereafter McCulloch Papers). She served the NAWSA from 1904 to 1911.

58. Catharine G. Waugh to Equity Club members, 30 May 1890, *WL*, 191.

59. Ibid., 191.

60. Catharine Waugh McCulloch to Equity Club members, 8 November 1890, *WL*, 192.

61. Ibid., 192. All quotations in this paragraph cite to this letter.

62. Wilson, "Catharine Waugh McCulloch," 36, citing to Catharine Waugh McCulloch, *Autobiography* (n.p.: n.d.), McCulloch Papers.

63. Ibid., Timeline Appendix, citing to December 22, 1897, case, *Wiedeman v. Keller*, 171 Ill. 93, 49 N.W. 210 (Supreme Court of Illinois). Catharine McCulloch was the seventeenth woman admitted to the U.S. Supreme Court bar. She apparently never argued a case before the high court.

64. Wilson, "Catharine Waugh McCulloch", 19-21 and accompanying notes.

65. See www.herhatwasinthering.org.

66. "Catharine W. M'Culloch: A Character Sketch." Newspaper item, n.d., McCulloch Papers. See also newspaper clipping from March 18, 1907, McCulloch Papers.

67. Wilson, "Catharine Waugh McCulloch," 13.

68. Ibid., 15.

69. "Mrs. McCulloch Elected a Justice of the Peace," *CLN*, April 6, 1907, 277.

70. Letter from Catharine Waugh McCulloch to Catharine McCulloch Spray, 1 November 1943, McCulloch Papers.

71. Wilson, "McCulloch," 27. Two similar versions of McCulloch's "Women's Rights Game" are archived in the McCulloch Papers. She lent the game to friends but never printed it because of the expense.

72. C. W. McC., "Shall Men Vote," 1. Lindseth Collection of American Woman Suffrage: Series I, Printed Materials, Box 3, Folder 4, Division of Rare and Manuscript Collections, Kroch Library, Cornell University.

73. Ibid., 2.

74. Boyer, "McCulloch," in *Notable American Women*, 459.

75. Ibid., 460.

76. Ibid., 460.

77. Ibid., 460.

CHAPTER 8

1. Mary A. Greene to Equity Club members, 5 April 1888, cited in *WL*, 98.

2. Ibid., 124.

3. *Chute v. Chute*, No. 2003 Mass. (1878).

4. Mary A. Greene, "Mrs. Lelia Robinson Sawtelle—First Woman Lawyer of Massachusetts," *The Women Lawyers' Journal* 7 (April 1918): 51.

5. Ibid., 51.

6. LRS, Receipt for Tuition, Trustees of Boston University, October 22, 1879.

7. Kathryn Johnson, "'A Pioneer Woman': The Scholar and Lawyer, Mary Anne Greene," Section 2, 6. Paper submitted to the Stanford Law School Women's Legal History Seminar, May 2006, available on WLH, citing to Homer Albers, *The Boston University School of Law, Boston Law School Magazine* 1 (1896): 7-9.

8. This paragraph draws upon Robinson's Equity letter of 7 April 1888, *WL*, 126-27.

9. Greene, "Mrs. Leila Robinson Sawtelle," 51.

10. Lelia J. Robinson to Equity Club members, 9 April 1887, *WL*, 64.

11. See *Lelia J. Robinson's Case*, 131 Mass. 376 (Mass. 1882). Robinson could conduct office business without admission to the bar.

12. "Lucia M. Peabody," http://www.herhatwasinthering.org.

13. Louis D. Brandeis to Alfred Brandeis, 30 January 1884, cited in Philippa Strum, *Louis D. Brandeis: Justice for the People* (New York: Schocken Books, 1984), 54-55.

14. Mary M. Huth, "Kate Gannett Well, Anti-Suffragist," *University of Rochester Library Bulletin* (1981): 3562. The legislature was considering a bill to allow women to vote in municipal elections, one that had been defeated through the efforts of several prominent men and women in 1882. Most members of Well's family strongly supported woman suffrage.

15. Henry James, *The Bostonians* (New York: Barnes and Noble Classics, 2005), 6. The novel appeared first in serial form in 1885-86, and was published as a book in 1886.

16. Communication from Professor Elisabeth Gitter, 15 July 2011.

17. Strum, *Brandeis*, 54. Brandeis changed his views on this matter around 1912. Ibid., 129-31.

18. Dan Ernst, "Lelia Robinson, Part 2," *Legal History Blog*, December 22, 2009. http://legalhistoryblog.blogspot.com/2009/12/lelia-robinson-part-2.html.

19. Sarah Killingsworth, "Lelia Robinson," 4, WLH, citing to Robinson, Petitioner's supplemental brief, 4. Copies of these briefs are found in LRS.

20. *Lelia J. Robinson's Case*, 131 Mass. 376. Elsewhere, courts cited this case

against other women lawyers who applied for bar admission, including the Oregon Supreme Court in the case of Mary Leonard.

21. Ibid. On the day that Mary Greene was admitted to the bar in Boston, Robinson told Justice Field "that she would have been much disappointed in the court if they had decided otherwise in her case, for she always considered the opinion a sound one, as the law then stood." "Mrs. Lelia Robinson Sawtelle," 51.

22. Massachusetts Statutes of 1882 c. 139.

23. Roberta Sue Alexander, "The Cult of Equal Opportunity versus the Cult of True Womanhood: Women's Efforts to Gain Admission to the Bar in the Latter Third of the Nineteenth Century" (unpublished paper, 2001, author's files), 29, citing to the *Original Papers of the General Court of Massachusetts, Order of the House*, January 31, 1882, Massachusetts State Archives.

24. *Boston Evening Transcript*, March 13, 1882, 3; *Woman's Journal*, March 18, 1882, n.p.

25. *Boston Daily Globe*, March 15, 1882, 4. Subsequent quotations in this paragraph cite to this article.

26. Robinson to Equity Club members, 9 April 1887, WL, 65.

27. Ibid., 65. Robinson does not describe how she paid for law school, or her law office. It is likely that her parents helped with these expenses, perhaps one reason she dedicated *Law Made Easy* to them. In this Equity letter Robinson refers to having had help "from my own people." Ibid., 66.

28. Ibid., 65.

29. Lelia Josephine Robinson to Equity Club members, 7 April 1888, WL, 125.

30. Statutes of 1883 c. 252.

31. Robinson to Equity Club members, 7 April 1888, WL, 121.

32. Lelia J. Robinson to Equity Club members, 9 April 1887, WL, 64-65. Robinson waited until 1884 to argue in court, taking the claim of a deserted wife for separate maintenance, and child custody, into probate court. Robinson, 7 April 1888, WL, 121.

33. Robinson to Equity Club members, 7 April 1888, WL, 121.

34. Ibid., 121. Robinson frequently observed that new male lawyers also had a discouraging wait for clients. Robinson to Equity Club members, 9 April 1887, WL, 65.

35. Robinson to Equity Club members, 9 April 1887, WL, 65. All quotations in this paragraph also cite to this letter. She wrote letters to newspapers under the nom de plume "Trimontaine." LRS. (Boston was called Trimontaine in the 1630s for the three hills around which the settlement was built.)

36. Robinson to Equity Club members, 7 April 1888, WL, 121.

37. On suffrage, see "An Act to Amend Section 3050, chapter 238 of the Code of Washington" (1883), reenacted in January 1888 as "An Act to Enfranchise Women."

38. Sandra F. VanBurkleo, "'A Double Head in Nature Is a Monstrosity': Recovering the Married Woman in Frontier Washington, 1879-1892." Paper delivered

at the Annual Meeting of the American Society for Legal History, Seattle, Washington, October 21-24, 1998, 1 and 9. This unpublished paper is not paginated. I have assigned page numbers to my file copy.

39. Ibid., 2. The next sentence draws on this article and page.

40. Mary Nicol, "Lelia Robinson Sawtelle: A Second Look," WLH, 4. Nicol is citing to the *Seattle Post-Intelligencer*, May 25, 1884. This paragraph draws on Nicol, 4-5. Clara Colby referred to her as "Mrs. Dr. Weed." See "Women's Rights in Seattle," *Seattle Daily Post-Intelligencer*, July 22, 1884, 4.

41. VanBurkleo, "'A Double Head in Nature,'" 2.

42. Ibid., 9.

43. Ibid., 9.

44. Ibid., 2.

45. Clarence B. Bagley, *History of Seattle from the Earliest Settlement to the Present Time* (Chicago: S. J. Clarke, 1916), 1: 316.

46. For a biographical sketch of Leonard, see Kerry Abrams, "Folk Hero, Hell Raiser, Mad Woman, Lady Lawyer: What Is the Truth about Mary Leonard?" WLH.

47. Nicol, "Lelia Robinson Sawtelle," 9-10.

48. Robinson to Equity Club members, 7 April 1888, *WL*, 122. She also notes that in New York and other large cities, women court stenographers were no longer a novelty, and often earned more than lawyers. Ibid., 126.

49. Cristina M. Rodríguez, "Clearing the Smoke-Filled Room: Women Jurors and the Disruption of an Old-Boys' Network in Nineteenth-Century America," *Yale Law Journal* 108 (May 1999): 1805. Rodríguez writes that "historically, suffrage and jury service for women have not been mutually-reinforcing entrances into the public sphere." Ibid., 1806.

50. Ibid., 1807.

51. Nicol, "Lelia Robinson Sawtelle," 6; VanBurkleo, "'A Double Head in Nature.'" In this paper, Van Burkleo presents an excellent discussion of the legal issues involved in women's jury service.

52. Lelia J. Robinson, "Women Jurors," *Chicago Law Times*, November 1886, 22.

53. Ibid., 31.

54. Ibid., 25. The next quotation also cites to this article and page.

55. Ibid., 26-27.

56. Nicol, "Lelia Robinson Sawtelle," 10; Robinson to Equity Club members, 7 April 1888, *WL*, 121.

57. Robinson to Equity Club members, 7 April 1888, *WL*, 121.

58. Ibid., 121.

59. Nicol, "Lelia Robinson Sawtelle," 13, citing to "Court Proceedings," *Seattle Post-Intelligencer*, October 10, 1884, 2, and "Won Her Case," *Seattle Post-Intelligencer*, October 18, 1884.

60. Robinson to Equity Club members, 7 April 1888, *WL*, 120.

61. Ibid., 121; Nicol, "Lelia Robinson Sawtelle," 15, citing to "The Smith Divorce Case," *Seattle Post-Intelligencer*, December 23, 1884, 1.

62. "Woman's Meeting," *Seattle Post-Intelligencer*, June 13, 1884, 2.

63. "Women's Rights in Seattle," *Seattle Post-Intelligencer*, July 22, 1884, 4.

64. Nicol, "Lelia Robinson Sawtelle," 18, citing to "Brevities," *Seattle Post-Intelligencer*, January 11, 1885, 2.

65. Robinson to Equity Club members, 7 April 1888, WL, 122.

66. Van Burkleo, "'A Double Head in Nature,'" 20.

67. For a short summary, see T. A. Larson, "The Woman Suffrage Movement in Washington," *Pacific Northwest Quarterly* 67 (April 1976): 49-62. In 1889-90 Washington women regained the right to vote in school elections, and to hold education-related offices. In 1910 and 1911, respectively, Washington women gained (again) full suffrage, and the right to serve on juries.

68. Robinson to Equity Club members, 9 April 1887, WL, 66.

69. Robinson to Equity Club members, 7 April 1888, WL, 122.

70. Robinson to Equity Club members, 9 April 1887, WL, 65.

71. Lelia Josephine Robinson, *Law Made Easy: A Book for the People* (Chicago: Sanitary Publishing Company, 1886), i. Reprinted in Kessinger Publishing's Legacy Series, and also available on Google Books.

72. Ibid., iii.

73. Ibid., v.

74. Ibid., vi.

75. Ibid., v-vi.

76. Robinson to Equity Club members, 7 April 1888, WL, 122.

77. Ibid., 122.

78. Ibid., 123.

79. Ibid., 124, 119.

80. Lelia Josephine Robinson, *The Law of Husband and Wife, Comp. for Popular Use* (Boston: Lee and Shepard, 1889). Reprinted by MLibrary (2011).

81. Robinson, for example, references Greene and her work at the beginning of her article, "Women Lawyers in the United States," *The Green Bag*, January 1890, 10.

82. Johnson, "'A Pioneer Woman': The Scholar and Lawyer, Mary Anne Greene," WLH website, section 1, 1, citing to *Mary Anne Greene, L.L.B: A Pioneer Woman*, 5, Duke University Library Biographical Collection.

83. Mary A. Greene to Equity Club members, 27 April 1887, WL, 52. The following quotations in this paragraph also cite to this letter, 52-53.

84. Mary A. Greene to Equity Club members, 5 April 1888, WL, 97.

85. Ibid., 98. Hemenway had been nominated by President William McKinley for a position on the U.S. Supreme Court, but after the president's assassination, Theodore Roosevelt nominated Oliver Wendell Holmes.

86. Mary A. Greene to Equity Club members, 22 May 1889, WL, 163.

87. Ibid., 165.

88. Gillett to Equity Club members, 27 April 1889, *WL*, 161.

89. Virginia G. Drachman, *Sisters in Law: Women Lawyers in Modern American History* (Cambridge, MA: Harvard University Press), 82. Robinson's name appears on the list of attorneys aiding the Union's Protective Committee.

90. *American Law Review* 24 (1890): 779; Lelia J. Robinson, "Women Lawyers in the United States," 30. For a list of Greene's articles before 1893, see "Mary A. Green," in Frances E. Willard and Mary A. Livermore, eds., *A Woman of the Century* (1893; reprint New York: Gordon Press, 1975).

91. Mary A. Greene, *The Woman's Manual of Law* (New York: Silver, Burdett, 1902). Reprint edition, Gale Publishing, MOML (Making of Modern Law Legal Treatises, 1800-1926), 2010.

92. Robinson, "Women Lawyers," 30.

93. Robinson to Equity Club members, 7 April 1888, *WL*, 118. The remaining quotations in this paragraph also cite to this letter, 118-19.

94. Mary A. Greene to Equity Club members, 14 May 1890, *WL*, 186. Robinson was also involved in starting the Pentagon Club, an organization for women lawyers as well as professional women in medicine, teaching, theology, and journalism.

95. Lelia J. Robinson to Equity Club members, 22 May 1889, *WL*, 170-71.

96. "Alice Parker," in Willard and Livermore, *A Woman of the Century*, 557.

97. Lelia J. Robinson, "Boston's Women Lawyers," *The Business Woman's Journal* 81 (1889).

98. Belva A. Lockwood, "Women of the American Bar," *The Illustrated American*, July 26, 1890, 45-47. Lockwood includes a page on the women admitted by this date to the U.S. Supreme Court.

99. Robinson to Equity Club members, 22 May 1889, *WL*, 171.

100. Lelia Robinson Sawtelle to Equity Club members, 18 September 1890, *WL*, 200.

101. Mary A. Greene to Equity Club members, 14 May 1890, *WL*, 186-87.

102. Item, "The Second Nationalist Club of Boston, Officers for 1889-90," LRS.

103. *Petition of Ricker*, 66 N.H. 207 (1890).

104. Greene, "Mrs. Lelia Robinson Sawtelle," 51. Many notices were published immediately after her death. See, for example, "Obituary Notes: Mrs. Lelia Robinson Sawtelle," *New York Times*, August 11, 1891, 4. This obituary included the label directions for the use of the belladonna, "Ten drops; may increase to sixteen," suggesting that the family wished the public to know it was an accidental death.

105. Greene, "Lelia Robinson Sawtelle," 51. Quotations in the rest of this paragraph cite to this article and page.

106. Johnson, "A Pioneer Woman," section 7, 3. Greene offered a class at the society about the legal status of women in countries where missions had been established.

107. "Women in the Law Reform Congress," *CLN* 25 (1893): 435. On August 3 and August 4, Greene, then Foltz, spoke at a meeting of women lawyers organized to coincide with the fair. Jill Norgren, *Belva Lockwood* (New York: New York University Press), 194-98.

108. Greene, *A Pioneer Woman*. In this autobiographical recollection Greene does mention regret at not seeking admission to the Rhode Island bar. She considered Rhode Island a very conservative state and, perhaps, feared that she would be turned down as the first woman applicant.

109. Greene to Equity Club members, 22 May 1889, *WL*, 164.

110. Johnson, "A Pioneer Woman," section 4, 18. My discussion of Greene's presentation draws upon Johnson's excellent analysis, section 4, 9-20. The published talk may be found at Greene, "Married Women's Property Acts in the United States, and Needed Reforms Therein," *Albany Law Journal* 48 (1893): 206.

111. Johnson, "A Pioneer Woman," section 4, 16-17.

112. Greene, *The Woman's Manual*, iii.

113. Ibid., iv.

114. Ibid., v.

115. Ibid., v.

116. Greene, *A Pioneer Woman*, 5-6; www.herhatwasinthering.org.

CHAPTER 9

1. Julia Hull Winner, *Belva A. Lockwood*, Number 19 of the Occasional Contributions of the Niagara County Historical Society (Niagara Falls, NY: Fose Printing, 1969), 94.

2. Laura de F. Gordon to Equity Club members, 26 April 1887, *WL*, 50.

3. Belva A. Lockwood to Equity Club members, 30 April 1887, *WL*, 57.

4. Ibid., 58.

5. Ibid., 59.

6. Ibid., 59.

7. Greene to Equity Club members, 22 May 1889, *WL*,164.

8. "Should a Woman Lawyer Wear Her Hat in Court?" Reprinted in the *Washington Law Reporter*, April 1, 1876, 47.

9. Ibid., 47; "Mrs. Lockwood's Hat," reprinted in the *Washington Law Reporter*, April 15, 1876, 71.

10. "Mrs. Lockwood's Hat," 71.

11. Robinson to Equity Club members, 7 April 1888, *WL*, 127.

12. Ibid., 127.

13. Ibid., 127.

14. Margaret L. Wilcox to Equity Club members, 1 June 1889, *WL*, 177-78.

15. Emma Haddock to Equity Club members, 12 May 1888, *WL*, 101.

16. Lettie L. Burlingame to Equity Club members, 22 April 1889, *WL*, 156.

17. Ibid., 156.

18. Ibid., 156.

19. Gillett to Equity Club members, 27 April 1889, *WL*, 159.

20. Catharine G. Waugh to Equity Club members, 26 April 1889, *WL*, 175.

21. Ada H. Kepley to Equity Club members, 3 July 1888, *WL*, 108.

22. Margaret L. Wilcox to Equity Club members, 20 April 1888, *WL*, 140.

23. Ibid., 141.

24. Lettie L. Burlingame to Equity Club members, 22 April 1889, *WL*, 156.

25. Florence Cronise to Equity Club members, 23 May 1888, *WL*, 95.

26. Florence Cronise to Equity Club members, late summer 1889, *WL*, 158.

27. Emma M. Gillett to Equity Club members, 18 April 1888, *WL*, 96-97.

28. "Mrs. Ada M. Bittenbender," in Frances E. Willard and Mary A. Livermore, eds., *A Woman of the Century* (1893; reprint New York: Gordon Press, 1975), 87. The Bittenbenders' partner in this venture was Clarence Buell.

29. Ada M. Bittenbender to Equity Club members, 10 May 1889, *WL*, 154.

30. Rebecca Edwards, "Mary Lease and the Sources of Populist Protest," in Ballard C. Campbell, ed., *The Human Tradition in the Gilded Age and Progressive Era* (Wilmington, DE: Scholarly Resources, 2000), 60. This sketch of Lease draws upon Edwards's research.

31. Joan Jensen, ed. *With These Hands* (Old Westbury, NY: Feminist Press, 1981), 158-59.

32. J. Ellen Foster, "Women in Politics," in Mary Kavanaugh Oldham, ed., *The Congress of Women: Held in the Woman's Building, World's Columbian Exposition, Chicago, U.S.A., 1893* (Chicago: Monarch Book Company, 1894), 668-69. Available at http://digital.library.upenn.edu/women/eagle/congress/foster.html.

33. At this time, a number of states had dram shop acts under which a person could sue bar owners and liquor dealers to recover damages caused by an intoxicated buyer. Richard H. Chused, "Courts and Temperance 'Ladies,'" in Tracy A. Thomas and Tracey Jean Boisseau, eds., *Feminist Legal History* (New York: New York University Press, 2011), 36 ff., and notes 16 and 22.

34. Elmer C. Adams and Warren D. Foster, *Heroines of Modern Progress* (New York: Sturgis & Walton, 1913; available on Google Books), 265-69. See also, Rebecca Edwards, *Angels in the Machinery* (New York: Oxford University Press, 1997) for discussion of Foster and Lease.

35. Francis Curtis, *The Republican Party* (New York: Putnam, 1904), 2: 251-53.

36. Adams and Foster, *Heroines*, 270.

37. My discussion of Stoneman draws on the research of Christine Sebourn in her Stanford Law School Women's Legal History Biography Seminar paper, WLH.

38. *In the Matter of the Application of Kate Stoneman*, 40 Hun. 538 (N.Y. 1886); *In re* Leonard, 53 *Am. Rep.* 323, 325 (Or. 1885); "A Lady Candidate for the Bar," *New*

York Times, May 8, 1886, 1; "The First Female Lawyer," *Albany Times,* May 20, 1886, 4; Judith S. Kaye, "How to Accomplish Success: The Example of Kate Stoneman," *Albany Law Review* 57 (1994): 961. Stoneman was aware that Belva Lockwood had applied, unsuccessfully, for bar admission in 1880, in Poughkeepsie, New York.

39. Mabel Jacques Eichel, "Miss Kate Stoneman, Lawyer, One of Our Pioneer Suffragists," *The Women Lawyers' Journal* 7 (1918): 35. In 1886 Stoneman was also appointed a notary public.

40. Lura McNall Ormes, "Our Washington Letter," *LDJ*, November 21, 1873, 2.

41. Ibid., 2.

42. For a discussion of the Women's Law Class and New York University's role in opening its law school to women, see Barbara Babcock, *Woman Lawyer: The Trials of Clara Foltz* (Stanford, CA: Stanford University Press, 2011), 184-88.

43. Grace Hathaway, *Fate Rides a Tortoise: A Biography of Ellen Spencer Mussey* (Chicago: John C. Winston, 1937), 107-8.

44. Emma M. Gillett to Equity Club members, 18 April 1888, *WL*, 96-97.

45. For a fictional account of this life, see Winston Churchill, *Mr. Crewe's Career* (New York: Macmillan, 1908).

46. This sketch of Senter's life draws on Karen S. Beck, *A Working Lawyer's Life: The Life Book of John Henry Senter, 1879-1884* (Clark, NJ: Lawbook Exchange, 2008).

47. Chused, "Courts and Temperance 'Ladies,'" 37.

48. Ibid., 38-39.

49. Ibid., 38.

50. Felice Batlan, "Legal Aid, Women Lay Lawyers, and the Rewriting of History, 1863-1930," in Tracy A. Thomas and Tracey Jean Boisseau, eds., *Feminist Legal History* (New York: New York University Press, 2011), 173. My discussion of these aid societies draws on Batlan's research. See also Felice Batlan, "The Ladies' Health Protective Association: Lay Lawyers and Urban Cause Lawyering," *Akron Law Review* 41 (2008): 701. New York produced another female-led legal aid organization in this period, the Arbitration Society. Short-lived, it was founded by Fanny B. Weber and Swiss lawyer Dr. Emily Kempin.

51. Batlan, "Legal Aid," 175-76.

52. Gwen Hoerr Jordan, "Them Law Wimmin: The Protective Agency for Women and Children and the Gendered Origins of Legal Aid," in Thomas and Boisseau, eds., *Feminist Legal History.* My discussion of PAWC draws on Jordan's research.

53. Ibid., 168.

54. Ibid., 168.

55. "Woman Gets Thieves after Police Give Up," *New York Times,* October 3, 1905, n.p.

56. "New Field of Legal Work among the Poor: A Woman Lawyer Who Stands

between the Ignorant and Oppressed and Those Who Take Advantage," *New York Times*, June 11, 1905, n.p.

57. Babcock, *Woman Lawyer*, 188, citing to Rosalie Loew, "Women Lawyers of the New York Bar," *Metropolitan Magazine*, June 1896, 279-84.

58. Babcock, *Woman Lawyer*, 188. In 1903 Loew married Travis Whitney and converted to Protestantism. For a short time, they practiced law together. Dorothy Thomas, "Rosalie Loew Whitney," *Jewish Women's Archive*, http://jwa.org/encyclopedia/article/whitney-rosalie-loew.

59. Felice Batlan, "Notes from the Margins: Florence Kelley and the Making of Sociological Jurisprudence," in Daniel W. Hamilton, ed., *Transformations in American Legal History* (Cambridge, MA: Harvard Law School, 2011), 2: 242. This sketch of Kelley draws upon Batlan's research. See also Kathryn Kish Sklar, *Florence Kelley and the Nation's Work: The Rise of Women's Political Culture, 1830-1900* (New Haven, CT: Yale University Press, 1995).

60. Batlan, "Notes," 247.

EPILOGUE

1. "Woman Suggested for the Vacancy on Supreme Bench." Unidentified newspaper, January 1912, author's files.

2. "Hobbs," at www.herhatwasinthering.org. If Hobbs did not serve, Catharine Waugh McCulloch would have been the first woman justice of the peace in Illinois.

3. Mary L. Clark, "Women as Supreme Court Advocates, 1879-1979," *Journal of Supreme Court History* 30 (2005): 47, 52.

4. Martha H. Swain, "Lucy Someville Howorth: Lawyer, Politician, and Feminist," *Mississippi History Now*, available at http://mshistory.k12.ms.us/articles/306/lucy-somerville-howorth-lawyer-politician-and-feminist.

5. Christine L. Wade, "Burnita Shelton Matthews: The Biography of a Pioneering Woman, Lawyer and Feminist," WLH.

6. Selma Moidel Smith, "A Century of Achievement: The Centennial of the National Association of Women Lawyers," WLH.

7. Wade, "Burnita Shelton Matthews," 12.

8. Nancy Gertner, *In Defense of Women: Memoirs of an Unrepentant Advocate* (Boston: Beacon Press, 2011), chapter 2.

9. Stephanie Francis Ward, "Female Judicial Candidates Are Held to Different Standards, Sotomayor Tells Students," *ABA Journal: Law News Now*, posted March 8, 2011, at http://www.abajournal.com/news/article/female_judicial_candidates_are_held_to_different_standards_sotomayor_tells.

10. Ibid.

11. "Women in Law in the U.S.," at http://www.catalyst.org/publication/246/women-in-law-in-the-us.

12. "Gender of All Federal Judges 1998-2009," at http://thinkprogress.org/justice/2011/08/01/284502/male-federal-judges-outnumber-women-three-to-one.

13. Ruth Bader Ginsburg and Laura W. Brill, "Women in the Federal Judiciary: Three Way Pavers and the Exhilarating Change President Carter Wrought," *Fordham Law Review* 64 (November 1995): 281, 289.

Select Bibliography

Allgor, Catherine. *Parlor Politics*. Charlottesville: University Press of Virginia, 2000.

Auerbach, Jerold S. *Justice without Law: Resolving Disputes without Lawyers*. New York: Oxford University Press, 1983.

———. *Unequal Justice: Lawyers and Social Change in Modern America*. New York: Oxford University Press, 1976.

Babcock, Barbara. *Woman Lawyer: The Trials of Clara Foltz*. Stanford, CA: Stanford University Press, 2011.

Babcock, Barbara Allen. "Clara Shortridge Foltz: Constitution-Maker." *Indiana Law Journal* 66 (1991): 849-940.

———. "Clara Shortridge Foltz: 'First Woman.'" *Arizona Law Review* 30 (1988): 673-717.

———. "Feminist Lawyers." *Stanford Law Review* 50 (May 1998): 1689-1708.

———. "Inventing the Public Defender." *American Criminal Law Review* 43 (Fall 2006): 1267-1315.

———. "Women Defenders in the West." *Nevada Law Journal* 1 (Spring 2001): 1-15.

Bakken, Gordon Morris. *Practicing Law in Frontier California*. Lincoln: University of Nebraska Press, 1991.

Batlan, Felice. "The Ladies' Health Protective Association: Lay Lawyers and Urban Cause Lawyering." *Akron Law Review* 41 (2008): 701-31.

———. "Law and the Fabric of the Everyday: The Settlement Houses, Sociological Jurisprudence, and the Gendering of Urban Legal Culture." *Southern California Interdisciplinary Law Journal* 15 (2006): 235-84.

Beck, Karen S. *A Working Lawyer's Life: The Letter Book of John Henry Senter, 1879-1884*. Clark, NJ: Lawbook Exchange, 2008.

Berger, Matthew, "Mary Hall: The Decision and the Lawyer." *Connecticut Bar Journal* 79 (2005): 29-58.

Biskupic, Joan. *Sandra Day O'Connor: How the First Woman on the Supreme Court Became Its Most Influential Justice*. New York: HarperCollins, 2005.

Bloomfield, Maxwell. *American Lawyers in a Changing Society, 1776-1876*. Cambridge, MA: Harvard University Press, 1976.

Bowling, Kristy, and Lynn Hecht Schafran, eds. *Women of the Courts Symposium*. Special issue of *University of Toledo Law Review* 36 (Summer 2005).

Brooks, Kim. *Justice Bertha Wilson: One Woman's Difference*. Vancouver: University of British Columbia Press, 2010.

Chester, Ronald. *Unequal Access: Women Lawyers in a Changing America*. South Hadley, MA: Bergin & Garvey, 1985.

Churchill, Winston. *Mr. Crewe's Career*. New York: Macmillan, 1908.

Clark, Mary L. "The First Women Members of the Supreme Court Bar, 1879-1900." *San Diego Law Review* 36 (1999): 87-136.

———. "Why Care about the History of Women in the Legal Profession?" *Women's Rights Law Reporter* 27 (2006): 59-66.

———. "Women as Supreme Court Advocates, 1879-1979." *Journal of Supreme Court History* 30 (2005): 47-67.

Cushman, Clare. "Women Advocates before the Supreme Court." *Journal of Supreme Court History* 26 (2001): 67-88.

Drachman, Virginia G. *Sisters in Law: Women Lawyers in Modern American History*. Cambridge, MA: Harvard University Press, 1998.

———. *Women Lawyers and the Origins of Professional Identity in America*. Ann Arbor: University of Michigan Press, 1993.

DuBois, Ellen Carol. *Harriot Stanton Blatch and the Winning of Woman Suffrage*. New Haven, CT: Yale University Press, 1997.

DuBois, Ellen Carol, and Richard Cándida Smith, eds. *Elizabeth Cady Stanton: Feminist as Thinker: A Reader in Documents and Essays*. New York: New York University Press, 2007.

Edwards, Laura F. *The People and Their Peace: Legal Culture and the Transformation of Inequality in the Post-Revolutionary South*. Chapel Hill: University of North Carolina Press, 2009.

Edwards, Rebecca. *Angels in the Machinery: Gender in American Party Politics from the Civil War to the Progressive Era*. New York: Oxford University Press, 1997.

———. *New Spirits: Americans in the Gilded Age, 1865-1905*. New York: Oxford University Press, 2006.

Epstein, Cynthia Fuchs. *Women in Law*. New York: Basic Books, 1981; 2nd ed., 1993.

Feld, Marjorie. *Lillian Wald: A Biography*. Chapel Hill: University of North Carolina Press, 2008.

Flanagan, Maureen A. *Seeing with Their Hearts: Chicago Women and the Vision of the Good City, 1871-1933*. Princeton, NJ: Princeton University Press, 2002.

Friedman, Jane M. *America's First Woman Lawyer: The Biography of Myra Bradwell*. Buffalo, NY: Prometheus Books, 1993.

Gardner, Deborah S. *Cadwalader, Wickersham & Taft: A Bicentennial History, 1792-1992*. Privately printed at New York: Cadwalader, Wickersham & Taft, Attorneys at Law, 1994.

Gawalt, Gerard W. *The Promise of Power: The Emergence of the Legal Profession in Massachusetts, 1760-1849.* Westport, CT: Greenwood Press, 1979.

Gawalt, Gerald W., ed. *The New High Priests: Lawyers in Post–Civil War America.* Westport, CT: Greenwood Press, 1984.

Gertner, Nancy. *In Defense of Women: Memoirs of an Unrepentant Advocate.* Boston: Beacon Press, 2011.

Ginzburg, Lori. D. *Elizabeth Cady Stanton: An American Life.* New York: Hill and Wang, 2009.

Gordon, Ann D., ed. *The Selected Papers of Elizabeth Cady Stanton and Susan B. Anthony,* vols. 1-5. New Brunswick, NJ: Rutgers University Press, 1997-2009.

Greene, Mary A. *The Woman's Manual of Law.* New York: Silver, Burdett, 1902. Gale Legal Treatises reprint edition.

Grossberg, Michael. "Institutionalizing Masculinity: The Law as a Masculine Profession." In Mark C. Carnes and Clyde Griffen, eds. *Meanings for Manhood: Constructions of Masculinity in Victorian America.* Chicago: University of Chicago Press, 1990.

Gustafson, Melanie Susan. *Women and the Republican Party, 1854-1924.* Urbana: University of Illinois Press, 2001.

Gustafson, Melanie, Kristie Miller, and Elizabeth I. Perry, eds. *We Have Come to Stay: American Women and Political Parties, 1880-1960.* Albuquerque: University of New Mexico Press, 1999.

Haar, Charles M., ed. *The Golden Age of American Law.* New York: George Braziller, 1965.

Hathaway, Grace. *Fate Rides a Tortoise: A Biography of Ellen Spencer Mussey.* Chicago: John C. Winston, 1937.

Haywood, C. Robert. *Cowtown Lawyers.* Norman: University of Oklahoma Press, 1988.

Hitchcock, Walter Theodore. *Timothy Walker: Antebellum Layer.* New York: Garland, 1990.

Horwitz, Morton J. *The Transformation of American Law, 1780-1860.* Cambridge, MA: Harvard University Press, 1977.

———. *The Transformation of American Law, 1870-1960.* New York: Oxford University Press, 1992.

Hurst, James Willard. *The Growth of American Law: The Law Makers.* Boston: Little, Brown, 1950. In particular, Section V, "The Bar."

Kaye, Judith S., and Anne C. Reddy. "The Progress of Women Lawyers at Big Firms: Steadied or Simply Studied?" *Fordham Law Review* 76 (2008): 1941-74.

Kerber, Linda. *Women of the Republic.* Chapel Hill: University of North Carolina Press, 1980.

Knight, Louis. *Citizen: Jane Addams and the Struggle for Democracy.* Chicago: University of Chicago Press, 2005.

Kroeger, Brooke. *Nellie Bly: Daredevil, Reporter, Feminist.* New York: Random House, 1994.

LaPiana, William P. *Logic and Experience: The Origin of Modern American Legal Education.* New York: Oxford University Press, 1994.

Lockwood, Belva A. "How I Ran for the Presidency." *National Magazine* 17 (March 1903): 728-33.

———. "My Efforts to Become a Lawyer." *Lippincott's Magazine* (February 1888): 215-29.

Miller, Perry. *The Life of the Mind in America from the Revolution to the Civil War.* New York: Harcourt, Brace, and World, 1965. In particular, Book Two, "The Legal Mentality."

Morello, Karen. *The Invisible Bar: The Woman Lawyer in America, 1638 to the Present.* New York: Random House, 1986.

Mossman, Mary Jane. *First Women Lawyers: A Comparative Study of Gender, Law, and the Legal Profession.* Portland, OR: Hart, 2006.

Nelson, William E. *The Americanization of the Common Law.* Cambridge, MA: Harvard University Press, 1975.

Nevins, Allan, and Milton Halsey Thomas, eds. *Diary of George Templeton Strong: Selections.* New York: Macmillan, 1952.

Norgren, Jill. "Belva Lockwood: Blazing the Trail for Women in Law." *Prologue Magazine* 37 (Spring 2005): parts 1 and 2. Available in print and online at http://www.archives.gov/publications/prologue/2005/spring/belva-lockwood-1.html.

———. *Belva Lockwood: The Woman Who Would Be President.* New York: New York University Press, 2007.

———. "Ladies of Legend: The First Generation of American Women Attorneys." *Journal of Supreme Court History* 35 (2010): 71-90.

———. "Lockwood in '84." *Wilson Quarterly* 26 (Autumn 2002): 12-20.

Pascoe, Peggy. *What Comes Naturally: Miscegenation Law and the Making of Race in America.* New York: Oxford University Press, 2008.

Reid, John Phillip. *Law for the Elephant: Property and Social Behavior on the Overland Trail.* San Marino, CA: Huntington Library, 1980.

———. *Legitimating the Law: The Struggle for Judicial Competency in Early National New Hampshire.* DeKalb: Northern Illinois University Press, 2012.

Roberts, Betty. *With Grit and by Grace: Breaking Trails in Politics and Law; A Memoir.* Corvallis: Oregon State University Press, 2008.

Robinson, Lelia Josephine. *Law Made Easy: A Book for the People.* Chicago: Sanitary Publishing Company, 1886. Available on Google Books and in Kessinger Publishing reprint edition.

———. *Law of Husband and Wife, Compiled for Popular Use.* Boston: Lee and Shepard, 1890. Available on Google Books and MLibrary reprint edition.

———. "Women Lawyers in the United States." *Green Bag* 2 (January 1890): 10-32.

Schechter, Patricia A. *Ida B. Wells-Barnett and American Reform, 1880-1930*. Chapel Hill: University of North Carolina Press, 2001.

Schier, Mary Lahr. *Strong-Minded Woman: The Story of Lavinia Goodell, Wisconsin's First Female Lawyer*. Northfield, MN: Midwest History Press, 2001. (A young adult biography.)

Schudson, Michael. "Public, Private, and Professional Lives: The Correspondence of David Dudley Field and Samuel Bowles." *American Journal of Legal History* 21 (1977): 191-211.

Schuele, Donna C. "In Her Own Way: Marietta Stow's Crusade for Probate Law Reform within the Nineteenth-Century Women's Rights Movement." *Yale Journal of Law and Feminism* 7 (1995): 279-306.

Scott, Donald M. "The Popular Lecture and the Creation of a Public in Mid-Nineteenth-Century America." *Journal of American History* 66 (March 1980): 791-809.

Sellers, Charles. *The Market Revolution: Jacksonian America, 1815-1846*. New York: Oxford University Press, 1991.

Sheppard, Steve, ed. *The History of Legal Education in the United States: Commentaries and Primary Sources*. Pasadena, CA: Salem Press, 1999.

Sklar, Kathryn Kish. *Florence Kelley and the Nation's Work: The Rise of Women's Political Culture, 1830-1900*. New Haven, CT: Yale University Press, 1995.

Smith, J. Clay, Jr. "Black Women Lawyers: 125 Years at the Bar; 100 Years in the Legal Academy." *Howard Law Journal* 40 (Winter 1997): 365-97.

———. *Emancipation: The Making of the Black Lawyer, 1844-1944*. Philadelphia: University of Pennsylvania Press, 1993.

Stansell, Christine. "Madame Candidate." *New Republic* 236 (April 2, 2007): 56-61.

Stanton, Elizabeth Cady, Susan B. Anthony, and Matilda Joslyn Gage. *A History of Woman Suffrage*, 6 vols., 1881-1922 (Ida Harper, vols. 5 and 6). Reprint edition, New York: Arno & New York Times Press, 1969.

Steven, Robert. *Law School: Legal Education in America from the 1850s to the 1980s*. Chapel Hill: University of North Carolina Press, 1983.

Strebeigh, Fred. *Equal: Women Reshape American Law*. New York: Norton, 2009.

Stuart, Nancy Rubin. *The Muse of the Revolution: The Secret Pen of Mercy Otis Warren and the Founding of a Nation*. Boston: Beacon Press, 2008.

Swaine, Robert T. *The Cravath Firm and Its Predecessors, 1819-1947*. Vol. 1, *The Predecessor Firms, 1819-1906*. Privately printed New York: Ad Press, 1946.

Teles, Steven M. *The Rise of the Conservative Legal Movement: The Battle for Control of the Law*. Princeton, NJ: Princeton University Press, 2008.

Thomas, Tracy A., and Tracey Jean Boisseau, eds. *Feminist Legal History: Essays on Women and Law*. New York: New York University Press, 2011.

Weisberg, D. Kelly. "Barred from the Bar: Women and Legal Education in the United States 1870-1890." *Journal of Legal Education* 28 (1977): 485-507.

Welke, Barbara Young. *Recasting American Liberty: Gender, Race, Law, and the Railroad Revolution, 1865-1920.* New York: Cambridge University Press, 2001.

Williams, Geoffrey, and Carole Novick. "A Woman Who Wouldn't Take No for an Answer: Kate Stoneman." *Albany Law School Magazine* (Spring 1992): 16-19.

Winner, Julia Hull. *Belva A. Lockwood.* Lockport, NY: Niagara County Historical Society, 1969.

Winston, Clifford, Robert W. Crandall, and Vikram Maheshri. *First Thing We Do, Let's Deregulate All the Lawyers.* Washington, DC: Brookings Institution Press, 2011.

Zagarri, Rosemarie. *Revolutionary Backlash: Women and Politics in the Early American Republic.* Philadelphia: University of Pennsylvania Press, 2007.

Index

About the Author

JILL NORGREN IS Professor Emerita of Political Science and Legal Studies, John Jay College of Criminal Justice, and the Graduate Center, The City University of New York. She writes on U.S. politics and law, with a particular interest in the history of American women. She is the co-author (with Serena Nanda) of *American Cultural Pluralism and Law* and *Partial Justice* (with Petra T. Shattuck), and the author of *The Cherokee Cases: Two Landmark Federal Decisions in the Fight for Sovereignty*. In 2007 she wrote *Belva Lockwood: The Woman Who Would Be President*, as well as a young adult biography about Lockwood, titled *Belva Lockwood: Equal Rights Pioneer*. Her books and articles have received awards from the American Society for Legal History, the United States Supreme Court Historical Society, and the American Library Association. With colleagues, she has created www.herhatwasinthering.org, a website featuring biographies of U.S. women who ran for political office before 1920. She is currently writing a book about trail-blazing women lawyers of the twentieth and twenty-first centuries.